THROUGH THE NIGHT

THROUGH
THE NIGHT

Helping Parents and
Sleepless Infants

DILYS DAWS

BasicBooks
A Division of HarperCollinsPublishers

To the memory of my mother and father,
Florence and Jack Kahn

Contents

PREFACE, 1993

FOLLOWING THE PUBLICATION three years ago of *Through the Night*, I have had many letters from parents and from professionals telling me of the emotional impact it has had on them; one is quoted on the back cover of this edition. Most have also told me some small bit of personal history that it has led them to recall. I am gratified that the book has helped to create an atmosphere in which people feel freer to think of emotional relationships in connection with their babies, and that so many readers have felt that the book was relevant for them. I believe it has enabled quite a few professionals to think about their own experiences first, either as parents or as children, and allowed them in turn to 'slow down' in their response to their patients and clients. It has perhaps given them the confidence *not* to offer immediate solutions to problems, but to help these parents tell the 'story' of their baby, and to help them discover what the links between experiences in their own lives and problems with their baby might be.

The issue that people have taken up with me most often has been that of separation. I have become aware how many parents these days keep their babies very close to them, by day and by night, for the first months or even longer. Some of these parents find that their baby has difficulty in getting to sleep; many do not. It seems that there is an ability in some parents and babies to enjoy their closeness, and at the same time, to let go of each other emotionally, enough for each to be free to go to sleep. Other parents and babies come to experience such closeness as a mutual torment of intrusiveness, and no one is able to sleep long and deeply. They seem also to get caught in the closeness and become unable to think about how to get more separate from each other. There are two important issues here. First, *all* babies need closeness and intimacy with their parents to develop a sense of themselves as individuals, as well as a sense of themselves in relation to other people. Second, all babies need at appropriate moments to take steps away from their parents, both literally and metaphorically, in order to begin to grow up.

It is fascinating to think about the interaction of these two vital needs, given the different personalities of parents and babies, different families with their idiosyncratic ways of doing things, different races and cultures. To some extent what we expect of our babies depends on what sort of adults we picture them becoming. We must beware of any over-simplification of the interplay between the processes of intimacy and those of separation and individualization. Any idealization of one or the other might lead us to suspect that some vital human emotions and feelings are being avoided. I particularly have in mind here *conflicts* of love and hate, the 'ordinary' life and death emotions which parents and babies may feel for each other. I have increasingly realized that in families where babies are desperately sleepless and crying, desperate emotions are there already; it is essential to recognize the strength of these feelings.

This book is not intended to tell anyone what to do. I hope it will continue to help parents work things out better with their babies. Perhaps it will similarly free professionals from the burden of feeling they need rush to give advice to the families who consult them. However, as parents or as professionals we need to be brave. The impact of newly discovered emotions is painful and very frightening. It is also liberating. 'The courage to be', to borrow the title of Paul Tillich's book.

ACKNOWLEDGEMENTS

This book is the product of what is now twelve years' work as a child psychotherapist with the families of infants. It has been carried out in two places in London, at the Child Guidance Training Centre, now merged with the Tavistock Clinic, and at the Child Health Clinic of a general practice, the Wigg practice, in the Kentish Town Health Centre.

I am grateful to colleagues in both places. Firstly, this is my opportunity to show publicly my appreciation of the doctors, health visitors and others at the Baby Clinic who have found a place for me to work alongside them and who have stimulated and shared with me thoughts about the problems of young families. The combination of the welcome that I have been given over my years there and the creative tension from remembering that I come from another discipline and another institution has, I think, allowed me the freedom to develop some original thoughts in this area. From them all I single out Caryle Steen GP, who first took the risk of introducing me to the practice, and Helen Utidjian, health visitor, whose friendly directness with families taught me much.

Secondly, I am grateful to colleagues at the Child Guidance Training Centre and now at the Tavistock Clinic who have supported me over the years of developing the work and recently writing this book. Alexis Brook, Marcus Johns and Adrian Sutton encouraged me early on. Margaret Rustin, tutor in child psychotherapy, Judith Trowell, Chairman, and Joyce Piper, Administrative Secretary of the Child and Family Department, helped in many ways, not least in enabling me to organize the time to write the book. Diana Bissett, Corinne Gibbons, Jane Rayner and Janice Uphill typed and carefully prepared the various stages of the manuscript and helped my confidence in it grow. Margaret Walker, librarian of the superb Tavistock Joint Library, Angela Haselton and Helen Oliver gave me enormous help in finding the literature for the book.

I am glad to thank many colleagues, students and friends who have generously given me ideas, new directions of thought or their own experiences to use. They include Mary-Sue Moore who, as Fulbright Scholar at the Tavistock Clinic, made a great difference to the scope of the book when she enthusiastically introduced me to the world of sleep physiology and psychosomatic ideas; Helen Bender for her ideas on premature infants; Lisa Miller and colleagues at the under-fives counselling service of the Tavistock Clinic for useful discussions, and Freya Davy, Peter Evans, Ann Haigh, Leslie Ironside, Jane Osborne, Maria Eugenia Cid Rodriguez, Pat Trayner and many others. I especially thank the families who have shared critical moments of their lives with me and allowed them to be used as illustrations here.

My very special thanks go to my friend Juliet Hopkins who helped me to think through the principles of this work and encouraged me to write about it. She and my husband Eric Rayner steadily gave me information, criticism and a chance to reflect on ideas and gave me the courage to put it all together. I also thank my children Sam and William Daws and stepchildren Sarah, Will and Ben Rayner for the mixture of interest and scepticism which kept it in proportion.

Finally I am indebted to Robert Young and Ann Scott at Free Association Books for their confirmation that this was an exciting subject to write about, to Selina O'Grady whose copy-editing enhanced the completion of the book and for all their knowledgeable and constructive help throughout.

I would like to thank Oxford University Press for permission to quote from Anne Stevenson's 'Poem to My Daughter', published in *Minute by Glass Minute*, 1982.

CHAPTER ONE

WHAT IS A SLEEP PROBLEM?

OES YOUR BABY SLEEP through the night?' parents ask each other. This book is about infants' sleep, with thoughts about the babies who do, as well as the ones who do not.

I will be primarily concerned about the relationship between parents and child within which sleep develops well or badly. This naturally involves an examination of the emotions between them which influence the baby's capacity to sleep. The backgrounds of parents' lives, their personal histories and relationships are the framework within which they bring up their families. I look at how these connect with their baby's development, of which sleep is a vital ingredient. I will not be categorizing kinds of sleep problems, nor systematically giving solutions, but I will be looking at the context and some of the causes of sleep problems.

This book is above all clinically based. It describes my own method of therapy for sleep problems, developed over ten years or so: brief psychoanalytic therapy with parents and infants together. I use many examples from this clinical work, both in order to demonstrate the method itself and also as illustrations of my and others' theoretical ideas. Many writers have found statistical connections between infants' sleep problems and other aspects of development or relationships and I describe some of them here. My purpose is not to add to these statistical findings but to illuminate their connections with clinical, that is, particular, individual experiences so that the nature of the findings can be better understood.

'Through the night of doubt and sorrow', as the hymn says; a highly-coloured phrase, but perhaps not too exaggerated a way to describe the long nights that sleepless crying babies and their parents endure. Sleep problems may punctuate uncertainties between parents and baby at any stage of the baby's development and bring out doubts in parents about their parenting abilities. They are among the most undermining troubles a parent has to deal with.

Sorrow is, indeed, also one of my themes, in particular how parents' losses and traumas, for instance the death of the mother's own mother or a birth experienced as disastrous, go on resounding inside the parent and colour such an apparently simple operation as putting a baby to bed. Separations in a parent's life, felt to have been unbearable, may make the small separation of putting a baby down in its cot also seem unbearable.

This book is not so much about how to make sleepless babies behave differently – in fact it is argued throughout that the problem is rarely in the baby alone – it is about how to think differently and more widely about the problem. The sleep disturbance can then be a jumping-off point for real creative thinking by a family about how they all – parents, baby and other children – interact with each other.

As I shall argue, the interchange between parents and baby about going to bed and getting to sleep is, like feeding, one of the crucial transactions between them. The way in which this is conducted may, firstly, influence the length and quality of the baby's sleep. Secondly, for an individual it may contribute one of the most powerful and influential memories of their childhood and thirdly, the emotional tone and precedent for negotiation may influence later transactions between parents and child even into adolescence. Further, sorting out aspects of what is going on between parents and baby *during the day* may be just as necessary in helping with the sleep problems as going head-on for the events of the night.

In the course of the book I cite various thoughts that parents have had about their babies' sleep and suggest that parents' dreams about their babies are one form of this thinking. In this vein, here, as an illustration, is a dream of my own; I think it shows how dreams can highlight vital aspects of the connections between parents and their children.

On the night before my younger son's first A-level exam I dreamt that he was a little boy again. We were staying in a strange place and I gave him a warm bath, pleasantly confident that he would fall asleep easily afterwards.

In this brief dream are several of the themes of my book. It examines the relationship between parents and baby within which a baby is able to sleep easily or not. It opens up the idea of how much the baby's sleep is a result of his parents' care or how much a 'letting-go' by the parent so that the baby can attain his own physiological rhythms. How does a parent appropriately follow the changing needs of babies and children at different ages? When a baby falls asleep, do he* and his mother experience this as a continuity between them or as a separation? How much does experience in the first weeks and months affect what happens later?

My dream about my teenage son was obviously in part a wish to 'mother' him inappropriately for his age. But perhaps principally it was a memory of the way he and I had negotiated in the past how I could help him towards what only he could do for himself. No one can fall asleep for someone else, and parents cannot take their children's exams for them! Parents are guardians of their children's sleep, in the words of the psychoanalyst Joyce McDougall (1974, p. 446) who echoes Freud's idea that dreams are the guardians of sleep (1916–17, p. 129), but paradoxically they can often do this best while asleep themselves. The parent who sleeps and dreams about her child leaves the child free to have his own dreams.

This is also a book about strong emotions. I hope to convey the desperation with which parents have told me about their baby's sleeplessness and the life and death feelings sometimes associated with this. In ten years of work with such families in a child health clinic and at the Tavistock Clinic in London I have, I think, been able to help many of them alleviate their situation. I will describe my method in the next chapter; in this one I want to give a context to the problems. This context is in my mind when each new family tells me their problem, their attempted solutions and the expectations about child-rearing that have informed their behaviour.

Some readers may be at times taken aback by the connections I make, with little apparent evidence, between parents' own experiences and their children's difficulties. I ask readers to bear with me as we look at this throughout the book. The parents I have worked with have often, I think, been relieved and supported by finding these links. It can be liberating for parents to look honestly at the intertwining between themselves and their child, not for blame or self-blame, but as a new chance to take the initiative in a more benign interchange with their child. Something falls into place and problems start to dissolve.

Looking at sleeping problems makes us aware of the complexity of the emotions involved in being a parent. We see how subtle is the process by which mothers and babies move from their early close-

* For simplicity I generally use the pronoun 'he' when referring to babies in this book.

ness to seeing themselves as two separate beings. Sleeping problems illustrate difficulties at every stage. Receptivity to the needs of a baby, sensitivity to their fears and spontaneous offering of comfort need to be tempered with a gradual setting of limits. Understanding of a baby's fears enables a parent to contain those fears; the baby gradually learns to manage them himself. A parent does not need to take on the baby's fears as though they are her own.

A SUMMARY OF THE CONTENTS

Part I examines ideas about how to work with families of infants with sleep problems. In Chapter 2 I describe the clinical method that is the foundation of this book. The work I do with families is psychoanalytically based (although it is usually very brief). By this I mean the approach of taking in and reflecting upon what parents tell me, so that an understanding and integrative process begins in my mind. A similar reflective understanding can then take over in theirs. I look together with parents at their baby, acknowledging the baby's uniqueness and so helping them to stand outside fixed ways of thinking and reacting. Although some of the success of this work derives from the experience of seeing many families with sleeping problems, it cannot be done in a routine way – the impact of each family's stress and bewilderment must be received afresh each time.

The connections I make between relationships in the family and parents' own early experience do also hinge on thoughts about immediate practical solutions. However, I actively suggest these solutions much less often than some of my colleagues working with sleep problems, although I always have in mind the many devices and practices that help a child to sleep better. I am much informed here by what other parents have told me works for them. Solutions are as much the province of parents as of myself; my task is to help them restore their ability to think effectively so that *they* can provide an answer for *their* child. In trying to evaluate the usefulness for families of this kind of brief work, I compare and contrast it with behaviour modification.

I hope that I convey some of my own astonishment and delight at the effectiveness in many cases of this work and also my reactions to the intensity of it. Families come bursting with emotion not only about their baby's sleeplessness but also about their ordinary hopes and fears for their children. At the risk of sounding sentimental, it is a privilege to be involved with such feelings. Baby clinics, as the health visitors and doctors who work in them know, are a concentrated experience of life and death feelings about pregnancy, birth and caring for vulnerable little babies. It is exhilarating but also exhausting to be confronted by these everyday dramas.

In brief focused work about a problem like sleeplessness families come distressed and confused and with a feeling of being fragmented. However, in most cases these are not seriously disturbed or problem families, they are viable ones, most of the time capable of looking after their own and each other's emotions. What they need is not to have the problem 'solved' or taken away, but for an integrative process to start to happen. This putting-together seems often to need an outside person to start it off. Perhaps one of the satisfactions of the work is that the therapist also benefits vicariously from this process of integration. There is a deep pleasure in being involved with the intense feelings of an ordinary baby's development.

Chapter 3 gives a case study of a family, the 'Armitages', who have allowed me to give a detailed picture of work with them (I have used pseudonyms for all my clinical examples). In this I pick out and underline some of the issues raised in the previous chapter.

This book is principally about people, although it also examines theories; perhaps it is mainly about people's struggle to work out their ideas. In Part I I describe my own efforts with families to sort something out from a confusion of thoughts and emotions, for the families who come to see me are themselves striving to make sense of their experiences and ideas.

In Part II I expand on the area of the theory of normal development and normal processes in infants, both emotional and physiological, so as to provide some essential background knowledge for thinking about sleep problems. Part II is also about my own particular struggle to put together two very different kinds of theories – psychoanalysis and physiology. I attempt to introduce some psychoanalysts and their original ideas about infant development. Most of this work has been familiar to me for many years, since training as a child psychotherapist. In contrast to this is the physiological data on the function of sleep for both adults and young children, and on the development of the baby's sleep states and other states, which was all new to me.

It has been fascinating for me to discover, albeit simply and naïvely, some of the neurological language for describing developmental processes in infants and I have tried to continue the work of writers who have already combined this neurological thinking with the psychodynamic way of describing the infant's emotional development. In this vein Chapters 4 and 5 describe the functions of normal sleep and the way in which the establishment of the baby's sleep rhythms and other bodily functions is influenced by the parents' handling of their baby, including all the routines of bedtimes.

Chapter 6 is a key chapter in the book. It describes the usefulness of dreams and nightmares, both in the physiological organizing function of REM (rapid eye-movement) sleep and in the creative imaginings of the mind in remembered dreams. Both of these are different ways of describing how the mind deals with and metabolizes the experience of the day. I show how dreams can illustrate both a person's individual thoughts and anxieties and also the connection between the minds of parents and child. Dreams are the dramatizations of the mind. The sleepless families I see have lost much of their time for dreaming. I think that the dramatic playing with ideas about crucial emotions in my meetings with them helps start some of them dreaming again.

Chapters 7 and 8 examine the central hypothesis that separation issues underlie many sleep problems. Here we look at the normal emotional development of a young infant in the context of his relation to his parents. We see how the infant builds up a loving and trusting relationship and from this is able to develop a sense of his own identity. Sleep disorders may be to do with something going wrong in this process and, surprisingly perhaps, it may be the parent who has the difficulty about separation. Putting a baby to bed may seem to vulnerable parents who have themselves experienced rebuffs as though they are rejecting the baby and a baby who closes his eyes and goes to sleep may seem to be similarly excluding the parent. But it is most important to realize that periods of being sleepless are part of normal maturation. New stages of awareness of themselves or of the parents' own relationship quite naturally produce anxieties that keep babies awake, or give them frightening dreams, or indeed may simply be a sign of a passionate involvement with all the achievements and pleasures of the day.

Part III takes specific topics and looks at their connection with sleep problems. In Chapter 9, on feeding and weaning, I note that the establishing of both sleep and feeding patterns is an essential part of what goes on between parent and child. Feeding and sleeping also influence each other and parents may be confused about whether or not a baby's waking is because of a need to be fed. Problems about feeding, especially in a baby who needs feeding constantly, day and night, can often be seen clearly as relationship problems. Problems about weaning may reflect a feeding situation that never quite got sorted out or may represent a mother and baby's reluctance to move on. Sleep problems often accompany these difficulties and, in particular when babies have only been able to go to sleep at the breast, mothers may be dismayed at the prospect of losing this when they wean their baby.

Chapters 10 and 11, on parents' own childhood experiences, the father's role, the parents' marriage and single and working parents, show how a range of personal experience both in the past and in the present colours how parents interact with their child. Many of these parents have had difficult relationships with their own parents or have been to some degree deprived. Several of the mothers I have seen had their own mothers die before the baby was born. They have not had confirmation of themselves as a mother from their own mother. This brief work can only touch on such experiences, but making the connection between their own experiences and their interaction with their child does seem to enable parents to differentiate themselves better from their children. Just as there is a drive towards development and integration in young children, so there seems to be a similar integrative thrust towards the development of parental capacity for most people even while carrying personal difficulties inside them.

The final three chapters discuss the way various states of health in parent or baby have an effect on the infant's sleep. Chapter 12, on sleep as a psychosomatic problem, shows how unexpressed conflicts can lead to confused handling of a baby or can turn into psychosomatic symptoms, including sleeplessness. I show how some mothers provoke such a process in their babies. I also show how a shortage of sleep can then exacerbate certain physical conditions.

Chapter 13, 'Mother's depression and other states of health', describes how mothers and babies normally communicate with each other. A depressed mother may be less able to respond to her baby and may miss some of the interactions with him that help set up patterns of sleep. In Chapter 14 I show how various disabilities or illnesses in the baby may themselves directly lead to sleep disorders or may inhibit or confuse parents' handling of the baby, with a subsequent effect on establishment of sleep patterns.

My argument throughout is that the setting up of a baby's sleep–wake rhythms is influenced by the interaction between parent and baby. It is also an aspect of the baby's own temperament and personality and of the stage of development it has reached.

It is also essential to note that having a baby sleep for very long periods is not the main aim of parenthood. New-born babies need long hours of sleep in which to grow and perhaps to recover from the experience of birth, but soon they are awake for longer hours and parents and babies use this time not only for feeding but for cuddles, looks, smiles and 'talking'. It is known that babies in institutions sleep for long periods, probably because no one is eager for them to wake up for this enjoyable play and loving interaction. Babies at home who sleep for inordinately long periods may also sometimes be in a situation where they do not feel that their company is sought; or alternatively they may be temperamentally apathetic or withdrawn.

Conversely babies who have slept well in the first months and later have difficulties in sleeping may be babies who are flourishing – their sleeplessness may be the outcome of their development. Towards the end of the first year many babies are fascinated by their discoveries of all that the world has to offer and are loath to shut this off and go to sleep. Babies who start to realize that their parents have a sexual relationship that excludes them may feel very cross about being put alone in their cots. Even the anxieties of the second year, which give many babies nightmares or develop into fears of tigers behind the curtains, are also signs of maturing minds and creative imaginings. In this book I am therefore thinking of sleep problems as ones that persist after parents have made allowance for such natural causes of sleeplessness.

DEFINING SLEEP PROBLEMS AND STATISTICAL RESEARCH FINDINGS

Sleep problems can tear a family apart, but it is only recently that sleep disturbance has been recognized as a major problem. In one study 30 percent of babies and children up to four had a significant problem (Lozoff et al., 1985). Do more babies these days have a problem; are parents less tolerant of broken nights; or is it simply that more are reported to easily accessible health visitors and doctors?

The definition of what constitutes a sleep problem is, however, variable. A baby waking in the night does not necessarily have a sleep problem. New-born infants wake as a matter of course to be fed during the night and parents usually respond instinctively to this need. If the baby only wakes once or twice during the night and falls asleep after a feed, it is likely to be a satisfying experience for both parent and baby.

At later ages babies may wake occasionally or regularly from physical cause or to seek comfort from parents. Change or stress in the family, or even the impact of their own developmental progress, may cause babies to wake in the night. Parents on the whole take this in their stride. A problem could be considered to exist when the baby's reason for waking is not understood; when the parent feels the waking up is not reasonable; or when an apparent reason has passed but the baby continues to wake as a fixed habit. All these can be thought of in terms of how parents and infant are getting on with each other in their managing of the baby's physiological state.

Naomi Richman (1981a) used a more specific definition in a questionnaire about one- to two-year-olds in Waltham Forest, London. In this a child was considered to have a severe waking problem if the problem had existed for more than three months and the child was waking five or more nights a week. In addition the child had to be doing one or more of the following: waking three or more times a night; waking for more than twenty minutes during the night; or going into the parents' bed. (There is disagreement among researchers as to whether going into the parents' bed is a problem or not.)

Such definitions give us specific criteria for establishing what is being described, so that useful comparable research figures can emerge. Zuckerman *et al.*'s (1987) definition of the problem was when an infant took an hour or more to get back to sleep after waking at night, was waking three or more times a night or where there was any problem causing severe disruption to the mother's sleep. This definition in fact allows for an evaluation of the mother–infant relationship in which the problem occurs. Their third category of disruption to the mother was included so that lesser problems, such as waking twice a night, would not be missed. In considering the problem in the context of how it is seen by the mother, Zuckerman *et al.* say that regular waking once a night, while considered a problem in older children, may reflect an ongoing comfortable adaptation for mother and child at eight months and should not be used to define a sleep problem at this age.

Lozoff *et al.* (1985) also have a definition with an evaluative component. Their criterion was that a problem existed if 'night waking involving parents or bedtime struggles occurred three or more nights a week for a month preceding the interview, accompanied by conflict or distress'. Here we see that the frequency of waking alone does not constitute the problem and that conflict or distress must be a part of the constellation.

It is also interesting that parents may not even be aware of how often their baby wakes, if he does not wake them. On the basis of video recording Anders *et al.* strikingly report:

> a sleep problem in infancy is usually so defined only when it disturbs the sleep of the parents. Some infants may awaken and call in the middle of the night, but its parents do not describe this as a sleep problem. Other infants may awaken for short periods during the night and not signal their parents. These infants have been assumed asleep by studies relying on maternal reports. Finally some infants may awaken before or after the conventionally defined hours (12.0 p.m. to 5.0 a.m.) and not be defined as night wakers by investigators. (1983, p. 163)

Anders *et al.* go on to say that mothers regularly report less night waking than is evident from video recording.

Isabel Paret (1983) also shows the fascinating evidence from video recording babies' sleep habits. She studied thirty-four mother–infant couples, where the infants aged about nine months were all crawling but not yet walking, and from these distinguished eleven night wakers from 23 night sleepers. The two groups were separated out by the mothers' own reports and validated by twelve hours of video reporting. The mothers' own reports, taken over five days, were reliable enough to separate the two groups of babies.

In distinguishing the wakers from the sleepers, Paret says that none of the twenty-three sleepers woke more than twice, whereas of the eleven night wakers 8 woke between three and six times and not one woke only once. Even more interesting, Paret shows that the total amount of sleep over a 24-hour day was the same for both groups, though the groups differed significantly in the distribution of their sleep. Wakers averaged many more naps during the day. They made up for their missing night's sleep not by taking longer daytime naps but by a greater number of naps. Thus even in daytime their sleep cycles were shorter than those of the other group.

The discovery that these particular 'waking' babies slept as much as 'sleeping' ones is indeed surprising and of course contradicts the belief of most parents of children with sleep problems. In fact many 'waking' babies do *not* sleep much during the day. However, even if they do, parents' impressions may also be intuitively correct in the sense that these frequent, short periods of sleep are of less use to an infant than a longer, continuous period would be. These crawling babies were of an age where, as we will see in Chapter 5, the periods of REM sleep have moved to the latter end of sleep cycles. With too short a time asleep an infant will have neither sufficient of the indispensable REM sleep nor of deep sleep for the restorative and consolidating processes of these stages to take place.

As well as this intuition that their infants' sleep is not physiologically efficient, parents' belief that their babies are not getting enough sleep may also derive from a feeling that there is something inherently emotionally unsatisfactory in such short periods of sleep. In addition they are viewing the situation from the position of the feelings stirred up by their own disturbed sleep.

SETTLING – DOES YOUR BABY SLEEP THROUGH THE NIGHT?

Anders *et al.* (1983) define 'settling' as sleeping through the night, measured from midnight to 5.0 a.m. To avoid confusion it should be noted that some other authors, such as Douglas and Richman (1984), use 'settle' to describe the process of getting to sleep.

In a pioneering paper on sleep problems Moore and Ucko (1957) touched on most of the issues that later research has expanded on. They described the settling process as a form of learning at the level of biological adaptation which requires no consciously directed training by the parents. Generally it takes its course and if disturbed by illness or change, will be resumed when the disturbance is past. If, however, the settling process is delayed beyond the fourth or fifth month, the automatic gravitation to the diurnal cycle will be lost and adjustment may then be very difficult to attain, perhaps because the organism has reached a point of stabilization on a different rhythm. According to Moore and Ucko about 70 percent of babies will have settled and ceased waking in the night by three months, another 13 percent by six months, and 90 percent by the end of the first year. (It should be noted that these figures probably apply to babies sleeping on their own. More recent work, for example McKenna *et al.* (1989), suggests that infants who sleep with their mothers wake more frequently during the first year.)

Although Moore and Ucko say that the settling process is a biological adaptation which cannot be influenced by consciously directed training from parents, we do see, from families who report their children's sleep problems, that parents have a very large part to play in either supporting and reinforcing this biological adaptation or in interfering with it.

Anders *et al.* (1983) made video recordings of forty full-term normal infants without sleep problems in their own homes. From these they were able to see what actually happens during the night in a family and how infants do settle. At two weeks of age *all* infants were removed from the cot during the night and 95 percent were removed between midnight and 2.0 a.m. At nine months only 10 percent were taken from the cot, but at a year this had risen again to 25 percent. In fact 55 percent of babies aged one year were seen by the videotape to have awakened, so that 30 percent had woken without disturbing their mother.

Other interesting findings in this privileged study of mothers and babies in their own homes was that 23 percent of two-week-old babies were put into their cots at some point whilst awake and 77 percent were put in awake at one year. At both ages it was more likely for babies to be put in their cot awake after awakenings that happened later in the night. The sleep latency time, that is, the time it took the baby to get to sleep, was similar over the age span and varied from nine to fifteen and a half minutes.

From these figures we can also see that settling to sleep at an early age does not guarantee future undisturbed nights. Anders *et al.* show from their small sample that babies who settle before five months of age have a fifty percent likelihood of developing night waking. Babies who settle later have less likelihood of developing night waking, at least before the end of the first year.

Putting these and Moore and Ucko's findings together suggests that five months is an important physiological landmark. It might appear that they disagree about the benefits of settling by this age. However, as Anders *et al.* observed, later night waking is not part of a failure in the physiological consolidation of sleep. Babies who start night waking later on are in the throes of a developmental stage where emotional anxieties and conflicts can be strong enough

12

to waken them. This waking represents a newly based disturbance from within an established sleep rhythm.

THE PREVALENCE AND CONTINUATION OF SLEEP PROBLEMS

What various studies have attempted to do is to show the number of children with sleep problems at various ages and to use their figures to look at the continuance of the problem. For example, Zuckerman *et al.* (1987) found that from a sample of 308 babies aged eight months 18 percent had a problem, according to their definition, while at three years of age this had increased to 29 percent, with a difficulty in getting to bed or to sleep or staying asleep. They relate their figures to children's development by saying that 41 percent of children with a sleep problem at eight months still had a problem at three years and that conversely only 26 percent of children without a problem at three months had developed a problem at three years.

In her Waltham Forest study Richman (1981a) estimated that between 13 percent and 20 percent of one- to two-year-olds in her sample population woke regularly and that between 6 percent and 10 percent had severe sleep disruptions. Taking the data retrospectively, Richman found that 46 percent of the wakers in her sample had had difficulties since birth.

Lozoff *et al.* (1985) took two samples comprising 96 white children between six months and four years of age and with their somewhat fluid definition (see pp. 9–10) found that in each group 30 percent had a sleep problem. This figure of 30 percent seems quite compelling and is much quoted by other workers. It makes sense if looked at over the period of early childhood; for example, Zuckerman *et al.* (1987) say that up to 30 percent of children have a sleep problem at some time during their first four years.

Guedeney and Kreisler (1987), who noted that 28 percent of the young patients referred to their child department for psychosomatic problems in 1985 were suffering from sleep disorders, suggest differentiating primary and secondary sleep disorders, depending on whether the trouble begins before or after three months of age. Richman (1981b) makes the useful point that the factors starting off a sleep problem may not be the same as those maintaining the problem. She suggests that some infants may have a predisposition not to fall asleep again after waking, because of high arousal determined by physiological factors or anxiety. Perinatal activity and early irritability, as well as family stress, are all important factors in this difficulty of going back to sleep.

WHO HAS THE PROBLEM?

Lozoff *et al.* (1985) cite five experiences which distinguish children with sleep problems from those without: an accident or illness in the family, unaccustomed absence of the mother during the day, maternal depressed mood, sleeping in the parents' bed and a maternal attitude of ambivalence towards the child. Some of these accompanying factors may be partially the cause of a sleep problem, but others, like sleeping in the parents' bed, as we will see later, may be connected with either the causes or the effects of the problem.

We are here looking at stressful or pathological circumstances which appear to be triggering off sleep problems in children. Sleep disturbances, however, are not necessarily seen as sleep problems by the children's parents. They may be understood as a reasonable part of the child's development. Crowell *et al.* (1987), for instance, show how children in their third year called out for their parents after being put to bed and expressed fears of the dark but that such behaviour was not necessarily thought to be a problem by parents. One of the tasks of parenthood is to help a child grow towards eventual independence and separation from the parents. Crowell *et al.* make the point that getting to bed and falling asleep mirror this separation process. Parents' own experiences affect how they help their children in getting to bed, including how bedtime was negotiated in their own families of origin. Giorgis *et al.* (1987) show that 16 percent of mothers of the babies they examined with sleep problems had had such problems themselves. Interestingly, 26 percent of the mothers had families with sleep problems, compared with only 10 percent of the fathers'. One wonders if the mothers' memories were better(!) or, more seriously, whether these figures show the greater influence a mother's experience has than does the father's on their baby's sleep.

THE CONTINUATION OF SLEEP PROBLEMS AND THEIR CONNECTION WITH OTHER BEHAVIOUR PROBLEMS

As we have seen, Zuckerman *et al.* (1987) found that 41 percent of children with a problem at eight months still had it at three years. At eight months 18 percent of the sample had some problem and 29 percent at three years. There was no connection at eight months with other behaviour problems, but at three years they were more likely to have temper tantrums and other behaviour problems. The one problem in the baby that was found to correlate with sleep disturbance at eight months was difficulty with teething. Zuckerman *et al.* speculate as to whether teething can cause sufficient discomfort to awaken the child during lighter sleep stages or whether a low sensory threshold for discomfort might explain both teething and sleep problems at eight months.

Opinions differ about whether sleep problems augur future psychological and behavioural difficulties. Giorgis *et al.* (1987) argue that it can be a momentary condition not indicative of future psychopathology. Lozoff *et al.* (1985), on the other hand, suggest that bedtime conflicts and night waking seem to be quantifiable and easily ascertainable behaviour patterns that could alert paediatric health professionals to the existence of other more pervasive disturbances in the child and its family. The mother's state of mind and state of health is obviously crucial to the baby's well-being. Zuckerman *et al.* found that the mother's depressed feelings were the most important psychological factor associated with sleep problems. What increasingly emerges from the research literature is the connection between infants' sleep problems and the quality of the emotional relationships in the family. I hope to develop the various elements of this throughout the book. We turn in the next chapter to my discoveries of this emotionality in meetings with families.

PART I

CHAPTER TWO

BRIEF PSYCHOANALYTIC THERAPY
FOR SLEEP PROBLEMS

I N THIS CHAPTER I will be describing the way in which I work
with families on their infants' sleep problems. The consultations are an interaction between myself and the family which
enables them to discover how some of the ways that they behave
with each other influence the baby's sleep. The process of the
consultation has in itself an integrative effect for the family. I
compare the principles of this work with those of behavioural
therapy and also discuss the various ways in which families may use
different approaches – either therapy, reading 'baby books' or
advice from elsewhere.

COMING FOR HELP

My own work with infants who cannot sleep is in the Child Health
Clinic of the Wigg general medical practice and also at the Tavistock Clinic, London. In both places I see families about problems
with their babies' or small children's development. When families
come with a sleep problem, it is always urgent and they need to be
seen quickly. Although they may have been suffering from one or
more sleepless children and apparently tolerating the situation for
some time, when they do get to the point of negotiating a referral
they often represent themselves as being 'at the end of their
tether'.

In spite of the urgency of the problem and often the distress of
all the family, I have found that as few as one or two consultations
may allow a change in the parents' approach to the baby that breaks
the deadlock between them. I usually find that if a change is going
to occur it does so after the first or second meeting; I then often see
the family several times more to consolidate these changes. As a
psychoanalytically trained child psychotherapist this is a departure
from longer-term intensive work and I will be examining the
principles underlying it.

It has been remarked that no one is ever the worse for having a

19

sleep problem cured. That may be so and sleeplessness, which can spread through a whole family, actually stops useful thinking by parents about what is going on in the family. Helping them think during the day can start off a process that enables them to manage the chaos of the night. When a sleep problem has been resolved, parents may then be able to deal more effectively with the normal run of the family's and children's developmental problems. However, curing a problem, without also having thought through its possible origins in the context of family relations, means at best that an opportunity for the family to look at their dynamics or their handling of their infant has been lost and at worst that the 'cure' may appear to confirm that the child alone was the problem.

Families come for help with their children's sleep problems bursting with emotion. They come in distress, in anger, overcome by helplessness. In looking at such problems with them, I have thought that the clue to the work lies within this emotionality. The strong feelings are not only the result of sleepless nights. They are also both a cause of the problem and a route into discovering how to alleviate it.

Sleep disturbances often illustrate what is going on in a family. Families need to be helped to discover for themselves what is being represented by the problem. Also, the issues uncovered between parents and children, or between the parents themselves, often lead back to parents' own experiences in their childhood with their parents. Repeatedly the theme of how to deal with and survive separations comes up; there will be more about this later.

I am about to describe the way I work, but I hope that the style of the book is itself evidence of this. It does not describe solutions and I do not myself immediately 'reassure' parents, declare the normality of their child's behaviour or give them advice, although some of this may happen during the work. In reading accounts of interchanges between families and myself, I hope that other professionals working with families with sleep problems, or parents themselves, will consider the issues that we have covered.

The strength of the book is, I like to think, in the anecdotal clinical illustrations. They are not intended to 'prove' that this method works. They are there to indicate how many different facets of people's lives can interlink with one symptom or disturbance, such as a sleep problem. Furthermore, it need not be daunting to take this on board in brief therapy. My principal hypothesis is that for the therapist to acknowledge and gather in for the parents all the relevant aspects of a baby's life and its relationship to them, within the brief framework of the consultation, is itself therapeutic.

With this in mind, the method that I use is to combine three different elements. Firstly, a structured questioning about the details of the baby's timetable: as I ask for the precise details of day and night, a vivid picture builds up in my mind of what actually happens in this family and their assumptions of what should happen. My mental picture also involves the physical placing of cots and beds and the permutations of who sleeps with whom and in which room. The questions themselves sometimes begin to clarify a confused situation as the parents both inform me and think about the logical connections of the questions. Secondly, a free-ranging enquiry into memories of the pregnancy, birth and early weeks: I tell parents that I need to know the baby's life-story to make sense of what is happening now. Thirdly, I ask questions about the parents' relationship with each other and with their own parents, so that we see the family context of this particular baby.

I start by letting parents tell me in their own way what the problem is, so that I do not lose the particular flavour of what they feel is the problem and its origin and also do not lose the chance to experience the predominant emotion with which parents begin their story. Once I have begun to ask questions, I am perhaps felt to be looking after them and intense emotions often subside. Whatever emotion comes out strongly in these first few moments is perhaps the same as what the baby feels is directed towards him during his sleepless nights, be it anger, anxiety or responsible concern. After the parents have told me the problem, I explain that I would like to ask them questions about the baby and the family in general, so that we can discover what links there may be. I start with questions of detail and then feel free to get into the general area of family relationships. (In later chapters I describe how these connect with the problem.) In every interview I have in mind a very specific body of information that I wish to collect. However, no two interviews are in any way the same. The order and the nature of my questions are always different, dependent, I hope, on my beginning to pick up the special and unique links in each family's story.

Who actually comes to the first interview varies. I always invite both parents to come, with their baby. If there is a good marriage, it does not seem to matter particularly for the effectiveness of the work whether Mother comes alone or whether both parents do. Most parents naturally bring the baby along with them. If not, I always ask to see the baby on the next occasion. It not only adds greatly to the information for me to see how mothers, fathers and babies interact with each other, as well as listening to what is reported, but as the work progresses it is *about* this interaction. Mothers are the ones who usually bring their children to the Child Health Clinic for routine check-ups. It often seems natural to them to come alone with the baby in the first place and bring their husband along the next time, if I have made enough sense to them in the first encounter!

The parents I see have usually been offered much advice already and often feel they have 'tried everything'. What I give them in the first place is simple – the ordinary psychoanalytic free-floating attention. As they tell their story, unconscious threads draw together and connections emerge. Because I do not at once offer solutions, they are less likely to react negatively. They are left able to free associate, that is, let their minds lead freely from one related theme to another. They may perceive me as interested, receptive and capable of holding on to a great deal of information. In this setting it is striking how parents can convey economically much focused information. It seems as though all ordinary parents have a 'story' to tell about their baby as dramatic and moving as any work of literature. What is also communicated, and confirmed by my interest, is the uniqueness of each baby and its family.

As this story unfolds, themes emerge about the nature of the family's relationships. For instance, the meaning of not sleeping may change with the age of the child. But underlying it at every stage seems always to be some aspect of the problem of separation and individuation between mother and baby, with feeding and weaning problems closely related.

SEPARATION PROBLEMS

Simplistically speaking, the problem for a mother in getting a baby to sleep is the basic act of putting the baby down, that is, of separating herself from her baby and the baby from her. Joyce McDougall (1974) describes how a baby needs to come to terms with the loss of the breast-mother and 'create psychic objects which will compensate for his loss'. His capacity to do this will be circumscribed by his parents' unconscious fears and desires. Through over-identification many parents tend to spare their children 'the inevitable confrontation with reality . . . The anxieties to which this primal separation give rise are usually qualified by terms such as annihilation and disintegration' (p. 438).

22

This conjures up for us powerful images of psychic processes. The consultations in which parents relate to me the details of their confused nights of wakings and feedings are a live illustration of the disintegration McDougall refers to. The fragmented experience which is conveyed to me starts to come together, as I listen to these details and make a more integrated pattern of them, initially within my own mind.

One extreme example illustrates this. The mother of Barnaby, aged four, and Clare, aged six months, had consulted many doctors, homeopathic practitioners, and so on, about many different complaints in herself and her children. She came in great distress about both children's sleeping problems. She talked non-stop about her many attempts to get help for this multitude of complaints and her confusion about what to attend to first. There was no dialogue between us and ten minutes before the end of the session I stopped her to point out that she was leaving no time for *me* to talk. I then said that I had had two thoughts while she was talking. One was that it was very difficult to bring up children. The second was that she had consulted many professionals and that they had all got it wrong for her.

This mother was very taken by these thoughts. Because I offered no advice, I was in no danger of getting it wrong myself! More seriously I had recognized that, full as she was with her many conflicting anxieties, she had no space to let in yet another opinion. The next week she brought her husband and both told me, very painfully, of their own difficult childhoods. I remarked that, as well as leaving them unsure of their individual ability as parents, their different childhood experiences had given them conflicting ideas of how to be parents and they had reinforced these with the contradictory ideas that they had sought and elicited from the many professionals they had consulted.

Thinking about this enabled both to be more effective with their older child. Barnaby's alarming temper tantrums went within the next week and his sleep problems slightly improved. Their attention then turned to the baby, Clare, who was waking frequently during the night and needing to be breast-fed by Mother. They repeatedly asked me, 'Should we leave her to cry?'

I described how there seemed to be no idea of any middle way between going to her every time and absolutely abandoning her. They then asked if it would make her feel insecure and damage her if she was left for a while. I said that perhaps we could turn the question around and think about how insecure it would make Clare feel if she thought that they *had* to come in to her every time she called out – that they could not trust her to manage for a while on her own and that they could not trust their love and care for her to carry on for a while from the last feed. The parents knew that this reversal of mine was not superficial and 'gimmicky' – that I had been moved by their accounts of their own childhood insecurity and that I knew they felt damaged by it. While seriously keeping in mind the dangers of insecurity, I was able to suggest that Clare's position was not the same as theirs – with two loving parents safely at hand *her* need was to experience herself as *separate* from them. They reported that when she cried they no longer went in, picked her up and fed her. Each time she cried they now would call out to her or go in and talk to her briefly, telling her to go to sleep. They said that her cries no longer sounded 'frantic'; they were 'indignant' or 'complaining' or 'sorrowful'. Having thought about the meaning of Clare's cries, they then perceived the sound of them differently and were then also able to respond to them less frantically.

Barnaby and Clare's parents found the three or four consultations they had with me helpful; both children were happier and slept better. What made the difference? My choice of this family as the first clinical example in the book comes from two elements in the work: firstly, that it was overwhelmingly evident that the parents' own past childhood experience underlay their present problem in handling their children; secondly, that they asked a question, 'Should we leave her to cry?', that seemed to call irresistibly for a straight answer. In the response to such a question we have the ideal chance to examine the differentiation and the common ground between myself and behaviour management colleagues who give more specific advice than I usually do.

COMPARISONS WITH BEHAVIOURAL WORK

Those who have well-structured programmes for parents to follow are of course also interested in and respectful of the relationships and situations of the families who consult them. But they may also be careful to define a cut-off point. For instance, Douglas and Richman suggest:

> In practice we have found that generally it is not useful to delve back into the past or into the parents' or the child's psyche to find out the cause of a sleep problem. It is more profitable to concentrate on the here and now of how parents are responding

at night-time and how that might affect the sleep pattern. (1984, p. 47)

It seems from this that professionals may feel reticent about going too far into a family's privacy and that too much attention to the family's history is intrusive and not particularly relevant. I do not think this is quite right, and that in fact there is a deep human need to be known about and understood. Sleep problems may often arise when families are having difficulty in straightforwardly understanding and responding to each other. Even brief work where families are really listened to may enable them to feel that something crucial about them has been understood. They may then be better able to understand and respond to each other.

From informal comparisons I gather that my own results in helping babies to sleep better, taken from the family's expressed satisfaction or otherwise, are similar to those of other workers. My impression is that in half of all referrals there is a noticeable improvement in the baby's sleep. I hope in future work to describe these results accurately. So far I have taken into account improvement claimed by the family to have happened at the time of the end of treatment. However, in taking this further and looking at whether improvements are held over to, for example, the year following treatment, complications arise. Two opposing factors must be taken into account: firstly, that many sleep problems 'cure' themselves over time without treatment; secondly, that new stages of development in babies may lead to difficulties in sleeping. For any method of treatment it therefore needs to be considered how much 'success' at the time should be held to imply non-recurrence of the problem.

In comparing differing methods it is interesting to speculate whether parents who are determined that they will solve the problem *now* can use whatever method is confidently offered or whether one method suits the personalities and needs of some families better. Several times I have seen parents who have previously had some behaviour management counselling and have then complained to me, 'They just told us what to do; they didn't *listen* to what *our* problem was'; but I suspect that as many parents have travelled in the opposite direction, complaining of me, 'She wouldn't give us any proper advice; she kept on asking us questions about ourselves'.

A psychotherapeutic method allows parents to work out for themselves important elements in their emotional relationship with their child. It seems that this might also help them deal with future problems. Behavioural work has equal, perhaps greater, success in alleviation of the problem, but less gain for the families in under-standing for themselves the psychological process involved and in thinking about the origins of the disturbance. There are diagnostic implications here in assessing which families are able and willing to take the responsibility for thinking about their family dynamics and which are not.

Here I must declare my debt to behaviour modifiers and the thought that they have put into the many questions that parents bring, such as, 'Should we leave her to cry?'. Douglas and Richman (1984), Richard Ferber (1985a) and Marc Weissbluth (1987b) are among those who have clarified very well the different aspects of sleep problems and management techniques for solving these problems. Ferber's chapter, 'What your child associates with falling asleep', is an extremely helpful exploration of both problem and solution. Richman (1981a,b) makes a useful differentiation between the causes of the sleep problem and the parental manage-ment which maintains it. Behavioural management addresses itself to this prolongation of a problem that no longer has a dynamic meaning for the child and its family.

What most workers in this field have in common is struggling with the essence of what a baby's waking and crying means in terms of expression of need and as a communication to his parents. What is less thought about is the way parents' hearing of their baby's crying is influenced by their own early experiences. Thus, 'Should you leave a baby to cry?' may in the first instance mean, 'Should I have been left to cry?'. The first consultation may, indeed, be a testing of how the therapist, of whatever orientation, listens and takes seriously the 'cries' of the family as a whole for some under-standing. The urgency of a baby's cries may stir up memories of similar infantile feelings of desperation in the parents themselves which then render them incapable of acting as adult, competent parents. They identify with the baby's cries and are powerless to change them.

All therapists are, then, faced with the problem of how to help parents use their adult competence to face their baby's cries. My colleague Juliet Hopkins has pointed out (personal communica-tion, 1986) that the parents who consult about these problems are the ones who do listen to their baby's cries. It is in fact one of the satisfactions of this work that although parents are often desperate, confused and angry about the problems they come with, they are concerned parents. Those who without a qualm can put their baby to cry itself to sleep in a room out of earshot and not notice whether there is a problem are by definition not the ones who consult us in this way.

It is, then, necessary to look at the mixture of both relief and antipathy with which we ourselves, or the parents we work with, may greet advice which includes the concrete suggestion of leaving a baby to cry. The apparently simple question, 'Should you leave a baby to cry?', contains parents' agonizing and deeply felt doubts about whether their impulses are in fact cruel and sadistic. When their own desperate feelings have been thought about, they may also, like Clare's parents, hear the baby's cries as being less frantic.

Behaviour management techniques also deal with parents' fears at this level by giving firm, sensible advice which tells them what is acceptable behaviour towards little children and what is not and in this way enables some parents to use their common sense with their children. However, it is also necessary to evaluate the logic behind these techniques. Among behaviour modifiers there is considerable debate about different methods. Douglas and Richman (1984), for example, suggest letting a baby cry without picking him up, but also emphasize the importance of checking on him and reassuring him of the parents' presence.

Weissbluth (1987b) dismisses this checking as delaying the resolution of the problem and advocates leaving the baby alone until he falls asleep, citing many successful examples. His reasoning is that the baby quickly 'learns' to fall asleep and stay asleep and that the baby's ability to sleep in itself improves the relationship between parents and babies. However, in looking at this method we can see that it does not address itself to the underlying relationship, although the change in the baby's behaviour may be a relief to all. Parents are switching from too much response to their baby to apparently none at all. Such an abrupt change of tactic could seem in itself as irrational as the previous practice. By contrast, with Douglas and Richman's technique, where the parents remain near and responsive, the parents can be said to remain responsible to the baby for their change in their management of him; the baby also has some choice in 'deciding' whether to go on crying, or give up and go to sleep, and is also able to express his feelings to them about what is going on. Parents and baby are able to communicate and work something out between them. Penelope Leach, in *Baby and Child*, very clearly shows the dangers of simply leaving a baby to cry without going back to reassure him.

If you did persist with this policy to a point where your child actually gave up crying when you left him you would have won your battle at a very high price. You would have convinced the child that you did not care enough about him or understood him well enough to take any notice of what he was trying to communicate to you. How can he feel like an important independent person in a world full of other important independent people if nobody listens to what he says? (1977, p. 299)

This is salutary advice, though of necessity somewhat over-simplistic. It does not take account of the ambivalent relationship which already exists between parents and children who have been listened to *too much*. Gordon Scott (1986) has a simple, direct and informative style which enables parents to work out for themselves what their problem is about and choose for themselves the strategy that might suit them best in helping to alter it.

A PARENT'S COMPARISON OF WAYS TO SOLVE THE SLEEP PROBLEM

One mother of three little girls described to me her first baby's sleep problem at five months, two months after she had returned to work. Bridget refused to settle for the first stretch of sleep in the evening before her eleven o'clock feed. Mother and Father were desperate to have their own meal and do the household chores and Mother decided to use advice from a book which according to her said, 'Let them scream'. On the first night Bridget screamed for three-quarters of an hour before falling asleep, on the second night for half an hour and on the third night for only quarter of an hour. After two or three more nights of screaming for quarter of an hour, Bridget stopped screaming and settled quickly to sleep. Mother, who had become exhausted, was relieved.

However, when her third daughter Anita also had a period of not being able to sleep, though at the later age of twelve months, Mother felt she needed very different attention. This little girl in fact used to get to sleep easily, but later woke screaming. Mother thought she suffered from nightmares and needed the reassurance and comfort of Mother's presence until she was able to fall asleep again in her cot.

It is interesting how differently this mother responded to these two babies' sleep disturbances. On the one hand she was responding intuitively to different aspects of meaning in the wakefulness of

28

the two babies. On the other, she also felt that her attitude to the younger child was coloured to some extent by what had happened between herself and the older one. Bridget's failure to go to sleep had indeed been cured very quickly, by leaving her to cry. Mother was very thankful about this at the time. She could not have coped with more disturbed evenings. Nevertheless she was left with an uneasy feeling of something unresolved between herself and Bridget, even though the 'cure' had not harmed Bridget. She was a secure little girl who coped very well with some later hospitalization, when Mother stayed with her.

The transition for the mother from having a very wakeful baby, perhaps demanding attention because of her absence at work during the day, to having a baby who went to sleep quickly was gratifying, but it was also very abrupt. It is possible that what was missing for this mother in the few days of successful action was the chance to think through the implications for her relationship with Bridget of this enormous change. Perhaps the unfinished nature of this business with Bridget was what partly led to her different treatment of Anita, besides being the appropriate response to Anita at the time.

READING BABY BOOKS – THE PITFALLS

Reading books can be extremely helpful and supportive. The limitation is that the parent/reader cannot challenge their own questions as they bring them to the books in the way that a therapist can do in an interview. The problem for parents in reading books giving advice for solving sleep problems is therefore whether the choice of what advice is taken fits in with and is reinforced by the type of child-rearing behaviour towards the child they are already using or whether they are released to try something different.

For example, Dr Benjamin Spock's (1946) advice to be sensitive to a child's needs came as a great relief to parents who had felt that earlier professional advice ignored the baby's own rhythms in favour of imposing an easily understood 'schedule' of feeding and sleeping. On the other hand Dr Spock's ideas could be interpreted by anti-authoritarian parents as a manifesto that any kind of discipline or limit-setting was bad for children. Some of these parents may have been communicating their repudiation of the authoritarian style of their own parents. What they may not have been getting any more right than their parents was a sensitive discovery of what their baby's actual needs were.

Similarly books that give very specific advice to parents about behaviour modifying schemes for getting children to sleep better may rescue some indecisive and confused parents from a feeling of not knowing what to do. The pitfall in the use of such books is when parents who are already insensitive to the meaning of their children crying use them as a charter to go on ignoring the meaning.

One mother told her health visitor that her year-old baby slept about twelve hours in the night and one or two during the day, but could not learn how to go back to sleep on his own during the night. He woke once or twice and Mother used to go in, give him a bottle, and stay till he fell asleep again. Mother had now changed to giving him the bottle and a musical toy, instead of staying with him. She next announced a further change. She said, 'Today it's going to be a traumatic day', because she would not give him the bottle any more. She would leave him just with the toy. She predicted that the baby would start screaming and she would come up after five minutes to stay with him. The next day she would come after ten minutes of crying. After a couple of weeks he would get used to it and not need Mother or bottle to help get him back to sleep. Mother then showed the health visitor the advice book she was using, looked through it and said to the baby, 'You need a transitional object', and handed the baby several different soft toys. The baby wasn't interested and reached for Mother's book and she then fetched him two of his own books instead.

In this account we see how a mother has decided to change the baby's behaviour without, apparently, any curiosity as to *why* the baby was still waking up in the night. At any rate she did not pass on any such speculation to the health visitor. It may well be that, for whatever reason the baby was waking, both Mother and baby were better served by an unbroken night's sleep, but even so one element would still be missing – Mother's *understanding* of the baby's waking, even while communicating that she was not prepared to tolerate it.

It was interesting that when Mother had an 'intellectual' idea that the baby needed a transitional object and artificially produced one, it did not work. However, she was sensitive to the baby showing her that the book Mother was using herself was important to him. Mother then brought the baby his own books. It may well be that the books did have a real transitional significance for the baby and as something connected with his mother were satisfying to him. This is what the essential nature of the transitional object involves; it is to do with an idea and memory of being with the mother that then enables the baby to be apart from the mother. This concept, developed by Winnicott, is described more fully in Chapter 7.

Looking at this moment of sensitivity by the mother, we see highlighted why she had felt that the day of withholding the bottle completely would be traumatic. The plan to remove the bottle from the baby, and hence remove the need for Mother to come in the night to supply it, seemed to be based *only* on the belief that the baby could manage on his own. Mother was expressing no satisfaction at what she and the baby had achieved together in the mutual feeding relationship: nor was she expressing regret that she and the baby might be losing something between them. Moreover there was no suggestion from Mother that the bottle itself might already have been partly a transitional object for the baby.

HOW PARENTS USE ADVICE

Psychoanalytic work allows parents to put into words their conflicts about what to do and how to listen to the advice given to them. It may take such parents further in gaining mastery over their fears of sadism and violence towards their children, by putting into words the feelings evoked by their baby crying. Paradoxically it is sometimes those parents who seem most inept and unable to set any limits who are most afraid that firmness might lead to cruelty. It is always vital to clarify what they are afraid of doing. Uninformed reassurance can be really dangerous. It can seem to troubled parents like a validation of their cruelty (which had not been recognized by the therapist) and might lead to them acting it out either passively, by leaving the baby for long periods, or actively, by physical means such as hitting or shaking.

Advice on bringing up children has always swung from one extreme to another, but no one is obliged to take it. It is therefore illuminating to look at the taking or ignoring of advice as an aspect of projection of the unwanted qualities of the self, such as cruelty. For example, getting a professional to recommend leaving a baby to cry is a way of getting someone else to take responsibility for worries about whether this is a cruel way of dealing with a baby. The parent is then free either to follow the advice without owning it or to repudiate it, attributing such advice to others and perhaps only looking at it in terms of cruelty and not, as in some contexts, useful firmness. In extreme cases parents can project their own unacknowledged aggression so effectively that the professional's own aggression is stirred up and advice is given that does involve cruel or insensitive behaviour towards the baby.

Selma Fraiberg's thoughts about parents looking at their own traumatic experiences are useful here: 'It is the parent who cannot remember his childhood feelings of pain and anxiety who will need to inflict his pain upon his child' (1980, p. 182). She describes how bringing the *feelings* connected with experience, not just the experiences themselves, back into conscious memory can break the chain of ill-treatment.

Whenever an apparently innocuous question by a parent is posed of whether to be more or less firm with a child, it is essential to think, 'Firmer than what?', that is, in what context is the question being asked? Surprisingly often some cruelty or neglect in the parents' own background is waiting to be revealed. But the telling of this is only the start. Is it the parents' hope that the therapist will condemn this cruelty, or collude with it and insist on repeating it, or dismiss it as irrelevant to present matters? All this has to be clarified. It need not be a lengthy business. These dilemmas have been carried around since childhood, but the therapist does not need to *solve* the problem for parents. Putting the present problem in its context may be enough to enable parents to go away and start thinking about it for themselves, possibly finding that other ways of dealing with the child have become open to them.

Taking these dilemmas one generation further, we see how children themselves, either as babies or later on in childhood, may have difficulty in knowing whether their parents have behaved cruelly to them or not. Juliet Hopkins (1986) describes how they have neither the experience nor the objectivity to evaluate their parents' behaviour towards them. It can be difficult to discriminate between their own impulses towards their parents, their perception of their parents and the real behaviour of the parents. It can take much effort in later life to sort this out.

THE CLINICAL SETTING

When working in a general practice baby clinic, referrals come to me from doctors and health visitors. They may have known about the problem for some time and been working with it. Many such problems are in any case transitory; my colleagues usually consider a referral to me for some time, so as not to hand on the family prematurely. There may be a moment, with or without this background knowledge of the problem, when the doctor or health visitor realizes that the family is desperate. Even so, when I am told about it, I do not usually feel that I should see the family immediately. A gap of a few days, knowing that they have an appointment, enables parents to think through the problem and come perhaps with a balance of vulnerability and defence, so that they can work with me as their adult parent selves, as well as convey to me some of their infantile desperation.

I do not find it helpful for parents to come to me the first time with a written chart of their baby's sleeping and wakings. This could detract from the impact of the 'evidence'. In behaviour management making such charts can be a first stage in dealing with the chaos in the family. But I prefer to meet the family first in their state of chaos in order to be able to comment on it and think about the implications of this state. It is, however, then vital to start making a structure from the information they bring, though one that connects with emotions. As mentioned already, I go meticulously through the details of what happens day and night with the baby and often take notes of such details in front of the family. Families may also wish to write things down between our meetings. These notes are sometimes the only way the family and I can remember, in later weeks, exactly how things were before and by what stages changes have been made. Otherwise it can be hard to retain more than an impressionistic memory of the original situation.

PARENTS' USE OF THE THERAPIST

I do not usually comment on my use for parents in the sessions; I take for granted that I am doing a kind of parenting to them by my interested listening. Perhaps I am a combined parental figure, providing what could be described in a shorthand way as 'maternal' receptivity and 'paternal' limit-setting. At other times it does seem necessary for me to spell out what is happening between us. I am more likely to do this with sceptical and hostile parents, where I may point out how little expectation of help from me they seem to have. Sometimes they will then link this to experiences with their own parents. With Simon's parents, as described in Chapter 9, it seemed necessary for anger to be experienced by parents and child towards me (and felt by me towards them) before anger could be comfortably dealt with in the family and the parents be freed to be ordinarily angry and firm with Simon.

The length of treatment may be an important issue in a situation where parents use my support to take bold steps in separating from their child. They may wish me to remain with them – feeling they can manage new phases in their relationships only if this support remains. In work which is intended to be brief this can indeed be a problem. One mother decided she no longer needed to take tranquillizers after I offered her some weekly sessions. This was a brave decision, but we needed to discuss whether the weekly times with me might become as addictive as she had feared the medication would be. Just as babies' use of their mothers can be addictive (see Chapter 12), so there was a danger that this mother might need my continuing presence instead of being able to take away for herself the new ideas we had worked out together.

The nature of the problem can influence the parent's use of the therapist when, for example, there is an acute weaning problem and difficulty in separation. A mother's inability to say 'no' to her baby and her constant fitting in with his demands may be passed on as an expectation of how the therapist should behave towards mother and baby, that is, that she should fit in with them. One such mother was feeding her one-year-old baby constantly, night and day. She felt he could not stand it if his needs were not attended to at once. She herself was unusually specific about what times she could manage to see me and when she could not, although she was not working. I found myself feeling very unreasonable in not making special arrangements for her, until I saw these demands as a communication to me of what was going on between the baby and herself, that is, she was fitting in with his unreasonable demands as well as with his appropriate ones.

It will have become clear that I generally do this particular kind of work on my own. Working with a colleague changes the situation for both families and myself and has, as one might expect, both advantages and disadvantages. What is gained is another mind, another set of thoughts about a problem, someone who may see through one's blind spots. The co-worker can be a support to the therapist or help the family feel better looked after by a couple that is in some ways analogous to a parental couple. The loss is, however, serious. It can be harder for two people to pick up the unconscious links that are emerging from material. Simply by being different, a second person may pick up different, just as valid, themes, but in doing so may cut through the unfolding of something else. The delicate business of putting everything together in the therapist's mind is perhaps impaired by having two minds at work. One solution to these dilemmas is for the co-worker to be present mainly as an observer in the first meeting, joining in enough to prevent the awkwardness of being a totally silent presence, saying enough for the family to have a sense of who this person in the room is, but not cutting across the train of thought of the active therapist. This usually leads naturally on to the co-worker becoming active in later sessions. Such a method has great advantages for therapists training to do this kind of work.

SIGNALS WITHIN THE FAMILY

Returning to individual work, one essential factor is to pick up parents' feelings that I am being critical of them. This may come up in a reverse way, that is, *they* are critical of *my* way of looking at their problems. These feelings influence me when I wonder how much to tell parents of what I observe going on between them and their child in the room at the time. It can be useful to show parents ways in which they have got stuck in interpreting their children's signals or it can be persecuting. It is sometimes hard to know beforehand how it will sound when put into words.

One mother came to me, complaining that her two-year-old daughter would not sleep and whined all day. She could not stand it any longer. Mother said all this herself in an irritated moan. I took my courage in both hands and commented on her way of talking, adding that Mother and the child were looking at each other with equally disagreeable expressions. At the end of the hour I asked Mother, rather doubtfully, if she would like another appointment; she said she would and I anticipated another hour of moaning. But both came next week, bright and smiling, and Mother said how much better she felt. It seemed as though my remarks were experienced as a willingness to take on her dis-agreeableness. She started to tell me about her low opinion of herself and her capabilities. Over the next few weeks she was able to get a part-time job and to start losing weight. As her self-esteem rose, she became more confident in her mothering; she and her daughter had happier times together and could sort out bedtime problems more freely.

Less successful was my attempt to show another mother whose child woke frequently in the night how I felt she misunderstood his signals. This fourteen-month-old little boy, John, fell as he explored my room. Mother swooped on him and picked him up with loud shrieks, before John himself had made any sound. John considered for a moment and responded by shrieking too. It seemed to me that John had neither been given time to work out his own reaction to his fall nor had any chance to deal with it himself. I thought it likely that something similar happened in the night, with Mother reacting immediately to any sound or stirring from John, before really knowing that the sounds were a communication to her to come to him.

I commented to Mother on the sequence I had observed and realized I had offended her; the rest of the session did not go well. I told the health visitor of my tactlessness and she reported John's mother as saying that I had told her off. The health visitor advised her (and presumably me!) to give it another try. Next week during our meeting John fell again. Mother said nothing. John looked around in surprise, waited and came to me for a response. Mother looked 'daggers' at me. I decided this was one family I was not going to be in tune with.

Equally daunting was Kevin's mother. She was a single mother with a two-year-old, Kevin; he had a one-year-old brother and she was again pregnant. Kevin woke frequently during the night. She and Kevin came into the room and Kevin jumped on a chair. Mother told him not to. I said I did not mind and Mother explained that if he jumped on the sofa at home, he could fall out of the window. I agreed that this was a serious matter and offered to fetch Kevin some more toys. Mother said, 'That's all right, he can jump on the furniture.' Kevin jumped and Mother said, 'Don't jump on the furniture.'

Surprisingly perhaps, this mother was quite happy for me to tell her how confusing I, and presumably Kevin, found this sequence and to connect it with what might be happening at night. With this 'double-bind' in force Kevin would be very unsure of whether he was supposed to stay in his bed or not. Mother, Kevin and his little brother came for several weeks; we played and talked together; Mother joined in and followed the children's play and both children became able to concentrate better. Unhappily this brief work was not enough – it did not last outside the room, life at home was still chaotic and Mother did not feel able to accept the offer of a place in a Young Family Centre for long-term supportive work with her and the children.

What these last three families had in common was a misunderstanding or confusion about how to use signals among themselves and what to do with negative feelings about them. With the first family my interest in them was enough to allow them all to make pleasanter allowances for each other; in the second the mother's misunderstanding of her son was compounded by her feeling that I also misunderstood *her*. In the third case there was a feeling that I sympathetically understood the confusion, though this was unfortunately not enough to change anything.

The common element in my work with all three families was the attempt to enable the mother to observe the baby and her own responses to it. This can be supportive, when a mother is helped to see the meaning of the baby's cries and is gratified by discovering her own response to them; some mothers even lack basic reassurance that their babies need and appreciate them. However, for some mothers it seems that the very acknowledgement of the baby's needs reinforces the problem. Mothers who have already felt alarmed by the life and death quality of an infant's basic needs, or by the strength of his emotional expression of them, will be additionally persecuted by having this pointed out. In such cases the brief work described here may not be appropriate.

Main *et al.* (1985) have shown how secure adults are able to perceive their baby's signals; insecure ones need to ignore them. Being unwillingly made to perceive a baby's signals may thus interfere with the parents' defensive attempts not to look at issues of dependence, so very painful in their own backgrounds. An important consequence of looking at the meaning of behaviour between parents and baby during the meetings with me is that the parents also have the chance to start sorting out what goes on between themselves and their baby during the day. This can then carry over into a better understanding of each other during the night. Difficulties in relationships may seem manageable during the day but quite out of control at night. The greater ability to think things through during the day, including during our meetings, may then be able to influence the nights.

Other workers confirm some of the elements I have found to be part of the consultations. Lozoff *et al.* (1985), studying the correlation between sleep problems and other disturbances in family life, reported: 'We had the impression that the interview itself was therapeutic for some mothers, as they reflected on their child's behaviour and family circumstances' (p. 482). Guedeney and Kreisler (1987) have noted how work with parents and child together brings out connections in their emotional states of being. These connections are also noted by Serge Lebovici (1980), who says that the consultation in the presence of the child allows elements of the mother's infantile neurosis to appear much more easily than in a more usual setting.

Guedeney and Kreisler notice (p. 316) three parts to their investigations: the child's activity, the mother's attitude and language and the interaction between mother and child. The investigator tries to correlate the emotional tone of what the mother says with the interaction observed in the room. In this context it is specially interesting to observe, if the baby shows his need to sleep during the interview, whether he fails or succeeds in getting to sleep. This is a privileged moment for seeing behaviour, affect and fantasy interact; it is easy to see that the investigator could be experienced as intrusive at such a time and Guedeney and Kreisler emphasize the need to be tactful.

Equally interesting is what happens when the baby starts to cry during the session. As Lebovici suggests, perhaps some of the mother's own infantile feelings are expressed through her baby's cries. Often babies, apparently too young to understand the actual words, cry as parents talk about traumatic events in their own lives. I have noticed, for instance, that babies cry as parents talk about difficulties in their marriage. Following from this, we might think that at times a baby's crying in the night is connected with such feelings in the mother or, at any rate, that the mother's inability to comfort the crying baby comes from unresolved grief of her own.

Babies may cry when their mothers would like to escape from the discussion. It often happens that babies cry and their mothers stand up to go at moments of looking at painful matters. Sometimes I think this is to spare *me* the impact of the painful subject. When I describe some of these possibilities, and suggest that we continue, many mothers are relieved and are able to console the baby enough for us to hear ourselves speak. Such an incident may also be an insight into a mother's use of her relationship with her baby as an escape from working out painful issues either in her marriage or in her own history.

Attunement and the failure of it is, indeed, one of the themes of the book. In fact the hard work of this method of therapy comes from the need for the therapist to be in touch appropriately with each set of individuals. In order to change something, it is first necessary to know what it is. A family comes in a certain state of mind about their child and his sleep problem. It is necessary for the worker to know and be in touch with this state of mind without also feeling that his own is the same as theirs.

THE ATMOSPHERE OF THE CONSULTATIONS

The worker who offers this receptivity is assailed by a jumble of information, emotion and memories. At first I thought of this bombardment as just an unfortunate way of behaving by people who are short of sleep. Ernest Hartmann (whose work is discussed in Chapter 4) states that 'sleep, and probably D sleep [rapid eye-movement sleep] specifically, may have a restorative function with respect to symptoms of focused attention (especially the ability to focus on one item while ignoring others)' (1973, p. 147), and from this we would expect parents deprived by their babies of sleep to be short of such attributes. In time, however, I came to recognize such 'bombardment' consultations as being often the ones that promised most resolution. It requires the use of another set of ideas to understand how this comes about.

Looking ahead to Chapter 6 on dreams and Stanley Palombo's (1978) description of the function of dreams as assimilating memories of the day into settled long-term memory, I see one of the main uses of the consultation as being akin to dream-work. For parents nearly always come in a distressed state, with a confused mass of information. What happens in the dream-work by the process of assimilation also happens in my consultations with parents: the scattered information they bring to me is brought together during the consultation. The essential ingredient, I believe, is that the information has to be integrated in my mind for the process to happen in the parents' minds also. I cannot just politely listen while they do the putting together.

Main *et al.* (1985) have shrewdly noticed that the manner in which parents talk about their relationships with their own parents enables prediction of how they get on with their babies. They describe how parents who are themselves insecure are 'incoherent' in talking about their childhood experiences. I think that what Main *et al.* have observed about their manner of talking is a facet of what I see as the confused and jumbled way parents bring their experiences to the consultation.

As well as including a mass of information, the sessions are usually very lively. Babies cry, toddlers have to be taken to the lavatory, turn lights on and off, threaten to put their fingers in electric sockets. There is ample opportunity for families to show as well as describe how they deal with difficult situations. But what usually comes across is the parents' sense of freedom to look at this present problem of a baby who cannot sleep across barriers of painful memories of all kinds. Many mothers cry as they describe the birth of their baby. They cry as they remember moments of pain, humiliation, relief and joy. Sometimes I am shocked to find answering tears in my own eyes as I listen, but at the same time there is a moment of knowing that real emotion has been recollected and connected with the present. I have then been entrusted with knowing about the depth of feeling between parents and baby, however well or badly things might have gone.

If there is no 'flash' of feeling, as Balint and Norell (1973) describe the exchange between doctor and patient when something important is communicated, I am doubtful that anything will happen in the interview. One mother came, having recently taken her daughter into hospital, complaining that she could not cope with the baby's sleeplessness. The hospital had kept the baby a couple of days and sent her home again. Mother came to see me, looking worried and tense. She had no story to pour out and answered my questions dutifully, describing pregnancy and birth blankly. When I asked her about holding the baby for the first time, I again got a non-committal reply. When I said, 'Can you remember the first time she looked at you?', Mother's face lit up in a smile. Suddenly she *was* remembering. This baby, who had become a worrying, persecuting problem, connected for a moment with the baby who had first looked at her mother at a few minutes old. The memory of this first interchange produced a brief contact with me, although it soon faded and this mother did not come to see me again.

As with all infant–parent work one of the main aims is to help parents see their babies more clearly, to look at them without the misconceptions that misreading signals or re-creating old relationships have led to.

Parents need to talk about themselves, their marriage, their childhood, their jobs, even why they feel their problems are the fault of their mother-in-law or their neighbours. When they feel I am really in touch I may be told a dream, as a way of acknowledging that what goes on in their own minds, conscious and unconscious, connects with their baby's mind. One father dreamt that his not-yet-talking son said to him, 'Why don't you show me how to get to sleep?' We will see in Chapter 6 how much thought this one-liner opened up.

THE BABY'S PHYSICAL SETTING AT HOME

As well as looking at the complexities of the family relationships, the actual physical details of the problem, plus the parents' attempt to solve it, have to be gone into in detail. Indeed one of the pleasures of the work is the problem-solving within a framework of physical objects and limitations – beds, cots, rooms, bath times – and the range of behaviours and activities that any set of parents feel is possible for them – lights on or off, doors open or closed, the availability of teddies, books, musical toys.

The way in which physical objects are described reflects the quality of the emotional relationships between parents and baby. If these are going reasonably well, parents treasure even their baby's clothes and blankets. Feelings about them spring from their feelings about the body they cover. Parents, of course, know minutely, and see meaning in, the baby's expressions and gestures and they 'know' what is in their baby's mind. Following from this, the baby's toys are imbued for the parent with the meaning they have for the baby. I in turn picture all this vividly. Parenthood thus involves enjoying and being utterly involved with small objects and routinely performed actions. Similarly it is necessary for me to have a mental involvement with the minutiae of what I am told of all this. Because I hear so many different versions, I am also aware of what is missing, of parents who are unable to create a routine or furnish their baby's environment with objects. I am then alerted to look at where this lack comes from, although I do not rush in to supply what is missing with my suggestions.

METHODS OF GETTING A BABY TO SLEEP

Barnaby and Clare's parents were quite typical, when they told me how many different methods for handling their children they had used. They had tried so many ways, received so much advice and none of it had worked.

Moore and Ucko (1957) show in their study that 'the group that received variable handling contains a significantly higher proportion of chronically waking babies'. They go on to suggest:

> While some of the wakefulness of [this] group may be attributed directly to inconsistent handling, which gives a child no firm basis on which to establish a regular sleeping rhythm, there may, too, be an indirect effect in that rapid shifts from method to method can be one expression of maternal anxiety, which probably communicates itself to the child through stresses and tensions during nursing, or in other ways, thereby affecting his ability to relax and sleep soundly. It must, however, be considered only rational in the parents of a persistently wakeful child to try a variety of methods. (p. 340)

The trying of many methods is often the background of parents who consult me. One result of this is that cause and effect may have got thoroughly blurred. Parents can't always remember where they have started from to see whether something new makes a difference. One strength of behavioural technique is the way it can be helpful in sorting out the logic of making any change, in a way that parents can understand.

Another strength comes from looking at how one kind of behaviour by the baby links with another. For example, Paret (1983), in a study of both waking and sleeping babies, shows that wakers could fall asleep only while being moved, held or rocked. In one sample ten of the eleven babies in the waking groups could not be put down in their cribs until they were already asleep, whereas only one of the nineteen good sleepers was rocked or moved to sleep (p. 174). Here we have some objective data showing that behaviour intended to help a baby sleep, that is, holding him until he falls asleep, does not also help him to stay asleep.

What difference does knowing this make to therapeutic work? I do in fact tell parents of this kind of connection and the conclusions it leads to. In particular Ferber (1985a) describes how a baby who falls asleep having been put into his cot awake then has the means to get himself to sleep again when he wakes up later. This is soundly-based, logical information and is useful, both for its own sake and also in the context of looking at the assumptions that have led up to whatever practice the parents have adopted, and now feel to be unsuccessful, and their doubts and fears about trying other methods. As we will see in later chapters, these assumptions might involve the mother's ability to permit the baby to reduce his dependence on her and have other forms of gratification instead.

An important aspect of family consultations is of course the presence of the baby or small child. This provides the invaluable opportunity to see how the members actually interact with each other. Not to be underestimated is the direct effect on the child of listening to the conversation. In fraught mother–baby relationships quite a small baby can appear to be responding to the therapist's attempts to 'hold' the mother and baby couple (Juliet Hopkins, personal communication, 1986). It is easily apparent that older children are listening and making use of the issues discussed.

One three-year-old, who according to his parents had never been able to settle easily to sleep, said on the evening after the family's first visit to me, 'The lady said I have to go sleep', and asked to be put to bed. It is touching that this little boy needed this simple 'instruction' so much that he had abstracted it from the conversation; I had not in fact directly addressed him in this way. What it allowed, in the following meetings, was a look at the dynamics of

42

why the parents themselves had been unable to supply this much-needed, simple precept to their son and had had to invoke my help.

In another example, also of a three-year-old boy, Terry, the parents told me that he had never slept well and had screamed for hours from the day he was brought home from hospital. Mother cried as she told me the details of his difficult birth and the fears she had had that, firstly, he would die and, secondly, that he was brain-damaged. (We will see in Chapter 7 the frequent connections between birth difficulties and sleep problems.) Three times during the account Terry asked to go to the toilet and three times his father anxiously took him. On the second and third occasions I commented on the fact that painful things were being talked about when Terry asked to go out. I was not meaning that he ought to stay in the room, but that his parents could start considering whether or not it would be helpful to Terry to hear his mother's fears about him openly stated. Meanwhile we had the evidence that Father's first instinctive way of helping Terry in anxious situations was to allow him a change of scene, not try to hold him in one place. The immediacy of this, happening in the room, adds greatly to the picture of what happens in another place and another time, that is, at home at night when Terry cannot settle down to sleep. We see also in this family a vignette of one constellation of relationships. A vital aspect of the father's role is how much he is able to limit a mother's irrational concern about the child. This father, if any-thing, intensified the mother's concern, so there was no respite for Terry from his parents' anxieties.

One basic factor in the sleep problem is the age of the baby when the family comes to seek help; the problem is very different with a three-month-old baby or with a three-year-old child. The issues of adjusting to the life and death demands of a very new baby are different from the negotiations with an older child. As we saw earlier, Richman (1981b) has pointed out also that the origin of a problem and the forces that have maintained it as an ongoing conflict need to be disconnected. In the clinical examples illustrating each of the ensuing chapters, I hope this will be made clear.

Also of interest is the basic personality of the parents and their assumptions of what babies should be like. Joan Raphael-Leff (1983, 1986) has made an interesting distinction between types of mother. She calls them 'facilitators' and 'regulators'. In defining them she says: 'The most crucial determination is whether they instigate a routine in the daily management of the baby' (1983, p.

382). According to Raphael-Leff, the regulators have more fixed ideas about how babies should fit in with their own lives and in fact have babies with fewer sleep problems; the facilitators have more of an idea of fitting in with their babies and these babies have more sleep disturbances.

In this chapter I have suggested that a baby's sleep ability is coloured by the parents' own experience, as well as their perception of the whole question of sleeping, and I have made the hypothesis that experiences such as difficult births have a connection with sleep problems.

With most families the presumed precipitating causes of the problem happened some time ago. What is often striking is that these families have already had a chance to talk over such events. Some seem to have forgotten that they have done so. What this suggests to me is that families who have had babies in intensive care or other traumatic experiences may need the chance to talk them through again at different moments in their baby's development. The continuance of a severe sleep or other emotional problem does not mean that talking through a difficult birth early on has not been helpful, but that it needs to be talked about again at different moments of the baby's continued survival and also needs to be talked about in the context of the parents' own childhood experience before it can be thoroughly dealt with.

One factor in perpetuating a family's apparent need for outside help may be that one vital element has not yet been taken up by any of the professionals prepared to listen. One such element may be anger with professionals for what has gone wrong at the birth or some other time and furthermore this anger may be displaced outside because of the parents' unbearable feeling of responsibility. A parent told me with scorn of all the advice doctors and health visitors had given her for her three-month-old son Patrick's acute colic. I said she did not seem to expect anything better from me. It took two or three meetings before I was able to show how she trapped unwary doctors into giving opinions that she could 'prove' did not work. This made sense, as she saw how it connected with her feelings towards me. There may also be anger with parents' own parents for not being more supportive during a traumatic time. In the logic of the unconscious, if the parents feel responsible for the difficulties with their own baby, then *their* parents must be equally responsible for what has gone wrong for them. Such 'irrational' connections do not often get put into words, but continue as a reproach. Parents go on perpetuating a communication that someone has got it wrong, which wears out professionals. Finding the origin of this is an enormous relief to all concerned.

Working through it, in terms of feelings towards the therapist now, also allows change to happen. Most families I see do not really need more advice. They need to look at the process by which they have found it difficult to use the advice which is freely available. Either they have felt a conflict within themselves about what to do or they have felt confused, not knowing which way to turn. In Chapter 10 we will look at the different types of childhood experience which might determine these responses.

Where simple 'advice' from me does appear to be needed, we may be seeing unparented parents needing a grandmothering view to make up for a real lack. At other times I suspect that when I am pressed to give advice, parents in conflict are trying to get me to support one parent's view against the other's, without having the conflict openly recognized.

Finally a warning: sleep problems are usually a sign of concerned parents who are perhaps just rather confused in what they want for their child; sometimes, however, they can be danger signs of disturbed or very ill parents who are unable to be appropriately in tune with their baby's need to be looked after – they must then be taken seriously as such.

CHAPTER THREE

A CASE STUDY
The Armitage Family

T HIS IS AN ACCOUNT of a family who were seen four times for their baby's sleep problem. In this time there was an improvement in the baby's sleep. The parents also used the opportunity to talk about their own family experiences. They spontaneously made connections between their own experiences and their baby's situation, though it was actually quite difficult for them to acknowledge that, in my opinion at any rate, this process was what enabled the improvement in the baby's sleep to get going. The first three times we met weekly. There was a gap of a month, while the family and then I were on holiday, before the fourth meeting.

Mrs Armitage had telephoned asking for help with her nine-month-old baby Gareth. She, her husband and Gareth came to meet Dr Julia Nelki and myself. Dr Nelki, with the family's permission, took notes during our meetings. It is important to recognize that although Dr Nelki was present initially as an observer and to record the session the family found her presence very positive. Probably they also responded to my own experience of her as supportive, although I usually work on my own.

This is a chance to see how themes emerge and develop in meetings with a family. I will give the gist of our conversations, as recorded by Dr Nelki (henceforth Dr N.); these include the remarks made at the time by her or myself to the parents. In italics are my additional thoughts, some from the time of the sessions or soon after; principally they provide an overview, connecting the material with my ideas of how the consultations worked and with theoretical ideas about some of the issues that arose.

FIRST MEETING

When we first met, Mrs Armitage was changing Gareth's nappy in the waiting-room. There was some confusion while Dr N. and I introduced ourselves and waited for the nappy-change to finish.

Mr Armitage carried Gareth, a big, alert, chubby and healthy-looking baby, down the corridor. Gareth looked and smiled at Dr N. on the walk down to my room.

As we sat down Mrs Armitage said, looking at Gareth, 'He's the naughty one.' Mr and Mrs Armitage sat down next to each other on the sofa, Mr Armitage still holding Gareth. Mrs Armitage is an attractive, dark, striking, Greek woman, her husband pale-skinned and precise in manner. Throughout the first interview Gareth sat close to his father and interacted more with him, except when fed from both breast and bottle by his mother.

Mrs Armitage began talking in a rushed and confused way about their difficulties with getting Gareth to sleep. At first it was hard to understand whether she was talking about a problem of putting him to sleep in the evening or of him waking late in the night. We gradually made clear that at this point they were talking about Gareth waking constantly, after he had got to sleep. He was at present sleeping in their room in his cot, as he needed constant reassurance. He woke every few hours and could be soothed sometimes by breast-feeding and at other times just by being cuddled.

The rushed and confused way that Mrs Armitage described the nature of the problem is a common feature in describing sleep problems. The word 'incoherence' has been used by Guedeney and Kreisler (1987) to describe these consultations. I think it is important not to interrupt this confusion too soon. Firstly, it is necessary to feel the impact of it before trying to sort it out. Starting to sort things out too soon could be experienced by the parents as an unwillingness to know the full extent of how dreadful the nights really are for them. Secondly, by listening to the emotions with which parents convey their description of the night, there is a chance to see what the baby experiences his parents as being like, when they deal with him in the night. The incoherence, anger or total loss of knowing what to do that is conveyed to the therapist as parents recall dreadful nights is likely to be a re-enactment of what they feel then.

Once this confusion and the quality of the emotions has been really registered by the therapist, it is time to ask questions so as to clarify the situation. These both highlight the fact that there is a confusion to be sorted out and also in themselves start to make some structure out of the chaos. I prefer families not to have made a chart of the baby's sleep patterns before our first meeting. It takes away some of the raw edge of experience. It is not that I want to delay the family's chance to start sorting things out for themselves, but comes from a cautionary idea that this structuring on paper might involve losing an opportunity to work out some of the meaning of the sleep disturbance. Some families, however, decide to keep a record after we have started work and this can be a very useful way of keeping straight what changes there have been. As I said earlier, it can otherwise be difficult to retain more than an impressionistic idea of what things were like before; it all gets blurred in memory.

Mr Armitage came in here, saying there was nothing at all wrong with Gareth, he was a healthy, happy boy, but could not go to sleep normally. He moans and fights sleep even if he is very tired, unless he is in motion, as when Mr Armitage walks around with him or puts him in the car and drives him around.

Here we see the initial 'fright' of parents who come to a child guidance clinic and are afraid that we will label their child as 'abnormal' or 'disturbed'. We hastened to say that one of our main functions was to help parents look at ordinary problems in their children's development. We also see here Gareth's conflict about getting to sleep and the way that being in movement does soothe him enough to get him to sleep. So far we have learnt that breast-feeding, cuddling and motion can all get him to sleep.

Mrs Armitage says that Gareth eats very well. In the preparations towards bedtime he has solids at about 5.0 p.m. and the bottle at 8.0 p.m. 'Sometimes it's like it's not enough', says Mrs Armitage. She then says that she and her husband disagreed over whether to leave him to cry or not, that Mr Armitage did not like leaving him.

I had asked Mr and Mrs Armitage to tell me first about the nature of Gareth's sleep problems and then about the routine of both day and night. Here we see that while Mrs Armitage attempts to give me an ordered account of Gareth's feeds during the day, leading up to the effect of this on his sleep, she diverts to the statement that she and her husband disagree about leaving the baby to cry. This is obviously a key issue, a major source of tension, and one we come back to during this session and in later ones.

Whether to leave a baby to cry is a major issue which we have looked at earlier. This is such a fraught subject, with so many possible interpretations of what 'leaving a baby to cry' means, before starting to think of whether or not it is an advisable thing to do, that it is no wonder parents often hold two opposing views from among the conflicting and confusing range of possibilities. For parents at odds with each other already this may be just another battleground, but for many parents this disagreement about their baby's sleep problem is stirred up by the peculiar confusions of the problem and can be an additional source of distress to them.

Gareth sat happily between Father's legs, playing with toys and keys and smiling and looking at Dr N. Mrs Armitage, a bit separate at this point from Gareth and his father, was thinking through the problem; she pulled a funny face at Gareth when he looked at her. She returned to the issue of leaving him to cry and, pointing to Mr Armitage, said, 'He can't leave him'. I asked them to tell me something of their lives, saying that we needed to understand the context of Gareth's sleep problems and that I was interested in finding out how they had all got to the present point. It was necessary at first to ask many questions, though gradually they talked more freely. They had met in England, while Mrs Armitage was on a visit. She said that although there were many children in her extended family, having her own had been very difficult and it was as if she knew nothing. She could not *talk* to her baby at first. She said twice that she had her baby 'by herself' and 'alone', although in fact her husband had been present.

> *This is the first hint that Mother has suffered by having her baby in a country away from her own family. Her own family experience – of being around small children – had, for the moment anyway, disappeared at this distance from them. Her inability to 'talk' to her baby is perhaps a sign of postnatal depression. It is also worth noting that her own language of intimacy from her childhood is not her husband's language or the language of the country she now lives in.*

The pregnancy and labour had been easy, with no problems at all. 'I saw him before you did', said Father, though Mrs Armitage held him first when he was put to the breast.

Gareth was now standing, held by Father. Mr Armitage said Gareth does not crawl but likes to be held in this standing position. He also uses the baby-walker at home.

> *I thought, but did not speak, about the possible confusing effects of baby-'walkers'. By allowing babies to move quickly across the room before they can really walk, are they having a physical experience before being psychologically ready for it? Does it take away from imagining being able to cross the room, if movement can magically be made to happen?*

'He is not very happy sitting down', said Father, adding, 'I'm speaking for him.' Apparently prompted by this Mrs Armitage said that Gareth was more like his father and that Mr Armitage chose his name. Mr Armitage said, 'I wanted a name that couldn't be shortened, not like mine.' (Gareth, of course, is not the baby's real name.)

This alerted us to thinking that Mr Armitage did not want Gareth to have some of the experiences he himself had had. Talking about the choice of name for a baby can often be a way for parents to bring in ideas about their relationship to their own families or their aspirations or fantasies about their baby before its birth.

Mrs Armitage now said that the beginning had been very difficult. 'Every time I was changing him he was screaming, I didn't know what to do. I couldn't relax. My husband said I was like a machine. After my parents had been, I realized Gareth had been aware of everything.' I said that it sounded as if Mrs Armitage had been helped by her parents' coming, at which point Mrs Armitage began crying. Mr Armitage did not appear to notice this. He was now very involved in the interview, sitting forward in his seat and talking freely. He said that he and Mrs Armitage had disagreed about how to get Gareth to sleep. Mr Armitage stands up to rock him. Mrs Armitage is too tired to stand with Gareth, but feels that if Mr Armitage does, then Gareth wants her to as well. Mr Armitage said he had stopped doing it to give Mrs Armitage a chance. He said they had disagreed in the past but 'Not now. I've no recriminations against her.'

We can see here the honesty with which the parents are struggling to let us know of the arguments between them about how to help their child.

Mr Armitage spontaneously said that he recalled being left to cry himself as a baby and being desperately unhappy at those times. His parents both had to work hard because money was short and were away a lot, leaving him in a large house in the care of his grandmother, who was too old to climb the stairs to see to him. His earliest memories are of *being left* and *crying*. He added later that the wind blowing through an aerial on top of the house made a whistling noise that terrified him, though nobody realized it for a long time.

He said he could not bear Gareth crying, even for ten minutes, and that they did try being firm for three to four days, but that these were the hardest times for him in Gareth's life. Gareth, still sitting in front of his father, gave one cry and Mr Armitage immediately gave him lots of toys.

Mr Armitage is illustrating one of the themes of this book, that parents' own experiences colour their interpretation of what their child is going through. Mr Armitage, with his memories of being left alone and unprotected, does not want his son to have to go through anything like that.

Mr and Mrs Armitage told us of their visit to Greece and Gareth's illness on their return two months ago. He had a chest infection and was admitted to hospital for a week and Mrs Armitage slept with him there and he slept well. He is now better and it was never clear what the diagnosis was.

Here we see that the hospital provided a respite for both Mrs Armitage and Gareth from whatever unresolved issue in their relationship, or other cause, was keeping Gareth from sleeping.

Mrs Armitage said she was 'full of confusions' and also sounded desperate at 'being 24 hours with him', which, however, Mr Armitage feels is extremely important for Gareth. Gareth started to moan and cry. Father picked him up and he struggled in Father's arms. I commented that in this state he did not look at either of his parents. Father gave him a toy, which he accepted and played with. Mr Armitage described Gareth as irritable, cantankerous and tetchy when going to sleep. Sounding rather irritable himself, he seemed to be still reliving his own experiences, saying that he was put to bed early and just left.

We see how Mr Armitage is using our suggestions to help him connect the present problem with past experience.

I asked how Gareth gets to sleep. Mrs Armitage said she would give him a bottle and hold him in her arms and he would fall asleep, before being put in the cot.

With so much essential thought about the past it was necessary for me to ask questions to anchor this to the details about the present.

Mr Armitage said Gareth does not go to sleep gracefully, but fights. He remembered how upset his wife had been in the early days after Gareth's birth. Mrs Armitage took this cue and said that her mother had not come until Gareth was one month old. This was because of an earthquake in their home town. Mrs Armitage told us that the earthquake happened two weeks before Gareth was due. It brought on her labour and for several days she did not know whether her parents, or the rest of her family, were alive or dead. She heard a few days later that they were safe, but it was a few weeks before her mother was able to come to this country. Mrs Armitage was very distressed not to have her mother there earlier. She said her pregnancy had only gone well because she knew her mother was coming.

Mrs Armitage's mother stayed three months, then Mrs Armitage went back home to Greece with her mother and Gareth slept well there until Mr Armitage arrived, though this coincided with the hotter weather.

I said it sounded as if the earthquake in Greece had been one for them too, that Mrs Armitage had been shaken up and worried about her family and had not got her confidence back until her mother came over. I went on to say that she had perhaps felt more secure and settled in her home country, as well as relieved to see all her family were safe, and that was perhaps why Gareth could sleep better there. Mr Armitage intervened and said that Mrs Armitage 'was dying to get home'. Gareth was beginning to cry and was handed to mother for breast-feeding. She was confident and relaxed with him. He settled immediately and soon fell asleep. As he fed, Mr Armitage said in reply to my questions that Gareth does not have teeth yet and is beginning to make recognizable sounds, such as 'Pa, Pa'.

We could speculate as to why Gareth cried at this particular moment – perhaps for his own internal reasons – perhaps he was picking up the painful emotions of the adults' conversation. We note how confident Mother is in dealing with him. Gareth has no teeth yet, so conflicts about biting have not yet arisen. When I asked about Gareth's words, Mr Armitage picks out for notice his saying the sounds 'Pa, Pa'. We were also able to see how Gareth is comforted by his mother's breast-feeding. Although he also has a bottle, he apparently has not yet got other self-soothing things to do.

I asked the parents what changes ideally they would like to happen. Mrs Armitage said she would like Gareth to sleep through the night, but did not mind where, though preferably in his own room.

Mr Armitage asked if we thought Gareth was hyperactive, he then observed that every child was different and there could not be pat solutions. He said several times that if we convinced him it was good to let a baby cry, he would of course accept it. The implication was that he wouldn't. I agreed with him that each family had to find their own solutions and said that it was important to recognize the difference between Mr Armitage's experience as a child and Gareth's experience now, with both parents around a lot, loving and available; and that to be left to cry in that situation could be different. It was also important to clarify just what we meant by 'leaving to cry'. We talked about the difference in giving a baby room to protest and the sort of abandonment Mr Armitage had undergone himself. I also said that if children get used to falling asleep in their cots, they are not as worried when they wake up there as when they have fallen asleep in someone's arms.

Mr Armitage said that Gareth was very sensitive and if they so much as moved in their bed, he would move or wake. I said that for Gareth his parents being present in the same room was perhaps comforting but also arousing. Perhaps he needed his own room now. Both parents seemed to agree with this.

As we ended, I suggested that the parents, Father in particular, think about the following:

1 What was so painful for him in his childhood that it was colouring the situation now?

2 How can Gareth be more independent?

I felt it premature to discuss any change in behaviour at this point. They were both keen to come again the following week.

Both Mr and Mrs Armitage came to this first meeting upset and agitated. They left in a much calmer mood. What happened in between? Looking over the events of this meeting, I find myself surprised that Mr Armitage, who had a very businesslike manner, quickly accepted our decision not to provide 'advice' as to what to change in his behaviour to Gareth. Both he and Mrs Armitage seized on the opportunity to talk about the personal issues that affected their relationship with Gareth. Mr Armitage needed to talk about his partly unhappy childhood; Mrs Armitage about being cut off from her happy one and the shock of the earthquake involving her family. Both got lost in these accounts. They also came to the session at odds with each other about what to do with Gareth. Telling us about this also seemed to help them to be more in agreement.

Mr Armitage's need to put himself first with Gareth was a crucial aspect of what we observed in this meeting. His emphasis on having seen Gareth first at his birth or Gareth's first words being 'Pa, Pa' were examples of this. It did not occur to me until later that Mr Armitage's feeling as a child at the times that he was left alone that he was not important to his parents made it vital for him to be important to his baby now, even if this meant sometimes competing with his wife. Mr Armitage, who had hoped for 'advice', was perhaps relieved not to get it. In fact he told us what advice he expected to hear from us, i.e. 'leave the baby to cry', and that this would be unacceptable.

Later I also noticed that the overriding catastrophic event of the earthquake, which sent Mrs Armitage into labour, was not told us until well after the middle of the first meeting. Although Mrs Armitage's parents survived, at the time she was giving birth to Gareth and for four days afterwards she did not know whether they were alive or dead. Mrs Armitage told us of this devastating experience in a hesitant, detached way, so that it was left to Dr N. and myself to exclaim at the awfulness of it. We could guess that this was partly the flatness of postnatal depression, perhaps brought on by the trauma, and also that not having allowed herself to know consciously how dreadful this experience was had left her more vulnerable to its consequences. Being out of touch with some of the feelings of what she had herself gone through made her prone to be out of touch at times with her son and his communications.

SECOND MEETING

We met the family a week later and they seemed much calmer. They said Gareth was settling better. Although they were quite hesitant and reluctant to admit it, it emerged that Gareth had slept well three or four times in the last week. Mr Armitage in particular seemed unable to acknowledge either any changes that had been made or any benefit that might have come from talking last week, or, indeed, that things really were any better. He said he was worried about how Gareth goes to sleep, that he fights it and is fretful and moans, though he now seems content with himself in the mornings.

I said that perhaps what we talked about last week had seemed rather nebulous; they couldn't see what connection talking about their own problems had with Gareth not sleeping, though it had felt to be making sense at the time. I also said that perhaps after our meeting they had felt rather embarrassed that they had said so much about themselves to strangers. They agreed and seemed to relax.

Mrs Armitage went on to talk more about when Gareth moans, that, just as we had seen last week, it is 'as if he is looking for something that isn't there' and they feel angry with themselves because they don't know what he wants. She said that since last week, when I had pointed it out, they had noticed how he doesn't look at his parents when he is in that mood.

Both parents talked about not having their own mothers around to help them. Mrs Armitage's mother is in Greece and Mr Armitage's died some time ago.

It did not feel right to use these remarks as an invitation to say that perhaps Dr N. and I were perceived as parents who could help them. If anything, we were being felt like the absence of their own mothers.
They were perhaps depicting feeling like Gareth when he moans, not knowing how to capture his parents' attention and look to them for help.

I asked what the parents felt about weaning Gareth. Mrs Armitage said the health visitor had advised her not to breast-feed, particularly at night, but she wanted to carry on for a long time still. I realized that the parents thought I was advising them to stop breast-feeding now and said this was not what I had meant.

We talked about what had happened during the week to make the difference to Gareth. Mrs Armitage said she had covered him with a blanket, perhaps that had done it. She then said she had left him in the crèche a couple of times, while she went to keep-fit classes. She said Gareth had enjoyed playing with the other children there. I said that perhaps our talk last week had enabled Mrs Armitage to think about being able to be separate from Gareth for a short time. Because she felt all right about leaving him, he could also enjoy it. Because he also found that she came back to him when she left him during the day, he might have realized that when he was put down to sleep at night his parents would still come back to him. It seemed as though Gareth had worried that he could not manage without his parents and was beginning to learn that he could. They said, however, that he can still only play with toys in his parents' presence and speculated whether his delay in crawling is because that also means more independence than he is ready for.

I asked if there was one thing they now thought they could change. After a silence Mrs Armitage said, 'Leave him to cry'. We emphasized that if they did leave Gareth, it was important to tell him where they were going and to come back within a few minutes. Mrs Armitage confessed she had left Gareth in the crèche without saying goodbye. We talked about the importance of saying goodbye, and about the difference between leaving Gareth for a few minutes and Mr Armitage's own childhood experience of being left for a long time.

Mrs Armitage said she always used to pick Gareth up when he cried; her mother had advised it because you would know that if he stopped crying when you picked him up he was not crying because he was in pain. It was clear that Mrs Armitage was now trying to sort out the consequences of this well-meant advice.

In this meeting it seemed that, having poured out their own stories last time, the parents were at first rather ashamed of having done so and therefore rather ill at ease. Perhaps they were afraid of being sucked into more revelations about themselves, beyond their usefulness for this piece of work. When I commented on this, they were relieved and able to work more purposefully this time on thinking about making changes for Gareth.

It is also very common to find that parents report a change in an offhand way, as though it has no relevance. It may be that they are worried that the therapist will count the change prematurely as success and stop seeing them too soon; or alternatively that even if they have not openly admitted it to themselves, they do actually see at another level that the connections they are making about relationships and about their feelings on separations are as important as the actual cure of the baby's sleep problem. This is not luring people into interminable therapy, but resolving important issues stirred up in the work, so that these issues can be comfortably left. It was also apparent in this meeting that the parents were more in agreement on how to think about and act for Gareth.

THIRD MEETING

Both parents seemed more relaxed this time. Last night they had had the best night ever with Gareth. The rest of the week had included a couple of bad nights but mostly things were better. Gareth was still enjoying the crèche and Mrs Armitage said she had been able to say goodbye to him. Father had also started to say goodbye when he went off to work in the mornings. It seemed also that Mrs Armitage was realizing the importance of preparation time. She had established much more of a bedtime routine for Gareth. The transition from waking to sleeping was becoming easier to think about, since the parents had stopped feeling so hopeless about it.

Gareth can still only go to sleep before he is put in his cot, usually in his mother's arms, but Mr Armitage said that once last week he had fallen asleep while lying on his tummy on their bed. It seemed as if Gareth was starting to take responsibility for his going to sleep. We suggested that they try to find a moment to say good-night to him before he falls asleep, to help him take account of being in this transition stage.

We talked about why Gareth doesn't look at his parents when he is tired. 'It's as if he's not looking to us for help', Mrs Armitage said. She added that when he gets in a state and she firmly says to him, 'Gareth, stop it', he does respond at once. However, she worried about saying it. I said that talking sharply was a way of bringing him to focus on his parents and enabled them to help him better.

I asked the parents to think ahead to when Gareth might be in his own room. The parents had thought they would need a two-way intercom, but then realized that they would be able to hear him from the next room without one.

Gareth was quite happy in this session and played a lot with his father. At one point he played with a toy telephone, which allowed us to think about how to keep in contact from a distance. Mr

Armitage said that Gareth now enjoys playing on a slide, allowing his father to let him go and trusting that he would be caught again. We talked about how this was a sign that he is beginning to separate and become more independent.

The parents again said on this occasion that they could not see how coming here had caused the changes in Gareth. This time I did take it up in terms of their relationship with Dr N. and myself and said there was a problem that if they felt there was a benefit in coming here, it would make it hard to separate from us after this brief piece of work.

It was noticeable that the parents had left after the second meeting torn about whether to leave Gareth to cry. They had achieved the better nights without having had to do anything that seemed drastic to them. In fact saying goodbye to herald separations during the day was what probably had the biggest impact on the symbolic separation of going to sleep at night-time. They had in no sense 'left him to cry'.

FOURTH MEETING

Dr N. is away on holiday. We had told Mr and Mrs Armitage, when we were arranging this meeting, but they are surprised at her absence. They report that Gareth is now in his own room. They have to stay with him for half an hour while he falls asleep in his cot. He wakes up once in the night and falls asleep again quietly. He wakes up again at 6.30 a.m., has a feed and goes back to sleep after it.

As the parents tell me this, Gareth crawls around the room, pulling himself up on the table. Mr Armitage says everything very mournfully; no hint from his voice that we are talking about considerable progress.

I guess that he is very put out by Dr N.'s absence. It was perhaps important that we had been there as a couple and was perhaps a mistake to resume work without Dr N. But the accident that the family, I and she, were all on holiday one after the other seemed to make too long a gap in what had started off as very urgent work.

It seems clear that the parents intend this to be the last meeting. Mrs Armitage says how delighted she is at their progress and thanks me. I say that they have worked hard. Mr Armitage says they don't begrudge Gareth the time.

This was a successful brief piece of work. In four meetings this little boy changed from being wakeful throughout the night to having a long night's sleep with only one brief awakening. He was also by the end sleeping in his own room. It was necessary, however, for Dr N. and I to hang on to our own optimism throughout this piece of work. These parents had to convey to us much confusion, indecision and hopelessness. By listening to their communications, we knew also what separation meant to them and why they found it so difficult. It can be tempting in such a case to think of keeping oneself at a distance and simply give out advice. Apart of course from this not being our way of working, both parents made it clear they could not have borne that. I really think that the only effective way to help these parents was to bear with receiving and understanding their feelings, so that we could then try to help them understand better how such feelings connect with behaviour.

I think it is significant that the ending of this brief work was painful for both parents, but especially for Mr Armitage. It seemed to me that he particularly felt Dr N.'s absence as a rejection, having suffered rejections repeatedly as a little boy. Mr Armitage's apparently narrow summing-up of the work, 'We don't begrudge him the time', has much more meaning than at first seems apparent. His parents did begrudge their time spent in thinking about his needs and his own receptivity to his little boy was a striking sign of his ability to be different from them. His initial distant way of talking covered considerable emotional feeling. These parents had both been affected by traumatic situations or events. This work was about their struggles to make sense of it all on behalf of their little boy.

Part II

CHAPTER FOUR

THE PHYSIOLOGY OF SLEEP STATES

F OR THE NEXT two chapters we are going to change gear, as it were, from clinical casework orientation to a more theoretical viewpoint, looking at the data on sleep, both in adults and infants, and other aspects of infant development. A reader who has studied physiology is likely to find my description rather naïve. As a child psychotherapist trained in psychoanalytic ideas my natural mode of work is that of clinical cases, as illustrated in the first three chapters, not the appraisal of scientific research. But during my time working on sleep problems I have come to be fascinated by, and see the vital importance of, sleep and dream physiology. So I hope to convey some of the excitement I have felt in discovering what for me is a new language to describe the processes of sleep and of infant development. I also attempt to put this together with what I already know from observing infants clinically. My sources are in fact mainly researchers who have helped me bridge the gap between physiological theory and clinical practice by having already put their own or others' biological data into a psychological framework.

Remember, even though this chapter is rooted in physiology, the development of sleep and other states is seen as inextricably bound up with the parents' handling of the baby. We will see the effect of this handling both on the baby's psycho-physiological state, that is to say, its feelings, and on the relationship between parents and baby.

It used to be thought that dozing off was a simple process and that sleep was a kind of negation of waking. However, recent research has shown how complex sleep states are and that there may be even more mental activity going on during sleep than during waking states. Perhaps the most accessible authoritative information on the psychology and biology of sleep comes from the work of Ernest Hartmann. He is an American psychiatrist who has collected together the results of his own research and that of others in the field during the past two or three decades. In his most recent book, *The Nightmare* (1984), he summarizes the characteristics of a night's sleep and the following account is taken from this.

ADULTS' SLEEP PATTERNS

Electroencephalograms, or EEGs, measure the changes in voltage in brain activity. These changes are rhythmical and of wave form. When awake, a person's EEG shows a regular pattern at a frequency of 8 to 12 cycles per second. These are called alpha waves. On falling asleep, the waves go through certain characteristic changes. Though the changes are continuous, they have been divided by researchers into discrete stages – 1, 2, 3 and 4. Stage 1 indicates the lightest form of sleeping and here there is a reduction in alpha waves, with the onset of low-voltage, desynchronized activity and sometimes regular waves of 4 to 6 cycles per second. After a few minutes at most this gives way to Stage 2, which shows 'sleep spindle' tracings at 13 to 15 cycles per second and also certain high-voltage spikes known as K complexes. A few minutes later Stage 3 begins to take over, with high-voltage activity at 0.5 to 2.5 cycles per second – these are called delta waves. Some time later the delta waves occupy most of the EEG record and this is Stage 4 sleep.

As I have said, this division into distinct stages is artificial, for the changes in rhythms are in fact continuous; moreover sleep rhythms are cyclical. After reaching Stage 4 and being in this state for a period of up to about half an hour, the rhythms move to a state similar to Stage 1. However, although the EEG patterns are the same as Stage 1, very different phenomena are also manifest. These are rapid eye-movements (REM) and many other characteristics, such as: irregular pulse-rate, respiration and blood pressure; the presence of full or partial penile erections (and presumably similar clitoral activity); generalized absence of muscle tone interspersed with sporadic movements of small muscle groups.

These periods differ from Stage 1 sleep, and from Stages 2, 3 and 4, in one further very striking way. Persons awakening during these periods very frequently (60 to 90 percent of the time) report dreams, whereas when woken from the other stages they very seldom report them. Because these specific characteristics have been repeatedly and consistently observed in dream research, these periods are now more or less universally regarded as a different state of sleep, termed D sleep, REM sleep, paradoxical sleep or active sleep. The other stages together are called S sleep, non-REM, orthodox or quiet sleep.

Normally there are four or five full cycles proceeding to REM sleep each night. These give up to about one and a half hours of dreaming in total. In between REM periods sleep proceeds regularly and reliably through the other stages. However, the deepest sleep, Stage 4, is usually reached only in the cycles early in the night. Later in the night the cycles only reach Stage 3 before proceeding to a REM period. Also the first REM periods tend to be the shortest, less than ten minutes, whereas later in the night these dreaming periods tend to be longer, up to forty minutes.

One last point to be stressed: Stages 1 to 4 can be termed lightest to deepest sleep based upon the arousal threshold in each stage. However, REM sleep, though having the EEG characteristics of Stage 1 (the lightest sleep), differs from it in that it does not have a low arousal threshold. This, among the other signs, indicates that it is definitely a different form of sleep from the other stages.

Summarizing, we see that for adults a night's sleep includes more REM sleep in the last third of the night and more Stage 4 in the first third. Each has its own particular function. To get the benefit of all these functions, a person needs to remain asleep long enough for each cycle to continue through to Stage 4 in the early part of the night and for the whole night's sleep to be long enough for the later REM periods to take place.

THE FUNCTIONS OF SLEEP

Having seen what the stages of sleep are, let us now look at their different uses. We know that the function of sleep in general is restorative and that the various stages provide different aspects of this. For example, it now appears certain that Stage 4 sleep is the one in which physical growth and the maintenance of the immune system are promoted. Subtle connections with other bodily systems have also recently been discovered, as we will see in Chapter 12 on psychosomatic problems.

Turning to REM sleep, or D sleep as Hartmann prefers to call it, he says (1973) that this seems to 'have a restorative function with respect to systems of *focused attention*' (p. 147). Thus the ability to focus on one thing at a time, to discriminate and pick out what is important, is dependent on REM sleep. Hartmann argues that the ability to maintain an optimistic mood, energy and self-confidence and the ability to adapt emotionally to the physical and social environment are also affected by REM sleep. We can see that this emotional adaptation and self-confidence are in themselves the base from which derives the ability to pick out what is important.

What is more, Hartmann discovered that sleep, and especially REM or D sleep, was needed in larger quantities after days of stress, worry or intense new learning, especially if the learning was in itself somewhat stressful. He crucially suggests from this that 'D sleep thus may have a role in *consolidating learning or memory*' (1973, p. 147, my italics). In emphasizing the importance of stress, Hartmann argues that those who need more sleep are not those who have had to learn new facts, but those who have had to restructure, stressfully, their way of doing things. He suggests, therefore, that sleep and D sleep may help in 'consolidating or reconnecting these important alterations made during the day' (1973, p. 147).

In the next chapter we will look in a bit more detail at the usefulness of the dream dramas that take place during D sleep. It seems that they help to consolidate learning and also, more particularly, are a way of putting into place in the mind emotional experiences through both unconscious and conscious levels of imaginings.

PARENTS' SLEEP

We have been looking at the general functions of sleep in adults. Particularly relevant for us are how these affect parents with babies. The consolidations happening in sleep are especially important for parents of new-born babies who are indeed going through emotional changes.

The experience of going through pregnancy and childbirth, having a new baby and following the many and astounding changes and leaps of development made in the first months and years has an emotional impact that could be called a form of stress, however enjoyable the experience is. Parents have the exhilarating but terrifying task of being responsible for a new life. Their experience of themselves and their relation to society changes radically; all this requires very great emotional readjustment.

One could say that new parents are the people most in need of a good night's sleep! We begin to see how, when disturbances in babies' sleep lead to loss of sleep by parents, their own ability to deal with the problem is in itself impaired. Focused attention and optimism, which are both affected by REM sleep, are the very qualities needed to help solve such problems.

In addition we can start to see how the actual process of waking can be difficult, either from the deep preoccupations of the dreaming period or from the deeply unconscious physiogical state of Stage 4. Parents woken by their babies at either of these stages may have difficulty in dealing with the baby. In a REM period they may be reluctant to divest themselves from their dream state, still caught in the necessity of working out their own stresses and anxieties. In a disintegrated state themselves their child's anxieties cannot be put into perspective. Parents who are deeply asleep in Stage 4 may awake shaky and confused, not easily in control of their bodily movements and not able to work out what their baby needs.

In spite of this, waking in the night in the early weeks to feed or attend to a baby does not of itself constitute a sleep problem for either parent or baby. Zuckerman *et al.* (1987) point out that 'regular waking once a night, which is considered a sleep problem in older children, may reflect an ongoing comfortable adaptation for mother and child at eight months' (p. 665).

As we will see, attunement to the baby's rhythms is more impera-tive for most mothers in the early weeks than following their own biological sleep–wake rhythm. Mary-Sue Moore (1989) shows that mothers of new babies do not in fact sleep deeply; they do not often proceed into Stage 4 sleep, because they wish to be able to hear their baby cry. McKenna *et al.* (1989) demonstrate that mothers' waking is not because they have already heard the baby's cries; they produce alpha waves during deep sleep which pull them up into light sleep again.

I myself would think that this is not so much to do with 'good' or 'unselfish' mothering as with finding the freedom for mutually satisfying exchanges of biological cues and signals between mother and baby. Inability or failure by a mother to respond to her baby's rhythms may be as deeply disappointing and disturbing to the mother as to the baby. This is our first glimpse of the intrinsic connection between biological and emotional processes and the way that the imperatives of parent–infant attachment can override the parents' personal physiological cycles.

INFANTS' SLEEP PATTERNS

How does infant sleep differ from our 'adult' description? Infants sleep for much longer than adults. It is obvious that these long hours are essential for both physical growth and maturation and for the consolidation of their emotional and cognitive develop-ment. As well as sleeping longer, infants' sleep patterns are also different from those of an adult. Let us now look at these and how they develop.

New-born infants sleep for two-thirds of the 24-hour period, that is, for sixteen to seventeen hours, but any period is for no longer than about three and a half hours. This gradually changes so that by six months they are spending half the time asleep and half awake. At first the periods of sleep and wakefulness alternate through day and night, but by six weeks sleep is more concentrated in the night and wakefulness during the day. However, the ability to remain solidly in either a sleeping or a waking state over a longish period and the synchronizing of these states with the 24-hour clock appear to be independent processes (Berg and Berg, 1987). It takes until twelve to sixteen weeks before the daily rhythm is clearly established, with daytime sleep now appearing as well-defined naps. At eighteen weeks the longest wakeful period has become non-random and by six months the longest sleep period follows the longest wake period (Coons, 1987). Seventy percent of babies are sleeping through the night by three months and 90 percent by nine months (Moore and Ucko, 1957).

The circadian rhythm is the innate daily fluctuation of physio-logical and behavioural functions including sleeping/waking (this was defined by the American Association of Sleep Disorders Center, 1979). It is generally tied to the 24-hour day–night cycle but sometimes to a measurably different periodicity (e.g. 23 or 25 hours), when light/dark and other time cues are removed. Some physiological functions, such as temperature, heartbeat or skin resistance, become entrained to this rhythm early on, while others become so later. Kidney function, for example, does not entrain until approximately two years of age.

The changes in the circadian distribution of the sleep and wak-ing periods are accompanied by changes within the sleep cycle itself. New-born infants go directly into REM sleep. By six months they are spending a quarter of a now shorter sleep time in REM sleep, so that it has lessened from five to six hours per 24 hours to four hours per 24 hours. As the baby's sleep/wake periods lengthen, there are naturally fewer sleep onsets (Coons, 1987) and consequently fewer times when the baby is falling into a REM sleep period. Somewhere between three and six months the nature of falling asleep changes and the baby goes not into REM or 'active' sleep, but into non-REM or 'quiet' sleep. As the baby matures, the proportion but not the total amount of 'quiet' sleep therefore increases.

There has been much interest in the function of the high amount of REM sleep for new-born infants. Roffwarg *et al.* (1966) have suggested that the infant organism has been programmed to seek stimulation, not to shut it out, because stimulation is necessary for development. In the first weeks when the infant spends so much time asleep, stimulation must of necessity mainly come during sleep states and REM periods are most likely to provide this. As the baby gets older, wakeful periods increase and sufficient stimulation from these times can then take place. It has been pointed out that this stimulation within the baby is necessary for behavioural and physiological activation (Emde and Robinson, 1979). The result is increased organization by both neurophysiological and psychic states. Protein synthesis in the brain is also a significant function of REM sleep at this time (Berg and Berg, 1987).

Emde and Robinson (1979) succinctly stress the importance of sleep states when they say: 'wakefulness is the time when novelty is experienced, when one's world is expanded, and when one changes and is most changed, and even though wakefulness is the time in development when most learning takes place, it may be sleep which holds up a more accessible mirror to the rapid organismic changes of early development' (p. 79).

However, another process, that of rhythmicity or sequencing, is equally important. Berg and Berg (1987) have shown how developmental changes are not simply the maturation of the sleep/wake cycle, but are also part of the developing interactions between a number of independent biological rhythms. For instance, they quote Aserinsky and Kleitman's (1955) important discovery that the cyclic alternations of active and quiet sleep in the new-born are manifestations of a basic rest–activity cycle (BRAC). Aserinsky and Kleitman have maintained that these cycles remain throughout development, lasting 90 minutes in adults as compared with 45 minutes in new-borns. In adults the BRAC is present both in the regular recurrence of REM periods during sleep (about once every ninety minutes) and also in cycles of alertness and efficiency during daytime wakefulness.

It is useful to think of these less alert periods while awake as times for losing focused attention and being reflective, which have restorative functions similar to REM sleep. The origin of this BRAC cycle has been shown in the foetus from three months on, but Emde and Robinson (1979) describe its presence in the first hours after birth.

We can thus begin to see how the BRAC interacts with the sleep/ wake cycle. For infant and adult it is seen in variations of activity both during sleep and in waking states. In infants quiet and active states within sleep are matched by similar quiet and active waking states, with crying as the most stimulated state of all.

67

Let us now take a closer look at the REM/non-REM sequence in a baby's sleep. Ferber (1985a) describes the baby's behaviour in different states of the sleep cycle, which is readily observable by parents. He says that REM sleep appears in the foetus at about six or seven months' gestation, and non-REM sleep at between seven and eight months' gestation. He then describes the appearance of REM sleep in the new-born baby. He vividly depicts the baby twitching, breathing irregularly, with eyes flickering under eye-lashes. In contrast, in quiet, non-REM sleep the baby breathes deeply and lies very still, occasionally making fast sucking motions or a sudden body jerk or startle.

Ferber also notes what we saw earlier, that after the first three months the baby falls straight into non-REM sleep and plunges rapidly through drowsiness and light sleep into Stage 4 within ten minutes. In youngsters this is an extremely deep sleep and waking a child from Stage 4 may be almost impossible. Ferber says that a child who is rocked to sleep in his parent's arms may wake if put down in his cot while still in an early light stage of sleep, but will not do so if put down after reaching the later deep stage. A child woken by parents during Stage 4, for example to urinate, will return to sleep instantly and have no recollection of the arousal in the morning.

These descriptions are useful in helping parents understand the physiological aspects of their baby's sleep cycles. Moore and Ucko (1957) also connect the outward signs of behaviour with sleep cycle phases. They show how at the end of the 'deep sleep' phase movements of body and eye suddenly occur, at which point the child may either wake or begin a fresh sleep cycle.

One of the most interesting issues is how individuals deal with the 'given' facts of their own sleep cycles, which include arousals, and how these are interpreted by parents on behalf of their babies. Many of us will easily recognize that as adults having a periodic arousal during the night, we can either turn over and go back to sleep, or can find that pressing anxieties pull us into wakefulness if the previous REM time has not dealt with these sufficiently to allow sleep to continue.

In the early weeks babies may wake to be fed at the times of these arousals. As they get older, waking may still signal such a need or it may simply be an arousal in the sleep cycle. It is easy to see how differently parents can behave at these times. Some, perceiving their baby to be awake, may let them drift back into sleep. Others, interpreting the arousal as a sign of some need, become party to waking the baby more completely. We shall look at this closely in later chapters.

Every new baby is, in an ongoing way, attaining and dealing with different psychological and somatic states. Parents attempt both to follow and influence these states. Daniel Stern (1985) has pointed out incisively how a baby needs an 'other' to help his self-regulation. The other is of course usually the parent. Let us now look at this in a little more detail.

CHAPTER FIVE

BABIES' PHYSIOLOGICAL STATES AND PARENTING

THE RELATION between parents and baby seems to play a vital part in the growth of the baby's physiological states. The handling of the baby by his parents helps him regulate his bodily states and has an effect on his psychological state, in other words it affects his feelings. This then has an effect on the feelings that build up between parents and baby. Sleep together with other states seem inextricably bound up with parents' handling of their baby; let us examine this more closely.

In looking at the development of the baby's physiological states, we can see that right from the first few minutes after birth there is an interplay between the baby's own state and that of his mother. If we looked only at a baby on his own we would be missing a lot. Mother and baby are open and receptive to each other. Kennell *et al.* (1979) have described how in the first hour after birth reciprocal interactions can take place between a mother, who is in a 'maternal sensitive period' at that time, and her baby, who is equally alert and active. During this time the baby's eyes are wide open and he is even able to follow objects with his eyes and hands (Desmond *et al.*, 1966). After that he falls deeply asleep for three to four hours. Kennell *et al.* describe how in this early responsive period the initial stage towards parent–infant bonding can take place:

> We hypothesize that during this early sensitive period a series of reciprocal interactions begins between the mother and infant which bind them together and ensures the further development of attachment. The infant elicits behaviours from the mother which are satisfying to him, and the mother elicits behaviour from the infant that is rewarding to the mother. These interactions occur on many levels – behavioural and physical. When the infant cries, his mother usually comes near and picks the baby up. The baby often quiets, opens his eyes, and will look at the mother and follow her with his eyes. During a feeding the mother may initiate the interaction. She may gently stroke the

infant's cheek, eliciting the rooting reflex which brings his mouth in contact with his mother's nipple. Nursing is pleasurable to both the mother and infant, and it stimulates the secretion of oxytocin which causes the mother's uterus to rhythmically contract. Simultaneously the infant receives immuno-globulins and experiences T and B lymphocytes in the breast milk, which, recent evidence suggests, may line part of the intestinal epithelium, providing protection against the enteric pathogens for which the baby receives little transplacental protection. Because the maternal and infant behaviours complement each other, the probability that interaction will occur is increased. These behaviours seem to be specific and programmed to initiate the process that bonds mother and infant in a sustained reciprocal rhythm. (1979, p. 796)

Kennell *et al.* are here describing this process as part of the way in which attachment forms between parents and baby. One of the purposes of their work (see also Klaus and Kennell, 1976) is to confirm the necessity in obstetric practice for procedures which enable mothers, fathers and babies to be as much together as possible in the early stages after birth. The sensitiveness of the early period means that not just the first few days or hours but even the minutes are precious. One implication is that the benefits of medication during labour have to be set against the effects on this sensitive period. Mothers or babies who are still very drowsy will partly miss out on this opportunity.

To put it in perspective it must be stated that the importance of this sensitive period is disputed by some researchers. Also the findings have to some extent become one of the 'bugbears' of current knowledge about babies. The bonding process can indeed get a good head start in those early moments, but the first hours after birth are *not* the only time bonding can possibly take place. Leaping ahead for a moment to clinical interchanges, mothers have several times told me with anguish that they have not been able to bond because their baby was, for example, taken away to an incubator for the first few hours. In such cases I say to them that what they have missed is *not* the only chance to bond with their baby, but a useful moment to start the long process of doing so.

However, we can see the dilemma that new knowledge always entails. On the one hand there is a chance to change practice for the better, in this case to maximize the time parents and babies spend together after birth. On the other hand it leads to worry, often unnecessary and burdensome. Mothers may obsessively pick out not having spent this time with their babies as the origin of all future difficulties.

When a mother and infant have achieved what Kennell *et al.* (1979) call a 'sustained reciprocal rhythm', how does this affect the baby's sleep? One of the ordinary universal tasks of a mother is to help her baby regulate his sleep rhythms. Léon Kreisler (1974) has remarked that of all the functions of the body 'sleep is without doubt the most fragile' (p. 96). A mother who has intuitively achieved a reciprocal rhythm with an adaptable baby will probably be puzzled by this comment. To others the fragility will be recognizable as an important characteristic and to them regular patterns seem unattainable.

We have seen how in the first weeks the sleep/wake cycle goes on irrespective of the time of day. It takes until twelve to sixteen weeks before day and night are clearly distinguished. We can now put the establishment of this day–night rhythm into a wider context. As well as being a physiological maturation, it is also a sign of psychological maturation (Ablon and Mack, 1979). For the baby this achievement is the product of innate biological factors, environmental stimulation, satisfaction and frustration. It is a vital aspect of his self-development. It comes as part of the relationship between mother and infant and their reciprocal exchanges of feeding, holding and playing. We can easily see how these affect the child's level of tension and hence his development of a stable sleep pattern. Here again we see a connection between parent–infant interaction and neurological processes. Sander *et al.* (1976) emphasize the significance of the first ten days of life for mother and baby in organizing the time and rhythm of the baby's sleep. They deplore the 'nonchalant separation' of mothers and babies in some maternity units, which is to the detriment of this process.

As the day–night rhythm gets established, so changes take place within the sleep cycle and the baby has a smaller amount of REM sleep. We have seen that REM sleep seems to be needed for auto-stimulation to promote neurological development in the early weeks, when the infant is awake for relatively little of the 24-hour period. However, when the infant is older and awake for longer, he receives stimulation both from other people and from his own explorations and therefore seems to need less REM sleep. He now has a higher proportion, though not higher amount, of time in quiet non-REM sleep. We can work out from this that a baby starts by providing the stimulation necessary for his physiological growth from within his own somatic workings, the long period of REM sleep. However, as the weeks go by some of this stimulating function is taken over by social relations, such as those between parents and baby. Thus the social relations of parent and infant affect physical development. Put another way, emotional growth mediates physical growth as much as vice versa.

Concluding our thoughts about the baby's sleep cycles, we can widen our view a little by mentioning Peter Wolff's (1974) simple classification of states a baby may be in. He suggests, rather crudely, three levels of sleep: regular, irregular and drowsy. In place of Wolff's first two terms we can use 'quiet' and 'active' sleep, which were discussed in Chapter 4. In waking states, Wolff likewise distinguishes three categories: alert inactivity, waking activity and crying, which is the most stimulated state. Our baby moves from one of these six states to another; our next question is, therefore, how and why he does this.

NEW-BORN BEHAVIOUR

We all know that babies are different from each other. The debate about innate characteristics and the effect of interaction with the environment has been developing over the years. Psychoanalytically based infant observations have accurately captured the way the infant and his parents interact through the early weeks and months. Recent behavioural research on the neonate has also been able to show subtle aspects of this 'nature–nurture' interaction from very early on. For example, Berry Brazelton's 'Neonatal Behavioural Assessment Scale' (1973) provides a way of assessing the temperamental variations in new-born babies and the effect they have on their caretakers. Als *et al.* (1979) describe the Scale as based on the concept that the infant is adapted to the environment in order to interact with it and elicit from it the stimulation necessary for his motor, emotional and cognitive development.

The Brazelton Scale assesses the infant's response to stimuli of various kinds and through this it looks at his capacity to recover from the demands of labour, delivery and exposure to a new environment. The examiner looks at the interaction between himself and the infant. He then measures his own reactions to the infant and evaluates them as the ones most likely to be elicited by that infant in his own parents. The infant's eliciting characteristics are then specified and include such everyday terms as cuddlability, irritability, consolability and self-soothing ability. Differences from one baby to another in tempo and style at birth and the way these might influence the new-born's parents are established. The sort of behaviour measured is, for instance, how an infant might bring his hand to his mouth to keep himself under control when upset. This would be noted along with how the examiner standing in for the parent might himself intervene to soothe the upset baby.

In their study of the Scale Als *et al.* pick out two major attributes which they call 'attractiveness and need for stimulation'. These measure how much initiative the new-born takes in the interaction with the examiner, or how much stimulation he needs, as well as how he is able to respond to the examiner's stimuli. Infants might vary from one who is stressed and unable to tolerate handling, even while being soothed, to one who shows periods of sustained responsiveness, while being able to maintain physiological stability and be available for social stimulation. With regard to a slightly different function, the examiner looks at the new-born's use of, and need for, stimulation in order to organize his responses. Many new-borns become more organized and stable as they are handled; while others are quite the opposite, they cannot tolerate handling and clearly give cues that they are better off alone. Yet other new-borns can deal with stimulation, but do not necessarily need it to become well organized.

These tests were originally designed to pick out infants at risk, to screen for handicaps and to see the effect of medication during delivery, but they have a wider interest for us. They alert us to the fact that the neonate's behaviour most probably affects parental response and we can then go on to see how varied the behaviour systems of a baby are that a parent has to become attuned to.

You will note that the Brazelton Scale criteria are a combination of the physiological and the social responses of the infant to whatever the examiner has initiated. The examiner, in turn, then responds to the infant. In 'real life', when the actual parent is picking up and responding to the infant's cues, she is doing so in ways she may not be directly aware of, that is, they are at an unconscious level. Brazelton's ideas of 'attractiveness' and 'need for stimulation' are perhaps similar to ways that psychoanalysts have thought of parents' intuitive and empathic knowledge of their baby's state of feelings.

In ordinary language parents describe their new-born babies' states in such terms as 'friendly', 'responsive', 'suspicious', 'bad-tempered', 'fussy', 'inconsolable', 'easy' or 'difficult to please'. They also speculate on which characteristics the baby was born with, whom he takes after or what in the environment has affected him.

Debates on babies' states are not only held in neurological or psychoanalytic language, they are also commonplace in practically every family. Nor are these debates just theoretical; they are not passive thoughts about a baby's state, they are practical discussions held while the baby is being actively responded to by his parents. Wolke and St. James Roberts (1987) state that parents' perception of their baby may be personally determined and not fit in with the 'objective' views of professionals. They then show how closely the parents' perception of the baby can influence its behaviour and argue that 'a mother who initially perceives her infant as slightly easier than an observer is believed to be more likely to positively interact and consequently influence infant behaviour than a mother who perceives her infant, in agreement with the observer, as difficult' (p. 65). Conversely, Nover *et al.* (1984), as we will see in Chapter 13, show that a mother's negative perceptions influence the baby's behaviour adversely.

PARENTS' INFLUENCE ON A BABY'S STATES

Daniel Stern is an American psychoanalyst and psychiatrist who has investigated these ideas about how closely the baby's physiological development is tied up with his relationship to the person looking after him and taken them further and in more detail than anyone else to date. In *The Interpersonal World of the Infant* (1985) he describes the interplay between babies and their caretakers and makes the point that babies need another person there in order to have the experience of their own bodies. The baby needs the physical mediation of another person to satisfy his hunger or deal with other physical states, such as getting to sleep. Stern says, 'others regulate the infant's experiences of somatic state . . . in all such regulations a dramatic shift in neurophysiological states is involved' (1985, p. 103).

Stern makes the further point that although the baby undergoes a dramatic transformation in his self-state through his interaction with this other person, he retains his feeling of being separate from that other person; he does *not* feel as though he has merged with that person. We will see later that this is in contrast to some other psychoanalytic thinking, where the baby is depicted as often feeling merged with the breast that is feeding it.

According to Stern 'strong feelings and important representations' come not just from the acts of being fed or put to sleep, but from the manner in which they are performed. He quotes Louis Sander (1980), who says that the infant's own states of consciousness and activity are ultimately socially negotiated states, affected by the other person who feeds and physically cares for the baby.

How does the infant experience within himself the 'social actions' of the other person and feel changed by what this other person does? One example is the way in which a bedtime routine affects what a baby feels about himself; this then has an effect on his somatic state. At its simplest, a baby who is cuddled and played with before being put to bed will have a different feeling about himself than one who has been perfunctorily put there. He will feel different about himself and also about the mother or other person who has put him there. These feelings will stay with him and, if he is in a cot or room on his own, the separation will be coloured by the feelings produced during the bedtime routine.

SLEEPING WITH PARENTS

The way in which a parent helps the child regulate his own sleep–wake state includes of course whether the parent actually sleeps at night with the child or instead helps the child to manage to be on his own. Here again physiological and relationship issues connect with each other.

James McKenna (1986) picks out the physiological aspects of parents sleeping with their babies and demonstrates connections between parents' and their babies' somatic processes. It must be said that McKena has very strong views on parents and infants sleeping together. He makes a synthesis of anthropological and physiological data on bodily contact with parents.

> It appears that in our enthusiasm to view the human infant as a competent pre-adapted organism which clearly it is . . . we have pushed too far the concept of the infant's physiological independence from the parent. For example, one inference that can be drawn from the cross-cultural and evolutionary data is that by having them sleep alone through the night and at very young ages we may be conditioning urban infants to sleep for artificially prolonged stages of the sleep cycle before their systems are best able to do so. (1986, p. 10)

McKenna talks of sleeping apart as being a sensory deprivation and suggests that parents and infants respond to each other's breathing sounds and movements. One effect is that a vulnerable infant can be 'reminded' to breathe by the sound or contact of the parents' breathing

76

For other mammal infants but especially primate infants, short-term separation leads to physiological consequences. This conclusion forces us to consider the possible effects of nocturnal separation on human infants who in Western and urban societies regularly sleep apart from their parents in separate rooms . . . Monkey and ape parents would no doubt regard this as a form of child abuse, as do peoples living in pre-industrial societies when told of parent–infant sleeping arrangements in urban settings. (p. 38)

McKenna is therefore suggesting that small infants are not neurologically independent enough to be separate from their parents and that to be alone throughout the night is a severe form of deprivation. He emphasizes the value physiologically, and by implication psychologically, of physical contact between parent and baby. (We come back to the emotional implications of this material in Chapter 8.) McKenna gives an interesting example of the connection between mothers' and infants' physiology, citing Smith and Steinschneider's (1975) study where infants born to mothers with low heart-rates slept for longer periods of time, fell asleep faster and generally cried less often than did infants born to mothers with higher heart-rates.

If we think of McKenna's argument as applying to the early weeks of infancy, it accords well with mothers' common feelings of anxiety and of being somehow incomplete when separated at all from their infants. When hospital practice is to remove new-born babies to a nursery to give mothers a 'rest', mothers may be confused by feeling that even after the arduous experience of childbirth they feel less in need of respite than of a confirmation through the baby's presence that he really exists.

As we have seen, sleeping with parents has an effect on the baby's physiology, but parents are of course rarely aware of this and their choice of whether or not they have their babies sleep with them derives from a range of cultural and personal reasons (see Chapter 9).

Other child-rearing practices also often have a calming effect on babies and this influences the baby's physiological state. These practices include swaddling, rocking and carrying of the baby; they consist of holding or movement, either on the parent's body or by other means. Similar also is the non-nutrient use of sucking, though this is more of a self-soothing mechanism, whether the baby finds its own thumb or whether the means is provided by the parent who gives the baby a dummy. (Sucking at the nipple or bottle-teat also fulfils such functions, in addition to the getting of milk.) Let us look at some of these practices in more detail.

SWADDLING

Swaddling affects the baby's physiological and emotional states and also the relationship between mother and baby. It can be an effective way of calming a 'fussy' baby.

Chisholm and Richards (1978) describe the use of techniques of infant restraint including swaddling, that is, wrapping the baby in bands or a tightly-folded blanket with or without the use of a board or cradle. They go on to look at the effects of this restraint on infant behaviour, citing Lipton *et al.* (1965), who 'found that infants who were swaddled slept more, had reduced levels of motor activity in response to stimulation, fewer startles and lower heart-rate variability than non-swaddled infants' (p. 259). When first swaddled most infants struggled for a minute or so, but 'gave up' long before muscle fatigue set in. Older infants struggled more. Chisholm and Richards also refer to Brackbill's (1973) thesis that tactile contact on the skin might be as important as motor restraint.

Chisholm and Richards also look at the Navajo Indians' use of the cradleboard. They report that babies go on the cradleboard for about sixteen hours a day in the first three months, decreasing to less than nine hours by the first birthday. The extent of use is determined by both infant and parent and, compared with European infants, Navajo babies spend more time in actual or potential social contact with adults.

The cradleboard appears in itself to calm the child and also affects the mother's responsiveness to the child. There is an initial protest at being put on the board, but part of the Navajo tradition of cradleboard use is the accepted wisdom that babies often fret when first put on the cradleboard and that one does not worry about this. Chisholm and Richards note that non-swaddled European babies frequently cry for at least a brief period when put down to sleep. Navajo infants do cry 'in order' to be picked up but mothers believe the cradleboard itself will stop the child's crying and do not respond with any behaviour within fifteen seconds. Chisholm and Richards then wonder whether, if the cradleboard and swaddling tend to reduce mutual responsiveness along with the infant's state and activity level, this is less than an ideal mother–child relationship. They answer this by suggesting that the opportunity for interchange may be as important as the interchange itself and that the social isolation of babies in some cultures is not experienced. The babies are near to adults much of the time. Walking is not delayed by the use of the cradleboard. Much of the actual time on the cradleboard is spent asleep, so that they are able to be active in their waking time.

After looking at the effect the cradleboard has on Navajo infants, Chisholm and Richards recommend its use for 'excitable, fussy' children. They say it would seem likely to have a beneficial effect, since its influence is to convert an awake, fussy time into sleep or a quiet, alert state. They quote Judy Bernal's (1973) study which showed that at sixty weeks about one third of a sample of 'normal' children were waking at night. As new-borns these babies had cried more than babies with no sleep problems and had remained in their cots for shorter periods. It was not clear whether they had a shorter time asleep or were more likely to cry if they woke. The implication of what Chisholm and Richards are saying is that if these new-born babies, described by Bernal as having heightened responsiveness, had been calmed early on by the use of a cradle-board or simple swaddling, the likelihood is that they would have slept more at that time and they would not have continued as sleep-problem babies.

Their observation of the Navajo mother's delay in responsive-ness when the cradleboard is in use is of great interest. This delay appears to give the baby space to 'protest' as part of a process of settling into sleep, without the confusion of being picked up again by the parent. The baby withdraws into sleep because of the lack of response by the parent; but this does not seem to be a pathogenic process of reciprocal emotional withdrawal. It is also not the same as 'leaving a baby to cry', as the parent remains within sight of the baby. It would be interesting to see the way in which mother and baby greet each other when the baby wakes from a long sleep on the cradleboard.

Wrapping a baby tightly in a blanket or shawl can have a similar effect to being on a cradleboard. One baby I observed being put to bed in the first few weeks was tightly wrapped in a shawl, with his arms inside. As he was 'wrapped up' each time, a peaceful look spread over his face; he would shut his eyes and fall asleep instantly. After a few weeks he struggled to have his arms out, though still liking his body to be closely wrapped. As he got older and his movements increased, the shawl soon worked loose and the calming effect lessened.

Perhaps the dilemma for some mothers with babies who have to be held in Mother's arms for long periods in order to fall asleep, and who tend to wake again when finally put down, might be solved by a cradleboard. In such cases the baby is in a sense using the mother as a 'cradleboard' – requiring her to go on holding him, without any acknowledgement of the mother's own need, that is, *not* to be holding him all the time. He is also not taking into himself any experience that could carry over to enable him to feel he could be put down. The neutral ground of the board might release both mother and baby from this impasse.

These thoughts must also be connected with the finding that babies given extra carrying in the early months cry and fuss less later on (Hunziker and Barr, 1986). Somewhere in all this is an issue about timing. Mothers who have to go on holding their babies to get them to sleep have somewhere missed the right timing in helping the baby regulate its *own* somatic states of sleeping and waking.

ROCKING

John Bowlby (1969) has described rocking as an effective way of terminating rhythmic crying. He notes that the effective speed at which rocking stops a baby crying is sixty cycles a minute or above. Sixty steps a minute is also the rate of a very slow walk. Bowlby makes the connection that when carried on his mother's back or hip, a young baby is rocked at not less than sixty cycles a minute and does not cry unless he is hungry or in pain. He suggests that although this may be a happy chance, it is more likely to be one of the selective pressures operating during the course of human evolution. To demonstrate the bodily effect that rocking has, Bowlby also shows that while being rocked the baby's heart-rate usually returns to near the resting level.

SUCKING

Sucking obviously has primarily a feeding function, but its non-nutrient uses are also very important. Judy Dunn (1977) summarizes some of the issues about sucking and shows how it stops a baby crying. Sucking on a dummy, for example, 'relaxes the movement of the guts and of the major muscles, and also reduces the number of eye-movements the baby makes when given something patterned to look at. While the baby is sucking in this way, not only is the stimulation from his mouth regular and rhythmic, but his random thrashing about is greatly reduced' (p. 28). Dunn questions whether the sucking reduces the active thrashing of arms and legs and so calms the baby or whether the calming effect of sucking reduces the movement.

Sucking also has great emotional significance as a way for the baby to be in contact with the mother through sucking at the breast. Sucking on, for example, a dummy can therefore also represent a memory of sucking at the breast and thus be both a way of keeping in contact through the mind and at the same time be a way of being separate in body from the mother.

CONCLUSION

We have seen that babies need considerable help in the development of their own neurophysiological states. It is obvious and simplistic to say that a helpless little baby needs to be fed by someone else. It takes a much more sophisticated thought to say that it is through another person's intervention that a baby has an experience of the workings of his own body and, what is more, that through this his body gradually becomes more organized. We have also seen how the parent's body, when near to the baby at night, has an effect on the baby's body. Further, it was noted how swaddling or wrapping the baby up tightly, while the parent also remains near, affects the state of the baby's metabolism.

All this help from the parent or caretaker is an essential service in promoting the baby as a viable being separate from others. Close contact with others starts a process which eventually enables the baby to look after the workings of his own body. Closeness facilitates eventual separation. In Chapter 7 we will see the parallel psychological process by which a baby needs intimate emotional contact with a parent, or substitute, within which to build up a sense of the self and that this is necessary in order to be able to separate from the parent. A baby's somatic functioning requires an interested other person's presence. It is also vital that the other person sees the baby as being separate from themselves, but we will come to this later.

CHAPTER SIX

DREAMS AND NIGHTMARES

EOPLE HAVE ALWAYS been interested in their dreams and believed that there was a 'meaning' to them. The telling of dreams to another person has also always been important. Sometimes there is an excited compulsion to relate the dream, the dreamer being preoccupied with it until the telling brings a feeling of relief. At other times there is a caution and reticence in the dreamer, who feels that telling the dream would be too revealing.

In early days, as we see from the Bible or from Ancient Greek and Roman literature, the 'meaning' of the dream was thought to be prophetic, the future could be foretold from it. Freud brought an entirely new perspective to this search for meaning. Freud, perhaps for the first time in history, gave his patients a great deal of time to tell him of their troubles and listened to them in very great detail. The method of free association, of letting thoughts flow freely so that connections could emerge, developed. In the course of this he found that his patients often dwelt upon their dreams because they seemed to carry great import. He realized that they seemed to be determined in part by present problems, but they also often led straight back to profound experiences at all stages of earlier life, even infancy, and were thus the 'royal road to the unconscious'. Freud looked in detail at his own dreams and those related to him by patients, colleagues and friends. In *The Interpretation of Dreams* (1900) he showed how present-day anxieties and conflicts intruded into sleep, disturbing it. He described how dreams seemed to include an imagined wish-fulfilment that apparently solved these conflicts and allowed sleep to continue. The dramatic action portrayed in a dream contained images that were disguised and condensed representations of present-day conflicts combined together with past memories. Many events packed themselves into one dream.

Psychoanalytic understanding of present difficulties partly in terms of past relationships and experiences evolved from this view of dreams. Even more important, it has given us all since then the opportunity to put our own thoughts, fantasies and dreams into the context of our own personal emotions and long-term life-events. Our dreams can be a useful way of checking our state of mental well-being. At its simplest nightmares are often understood as a sign of turbulence and stress in the mind. At times of change in life dreams, the linking of events from childhood with present-day occurrences, are a way of learning from and using past experience, consciously or unconsciously, or of seeing common themes in a life-history. We know ourselves from our history. Ella Freeman Sharpe (1937) compared dreams to works of art. In both, forgotten exper-ience becomes accessible in some way and is used, though without conscious awareness, as part of the creative imagination.

Recent work has confirmed how right Freud was to point out that what is remembered in dreams is about disturbances to sleep and that it also helps us to link present and past. Neville Symington (1986) is helpful in putting this into the context of later work on dreaming. Charles Rycroft (1979), perhaps more clearly than anyone else, has stressed how dreams may perform the very efficient function of 'internal' communication, that is, from one aspect of a person's mind to another. What Freud did not know was that the function of dreaming is much more than a protection of sleep, solving conflicts and thus allowing sleep to continue. It also serves to assimilate current experience into long-term memory, and, as I suggest later, performs a psychologically integrating function, whether or not the dream is remembered or the 'mean-ing' is consciously understood.

Donald Meltzer (1983), a Kleinian psychoanalytic writer, takes further Freud's connection between residues from the day before the dream and their links with infantile experience. He picks up Freud's point that in dreams 'some particular link to infantile experience was necessary for a daytime event to qualify for dream representation'. Meltzer develops this to suggest that in fact infan-tile experiences are ongoing and underlie the waking, conscious experiences of the day.

> The unconscious processes of dealing with the emotional experi-ences, that is the aspects of experience which bear significance of intimate human relationships as against the practical matters involving human or non-human objects in the outside world, would indeed appear from analytical experience to form a con-tinuum . . . We would consider dreaming to be as continuous in the mind as is digestion in the body, but concentrated more fully on its task when the other mental processes of dealing with the outside world are in abeyance during sleep. (1983, p. 88)

Here we see dreaming described as an extension of the unconscious phantasies that underlie our waking thoughts.

D OR REM SLEEP

Let us now look at dream-time from another point of view, in the context of the theory of D sleep as explained by sleep researchers.

Hartmann (1984) has described the biological progression of the stages of sleep, including D sleep in which dreams occur. Recapping from Chapter 4, it is worth quoting Hartmann:

> There are four or five D periods (REM) or dreaming sleep during the night and the total time taken up by them is about one and a half hours, a little more than 20 percent of the total sleep time . . . The cyclical nature of sleep is quite regular and reliable; a D period occurs about every ninety to one hundred minutes during the night. The first D period tends to be the shortest, usually lasting less than ten minutes, the later D periods may last fifteen to forty minutes each. Most D time occurs in the last third of the night whereas most Stage 4 sleep occurs in the first third of the night. (1984, p. 17)

As we have seen in Chapter 4, Hartmann goes on to show that whereas S sleep (synchronized or non-REM sleep) can be neatly organized in successive stages of depth, with Stage 1 as the lightest and Stage 4 as the deepest, D sleep (desynchronized, dreaming or REM sleep) does not fit into the same continuum. As measured by arousal thresholds or EEGs, D sleep is neither truly light nor deep sleep. Because of these opposing features, which make D sleep appear light in some ways and deep in other ways, D sleep has been called paradoxical sleep. In some ways it resembles active waking more than it resembles S sleep. Describing the function of D sleep in biological terms, Hartmann (1973) concludes from studies of sleep deprivation and tiredness that sleep, and D sleep specifically, is needed to restore focused attention, in particular the ability to focus on one item at a time and the ability to maintain an optimistic mood, energy and self-confidence. More D sleep is needed when there have been emotional changes or new learning to absorb, especially when there is stress involved in the impact of whatever is new. He concludes that D sleep may have a role in consolidating learning or memory and in reconnecting the important changes made during the day.

We see from this the importance to both parents and baby of

achieving enough time in D sleep. Its restorative functions are particularly relevant both to the situation of a baby developing and trying to master the implications of its own learning processes and to parents who are having to make changes in themselves to be in tune with the physical and emotional changes taking place in their baby. We also can see that, if their sleep process is interfered with, parents whose systems of focused attention have become impaired will have less ability to solve the sleep problems of their baby. Parents in this situation know only too well that systems that maintain optimism, energy and self-confidence are indeed impaired by lack of D sleep!

It is important to notice that the cyclical nature of sleep and the point at which D sleep occurs during the cycles affect the quality of sleep of parents who are woken by their babies, as well as that of the babies themselves. New-born babies plunge straight into a REM sleep. Older babies and adults go into D sleep later in the cycle. So an older baby who wakes frequently during the night may be waking both himself and his parents at the stage in the cycle before there has been a significant amount of D sleep. For both baby and adults the periods of continuous sleep during the night will not be long enough to allow sufficient D sleep for the vital restorative processes to take place. Noting that D sleep happens principally towards the end of a night's sleep, parents (or anyone else for that matter) woken in the middle of the night are, in fact, at their lowest ebb in a 24-hour cycle before the renewal of the D sleep period.

Palombo's recent work (1978) on dreams is exciting. He builds on Hartmann's theory, when he states that 'the dream itself . . . and not merely the interpretation of the dream – plays a positive integrating role in normal emotional development' (p. 6). Palombo illuminates what may be a crucial occurrence in dreams. He convincingly suggests that dreaming plays a central function in assimilating memories of the day into settled long-term memory. Thus if dreaming is insufficient or interrupted, the consequences are very serious for child and adult alike – they are left with a jumble of unassimilated memories.

Here it is worth differentiating between the function of the dream itself and the memory of the dream. Unremembered dreams perform the co-ordinating function for the mind, described by Hartmann and Palombo, without the dreamer being aware that this has happened. Remembered dreams have an additional function for a reflective person of illuminating in symbolic form present conflicts, choices, changes, and connecting these with experiences from the past. The dreamer has a chance to ponder over these images and symbols and the memories they release.

It has occurred to me that what goes on in my consultations with parents is somewhat akin to the co-ordinating aspect of dream-work. As I have said, parents nearly always come in a distressed state, with a confused mass of information. It seems to be compulsively necessary for them (and equally fascinating for me) to tell me the fullest details of the baby's behaviour through the day and night. All this is set in the framework of relationships and emotions. I think that an integrative process comparable to that of dreaming is set in motion by my listening to all of this and, to begin with, putting it in place in my mind. I think that I then help the parents to start to think and then dream it over; this then leaves the baby freer to have his own dreams.

PARENTS' DREAMS

Luke and his mother illustrate this well. The mother and her six-month-old baby (described further in Chapter 9) came to see me, agonizing over the process of weaning. Mother had to return to work in two months time, but was still breast-feeding Luke night and day. The coming separation felt arbitrary to her and this made it difficult for her to sort out whether Luke still needed her and her breast or whether both of them were ready to be more separate from each other.

When Mother had got to the point of being able to own natural feelings of *not* wanting to be with her baby all the time and was becoming ready to stop breast-feeding, I asked if she had had any dreams about it all. She laughed and said, 'I don't get to sleep for long enough to dream.' Then she recalled a dream a week previously, just after Luke's christening. In the dream she was wearing a white dress with buttons down the front. One button was open and the baby's godfather had done it up for her. The economy of this dream is quite startling: the allusions to this mother beginning to button herself up from breast-feeding and the associations to sexual feelings and a wedding brought together the themes of our work. She had begun to speculate whether her extreme closeness to Luke had caused her to feel more distant from her husband. She was starting to think about whether a more appropriate space between her and Luke would enable her marriage to come back to life. The white dress perhaps alluded to a new 'wedding' with her husband. The christening, a ceremony of recognizing Luke as an individual, was well timed for this family. I pointed out to Mother that this dream was a going-over in her mind, a commentary, on all these issues.

Wilfred Bion (1962a) has described how the mother's thinking about her baby helps him to deal with his confused emotional experiences in a way that enables him to start thinking and dreaming. I would add that the mother's dreaming is part of this process. This mother's dream seemed to have helped her prepare for the partial weaning process later in the week. Luke, in turn, was set free to sleep and dream.

Dreams can be a way of anticipating progress before it has been openly achieved, not as a form of 'prophecy' but as an acknowledgement of mental work. Parents' dreams may herald progress in dealing with the problems between them and their children. One father (already mentioned in Chapter 2) dreamt that his little son Stanley, who could not yet talk, asked him, 'Why don't you show me how to get to sleep?'. This released into consciousness memories that helped Father connect what was happening now with similar problems from the generation before between his own father and himself. This dream thus linked the past with the present, reminding Father of his own childhood difficulties and apparently informing him that *his* father's failure to help him was part of the background of his own failure to help his son now. However, I think Stanley's words in the dream, 'Why don't you show me how to get to sleep?', actually came from a dawning ability by Father to do just that. The words in the dream show that Father is beginning to imagine himself as being able to help his son.

In a sense, therefore, parents' dreams are one of the many aspects of caring for their children. The first example of this may be dreams in pregnancy. These are one of the routes of the psychological preparation that is a major task of pregnancy.

Dreams in pregnancy enable the mother to absorb the changes taking place in her own body and in her position within her family and her wider community. These dreams can provide a shape to her fantasies. Some may be an extension of her day-dreams about what the baby will be like, its sex, appearance and character; others may be a symbolic expression of disturbing fantasies about what the being inside her is doing to her body; and others may be a representation of anxieties as to whether the foetus is developing normally. In particular, anxiety-dreams about the impending childbirth may be one means towards mastering this anxiety. The turbulence of the actual experience of the birth may be demonstrated later by highly disturbing dreams, which may both denote a mother at risk and be a way of absorbing the psychic stresses.

Moving on to after the baby has been born, one mother, whose baby had colic and slept badly, dreamt that she took the baby's penis into her mouth. It seemed as though this was partly a reversal of the breast-feeding experience of *her* nipple going into *his* mouth. We see from this simple example how disturbing and exciting new bodily experiences like breast-feeding can be; they can arouse 'forbidden' sexual feelings in the mother towards her baby. Shocked by this dream, although able to confide it to her husband, the mother found the breast-feeding awkward. It was not until she told me the dream, and could make the conscious connection between it and breast-feeding, that she was able to get more comfortable with these disturbing fantasies.

Later the mother dreamt that her baby turned into a small furry animal with big teeth. I commented to her that this seemed to represent fantasies that she was breast-feeding a small biting animal and that this might be affecting her way of feeding him in such a way that it produced pain in him. Perhaps she strained away from this fancied biting, so that the baby took in gulps of air as he sucked, or something else fraught between them may have affected his digestion of the milk. This is one possible sequence of events, which can only be a hypothesis (in Chapter 9 we look at some of the explanations for colic). Given my explanation, the dream illustrated Mother's fear of being bitten, which then indirectly caused the baby's pain. Another possible chain of events is that the baby's pain was what precipitated the dream – perhaps the screaming of the baby was experienced by the mother as a kind of biting into herself, so that she pictured him in her dream as a biting animal.

Parents may thus dream about their children in many ways, ranging from dealing with their own trauma in having babies, and differentiating themselves out from these babies, to a mature ability to dream altruistically on behalf of their children.

PARENTS' UNDERSTANDING OF CHILDREN'S DREAMS

How can parents help their children with their own dreams? Palombo (1978) suggests, 'Parents are in reality the original "interpreters" of dreams' (p. 164). This should not be misunderstood as meaning parents should act as 'therapists' or enquire intrusively about dreams.

The repeatedly reassuring presence of his mother or her substitute after the experience of an awakening dream is a crucial element in any infant's learning to distinguish between his inner and outer worlds . . . The child just beginning to talk brings his awakening dreams to his parents both for reassurance and to take advantage of their ability to translate his strange experience into words . . . The parent's failure to supply what is needed at this point may have a serious effect on the later accessibility to the child of his early memories and of fantasy material in general. (Palombo, 1978, p. 164)

Through dreams and nightmares in children we can, in fact, see revealed the progressing stages of emotional and psychic development. These are conveyed both in the dreams that wake the child and those that do not. What are the differences between these dreams? W. Clifford M. Scott (a Kleinian analyst who was actually Melanie Klein's first student) puts it neatly:

When Freud began to listen to patients' stories of their lives their dreams were naturally part of the story . . . He discovered that dreams showed disguised attempts to fulfil wishes which often dated from infancy . . . These wishes were disguised in such a way that sleep was preserved or protected, unless the emotion connected with the attempted wish-fulfilment was so great, or the dream was repeated with such increasing emotion, that continued sleep becomes impossible. (1975, p. 253)

With young infants we can only guess at the content of their REM states, using the clues we observe of sucking mouths, crying out, and so on. But these clues can be very persuasive. One mother said to me spontaneously of her sleeping two-month-old: 'He's dreaming of sucking'. When a crying baby wakes in distress, not seeming to need food, parents may empathically guess at a 'bad dream'. It becomes much easier when a child who can use words is able to recount a frightening dream at the time of waking or obtain the relief of telling in the morning the memory of one that did not wake him. However, when Palombo (1978) talks of the seriousness of the need to understand a child's dream, we must include in this the need for empathy with the dreams, and the anxieties that lie behind these, of the pre-verbal child.

Joanna's mother (see also Daws, 1985) showed me how hard it can be in reality to be an interpreter for a child's dream. Joanna, aged one, would cry out during a nightmare, but when her mother went into her she was rejected, that is, treated as a part of the nightmare. Joanna slept badly, had many of these nightmares and frequent temper tantrums during the day. Joanna's mother vividly described feeling that her baby saw her as a 'witch' in the night.

It seemed appropriate to go quite explicitly through a simple Kleinian version of child development and talk about the child's difficulty in managing her own aggressive and destructive impulses, and her need to project these into her mother. This mother was interested intellectually, but also responded instinctively. The sleeping difficulties had started at six weeks, after a brief period when Father had to go away. We connected the sleeping difficulties with Mother's own panic at this separation and her resentment with Father for not being there to support her. After ten months of bad nights Joanna slept through the night for two weeks. After that there were some broken nights, but the relationship between Mother and daughter changed dramatically from mutual fury to a loving, teasing one. By understanding the nature of her baby's fears in the night, Mother was better able to respond to them. The baby now had the experience of being understood and was comforted by this understanding. She no longer needed to wake repeatedly to seek it.

W.C.M. Scott (1975) described what can happen later on when parents have not listened to their children: 'Patients may fear boring the listener by telling their dreams. They may instead have become identified with aggressive parents who once rejected or forgot their children's dreams and they in their turn began to forget their own' (p. 327). Scott's comments on sleep research have a special relevance to this chapter, where we have used some of the results of sleep researchers. He says: 'Researchers who awaken patients after REM sleep and ask for dreams may be doing something similar to the opposite of what happens when a child awakens after a dream and wants to be with the person who was with him when he went to sleep. He may wish to do something analogous to telling the dream' (1975, p. 328). It must be noted that Scott is making somewhat of a generalized assumption that parents don't listen, but of course many parents do. However, it is relevant to recall Hartmann's finding that laboratory subjects may remark that they can sleep better there and that nightmare-sufferers have fewer nightmares in the sleep laboratory because they feel safe, watched over by the researchers.

In 1910 Ernest Jones, the first psychoanalyst in Britain, wrote *On the Nightmare* in which he argued that in nightmares, and also other forms of anxiety-dreams, 'the latent content represents the fulfilment of a repressed sexual wish, usually an incestuous one'. This idea – that nightmares are deep and unacknowledged wishes in the self, sexual, aggressive, and so on, and that these wishes are usually directed towards the most important figures in the child's life – was courageous and startling when written in 1910 and is still a crucial part of our thinking about nightmares. It helps explain why it is so essential for the parents themselves to understand these frightening dreams. The child needs the parents' understanding, firstly, as a recognition that he is experiencing strong emotions and secondly, so as to receive an unconscious, unspoken acknowledgement from the parents that they themselves may be the focus of these nightmares. The parent who knows this does so from his own self-knowledge; his childhood dreams and nightmares were like that too. On the other hand parents often have to struggle to differentiate their own fears and anxieties from those of their children.

All this activity through the night is as universal and matter of fact as the parents' ability to tolerate the small child's daytime outburst of 'I hate you', which stems from the same instinctual source as the equally passionate 'I love you'. The significance of the child's confiding his nightmares to his parents is thus that they give him both protection over the strength of the impulses and anxieties that the nightmares represent and that there is an unspoken 'forgiveness' by the parents for themselves being at least in part the focus of these impulses.

One mother told me in some distress that she felt she was the cause of her two-year-old daughter's nightmares. After an angry outburst where she shouted irrationally at her, her daughter dreamt about an angry witch. She felt her daughter was putting this real encounter into symbolic form. It is important to differentiate between actual events which are dealt with psychically through our dreams and the grappling with emotions that also fills children's dreams with witches, monsters, and so on. These witches and monsters can be both the child's own impulses and the feared retaliation from parents for these imagined attacks.

THE CHILD'S CONFLICTS
In this book I have dealt at length with the effect of parents' pathology on the child's ability to sleep, suggesting that at times the child's disturbance is a direct reflection of the parents'. Secondly, I have shown how a child's own difficulty in sleeping can be eased or

not by the parent. Humberto Nagera (1966) distinguishes between sleep disturbances, which are 'service symptoms' due to a collusion with a parent's psychopathology, and those due to conflict within the child himself, which may give rise to sleep problems and be illustrated by dreams and nightmares. We will start by looking briefly at the connections between the physiological development of sleep, including REM or D states, and emotional growth.

David Metcalf (1979) describes how EEGs have shown that in the first three months of life (for full-term infants) the infant falls asleep directly from full waking to the REM state. After three months the more 'mature' method of falling asleep takes over and sleep proceeds electrographically from the awake record through Stage 1 non-REM to Stage 2, gradually progressing to a deeper slow-wave sleep and finally rising to REM sleep.

Metcalf suggests that both physiologically and psychologically the psychic precursors and prototypes of dramatic dreaming commence during this period of switch-over in sleep patterns at about three months. As the central nervous system matures, so the physiological possibilities of the nature of dream states become more complex.

This change in sleep physiology coincides with psychological change in the infant. His developing physical attainments are matched with a growing sense of his self and psychological differentiation from the mother. Developing at the same time are memory and anticipation. We may speculate that emerging dreams are facilitated by these. It can only be hypothesis as to what the content of an infant's REM state is, but like the mother who said of her two-month-old, 'He's dreaming of sucking', we are using something of our own experience when we speculate that an infant's dreams are memories and desires of states he has experienced, re-enactments of present gratification or unfulfilled states.

We will look in more detail at the psychological development of babies in the next chapter, but meanwhile we must note that the various anxieties that emerge at the different stages of development produce their own effects on sleep. As we will see in Chapter 9, the stage of weaning, both actual and 'psychological', and stranger-anxiety are important examples of a potentially stressful developmental stage. Babies who have slept well previously may now have sleep disturbances under the stress of this period. The dreams of this time probably reflect the internal preoccupations of the baby. Melanie Klein (1959), for example, vividly describes the concern of the growing infant for the mother, with the infant now *worrying* about how his impulses have affected the mother and how to deal with his aggressive feelings. This stage is called by Klein the 'depressive position'; it does not mean that the baby is depressed, but implies sensitivity and concern for others. This is also the age of teeth coming through. What is the psychological meaning of the sensations in gums, of the presence of these hard, biting new bits of the baby? Does the baby experience this as pain and suffering within his own body or as a tool with which to enjoy biting into hard rusks, teething rings, and so on? Does he feel joyfully sadistic or depressively guilty when he bites his mother, inadvertently or on purpose? And what does he make of all this in his dreams? No wonder parents of babies of six to nine months or so, intuitively aware of so much going on, are not surprised at anxious cries in the night.

Dreaming does not always herald anxiety. It is also a vital part of the attainment of psychic individuality. Frances Tustin (1972) writes of the stage where

> identification with a mother who can bear the pains of bodily separateness begins to take place . . . Thus the capacity for representations and the use of skills develop. Dreams begin to take the place of random discharges and bodily movements. Innate forms begin to be transformed into thoughts and fantasies. The psyche as we know it begins. The child becomes psychologically viable and continent. (p. 61)

As the baby gets older and is able to talk, he may then tell his parents of the content of his dream. As with adults' dreams, the manifest content may simply be an illustration of the themes underneath. For example, the monsters and wild beasts in many little children's dreams would seem to depict aspects of themselves or of their parents. Perhaps oedipal feelings, that is, jealousies of parents and also jealousies of new babies, may account for some of these dreams.

The book *Where the Wild Things Are*, by Maurice Sendak (1963), can have an amazingly therapeutic effect on children in the grip of these feelings. Max, the hero of this book, makes so much mischief that his mother calls him a 'wild thing' after he says to her, 'I'll eat you up', and is sent to bed without his supper. In bed he dreams that he goes to where the Wild Things are, tames the monsters and becomes their king. After a year of this he becomes lonely and goes home to 'where someone loved him best of all'.

What seems to work in this story for a small child is the acknowledgement of the wild feelings inside himself, making friends with them and overcoming them within himself and getting back to a loving relationship with his mother. Having this book read to them may often help children manage their nightmares, as also may patient listening by parents to children recounting the content of these dreams. The parents' task is to listen and help children deal with the forces of their dreams – the actual having of the nightmare may be a useful path to self-awareness for the child about the fierceness of his own emotions.

DREAMS AND PLAYING

We have looked at dreams and nightmares as ways of expressing and communicating anxieties and conflicts. The dreams may also help to resolve these conflicts. We have also noted that through the images that symbolically represent conflicts, an individual may be able to make connections, consciously or not, between past and present issues. We have also seen that the dream itself has an integrating function and helps sort out, make sense of, and put into memory, our continuing daily experiences.

Meltzer (1983) describes the dream process as continuing in our waking lives with our underlying thoughts. In children this continuous process can best be seen in their play. Children can often be seen engaged in reflective 'dreaming' play and, in a more active state, in playing out some phantasy or make-believe. This can easily be thought of as a carry-over from the work of dreaming. Anna Freud observed that children could relate their dreams, but not go on to talk about the meaning of their images. Both she and Melanie Klein evolved (though from very different theoretical standpoints) methods of therapy with children that involved understanding their play as a communication of some of the thoughts and phantasies underlying everyday ones.

Just as some children cannot easily relax into sleep and dreaming, so some children are unable to play. Andrea Pound (1982) has shown how some children of depressed mothers cannot relax their vigilance enough to turn their attention to play.

Children's nightmares follow the pattern of their emotional development. Babies becoming independent may appear to dream of feelings of abandonment, judging by their 'sorrow on arousal', to use Lenore Terr's poignant phrase. Toddlers struggling with their impulses may create daytime waking symbols of their fears and then produce these same symbols in their dreams. For example, fierce dogs, feared in the street, may represent newly acquired biting impulses. They may appear unchanged in dreams or get changed into even fiercer 'Wild Things'.

Terr (1987), looking at how children's nightmares progress developmentally, remarks on how the acquirement of language enables the child to tell his dreams. She suggests that 'the absence of language to label emotions may actually predispose' the toddler to nightmares. We can see from this that the organizational effect of having words in which to express feelings may start to get them under control. 'Nameless terrors' are less likely to remain so when a child has words to name them. We have seen earlier the therapeutic benefit of a child telling his parent his dreams.

David Foulkes (1983) describes how the manifest content of the dream changes as the child's cognitive capacities develop. Dreams become more complicated: for instance, small children dream of small figures such as rabbits, while school-age children dream of their peers. We see how the resolution of the Oedipus complex takes children out of the home in their dreams, as it does in waking life!

NIGHTMARES AND NIGHT TERRORS

Hartmann (1984) describes nightmares vividly. He defines the nightmare as 'waking up from sleep terrified (without an external cause) or something from inside that awakens a person with a scared feeling' (p. 10). He says that the typical nightmare occurs in the later part of the night, during a period of D sleep. 'The nightmare is definitely a dream, a long frightening dream which awakens the sleeper, and is clearly remembered as a very detailed, vivid and intense dream experience' (p. 19). A nightmare can last between five and thirty minutes and on waking the person may recall a long, detailed, frightening dream. The awakening is not in itself frightening.

By contrast the night terror is not a dream, but is in itself an unusual awakening, called by Broughton (1968) a 'disorder of arousal'. The night terror is a different biopsychological phenomenon from the nightmare, that is, it is generally triggered out of deep (slow-wave) sleep, not REM sleep. Hartmann (1984) observes that it happens early during the sleep period, usually in the first two hours during what is normally our deepest sleep, and that it consists of a simple awakening in terror, most often accompanied by a scream, by sweating, by body movements and sometimes by sleepwalking. 'Sleepers do not remember the night terrors as they might a dream. Either they recall nothing at all, and are only aware of the episode because they are told of it, or they are aware of a single frightening image, "something is sitting on me", "I am choking" ' (1984, p. 18).

By asking, 'Are your nightmares dreams?', Hartmann says he can almost always find out clinically whether patients have night-mares or night terrors. The question seems obvious; 'Of course' or 'Of course not' follow. 'The person . . . who sits upright in bed, or gets out of bed, screaming, with a glazed expression on his face, is a person having a night terror, not a nightmare' (1984, p. 21). This description will be familiar to many parents. Hartmann says night terrors in children are most commonly reported between the ages of three to eight. Parents often describe the child as screaming and then either returning to sleep or entering a sleepwalking episode with a glazed expression from which it is difficult to awaken him.

Ferber (1985a) describes how different a child appears to his parents if he is having either a nightmare or a night terror. A child waking from a nightmare can report a dream if he is old enough. He will cry or call for his parent, will recognize the parent and want to be held and comforted. He will remember the dream on waking and also in the morning. A child having a night terror is not awake. He may cry out, talk, moan, in a seemingly nonsensical way. He will not recognize his parents or allow them to comfort him and he will not remember the episode upon becoming fully awake or in the morning.

One of the interesting consequences of the differences in remembering nightmares and night terrors is that after a remem-bered nightmare a child may be frightened to go to bed or to sleep. After a night terror he does not have this fear. Ferber notes that on waking from a night terror the child will relax and be able to return to sleep quickly; with no memory of the night terror, he is not afraid to go to sleep on other nights.

A particular difficulty for parents in dealing with their children's night terrors is the sudden arousal that is a characteristic of them. This sudden arousal also rouses the parents with alarm and no warning. Their ability to deal calmly with the child is affected by their own psychological and physiological response to this awakening.

Hartmann (1984) says there is a tendency for night terrors to run in families and some children may have a genetic susceptibility to them. Night terrors can be considered a minor abnormality in the brain's sleep–wake mechanisms, producing unusual arousals.

However, night terrors can also be influenced by environmental or emotional factors. A child susceptible to night terrors may have them whenever there is stress or a difficult period in the family (Ferber, 1985b). Since sleep deprivation and extreme tiredness aggravate night terrors, keeping to a regular sleep schedule may in itself be a partial cure. Hartmann also suggests that reassurance both to parents and by parents is helpful and that short-term psychotherapy can be useful. It may reduce stress by helping parents handle potentially stressful events in new ways and gives them an opportunity to examine their own dangerous emotions – anger and rage – in a safe daytime setting. Magagna (1986), in her paper on older children, has described night terrors in latency as being a way of expressing unacknowledged hostility within families. Dangerous matters that cannot be openly talked about may be expressed in this way.

Now back to true REM nightmares. 'Is your nightmare a dream?', Hartmann asks his patients and, 'of course', some of them reply. That means it may be remembered and the possible meaning of it thought about. Nightmares, as frightening versions of dreams, are an opportunity to express and work out the conflicts and anxieties of waking life and its relationships. One major anxiety may be the fear of retaliation for one's own angry impulses. Nightmares are especially frequent in young children and increase during times of stress in older children and adults, especially in conditions involving feelings of helplessness.

NON-SYMBOLIC POST-TRAUMATIC NIGHTMARES
Mary-Sue Moore (1989) has highlighted, using some of Hartmann's findings, a connection between a significant reduction in Stage 4 sleep and a type of recurrent non-symbolic 'nightmare' that occurs at another stage of non-REM sleep. Moore tells us that these traumatic nightmares differ from REM dreams in very significant ways. In particular such nightmares are virtually non-symbolic, unlike true REM-sleep nightmares. They are arousals out of Stage 2 sleep and are repetitive memories of a traumatic event. The individual frequently awakes from these nightmares in a highly aroused state.

Moore shows that if depressed or anxious individuals feel vulnerable to external threats, they are less likely to go deeply into Stage 4 sleep. The urge to self-preservation keeps them from becoming deeply unconscious. Such individuals also experience fewer REM dreams or ordinary nightmares that would follow after

Stage 4 sleep and are deprived of the reparative work that a REM dream or nightmare could offer. When such anxious individuals have also suffered a traumatic event, they often experience nightmares coming out of the lighter Stage 2 sleep. During these Stage 2 nightmares, traumatic memories or situations are played over and over again, with little symbolic alteration. However, there may be some REM nightmares at the same stage which do help the person deal with the perceived dangers. As the traumatic experience is gradually integrated, fewer Stage 2 nightmares occur and REM dreams become less frightening.

Terr (1987) similarly describes children after a traumatic kidnapping having an exactly repeated, recurrent nightmare. As time went on the children were able to add current material from their lives to the nightmare. The dreams became 'modified repetitions' and became increasingly disguised with symbolism. Moore points out that in a post-traumatic dream the people involved are portrayed as themselves, not as someone symbolically standing in for them. As the dream begins to play a part in the recovery process, the dream itself gradually changes and settles into the context of other experiences. We are straying here into ideas derived from children older than those discussed in this book, but this available material sheds light on processes also pertaining for younger infants.

Moore (1989) also shows that night terrors which come out of Stage 4 deep sleep, rather than Stage 2 or REM sleep, may be understood as a conflict between two ways of surviving. When the anxieties of the night terror appear, the individual has a 'choice' between two ways of defending the threat to the self – either going into deeper unconsciousness or arousal. The disturbed arousal from a night terror where the child does not properly awake is the result of this unsolved conflict. The child wakes screaming and does not recognize the parent; the parent also becomes terrified by the child's state.

WHO HAS NIGHTMARES?

Hartmann (1984) tells us that adults with a lifelong history of frequent nightmares are usually open and independent in their mental structure, with a tendency both to mental illness (schizophrenia) and to artistic expression. He intriguingly suggests that people who suffer from nightmares are those with 'thin or permeable boundaries' (p. 104). They do not keep things pigeon-holed between rigid partitions; they 'let things through'. Using boundaries in many different senses, these nightmare-sufferers' dreams are not bounded in the usual sense: the nightmares themselves can be seen as a failure to keep dangerous and frightening material out of dreams in a way that most of us are able to do. Their sleep–wake boundaries can be considered permeable in that often they are not certain they are awake for quite a while after waking. Arguing that fear of retaliation for one's angry impulses may produce nightmares, Hartmann concludes that these are not people with an excess of aggressive drive or of hostility, but rather individuals with thin boundaries, such that normal fears or anger 'get through' more and become more vivid and frightening for them than for most of us.

In formulating this, Hartmann makes the fascinating observation that nightmare-sufferers see themselves as having been 'unusual' in childhood, that is, 'sensitive'. 'The word sensitive occurred frequently; referring sometimes to perceptual sensitivity – to light and sound, for instance; sometimes to interpersonal sensitivity – empathy, awareness of other's feelings; and almost always to being themselves emotionally sensitive – easily hurt by others. They saw this personality characteristic as having been present more or less from birth' (1984, p. 70).

Why go into details of adult nightmare-sufferers in a book about infants? Children do have more frequent nightmares than do most adults; it is a developmental phase and may really be one of the things most people 'grow out of'. As Hartmann says, the sensitivity of the adult nightmare-sufferer may presage mental illness or artistic creativity. However, the retrospective discovery of the 'sensitivity' of the nightmare-sufferer has an important bearing on how parents deal with childhood nightmares. The paradoxical solution is, I think, that facing the content of the nightmare commonsensically with the child may reduce this over-sensitivity – that a child need not go on being so sensitive and feeling special if the universality of his terror is acknowledged. We all have demons within us – sharing them by recounting our dreams can make them manageable. Nothing could be more robust than the monsters in *Where the Wild Things Are* or than Max in his way of dealing with them.

One mother described how her baby's father, since diagnosed as schizophrenic, used to wake her up in the night by thumping her for no apparent reason. When the baby, Jerry, was born, the father sat by his cot and woke him repeatedly, saying it was to check that he was still alive. Mother left Father, went back to him and, after several occasions when he violently beat her up in front of the baby, she finally left. At three this little boy woke repeatedly in the night, often with night terrors, screaming, being hard to rouse, and unable to tell Mother what was frightening him. Mother was terrified that he was taking after his father, ·that is, becoming schizophrenic. I talked with her about the need to understand with Jerry what the terrors in the night were about – that they were about the traumatic events he had seen and his own internal fears about them, and that these events had happened before he had words to describe them in. It seemed to me that the mother's attitude now was vital for Jerry's future mental health. Thus if she could convey to him that she *understood* the nature of his terrors, even without exactly knowing what they were, a process of gathering them together could happen for him that could enable him to deal with them. Jerry's mother had felt that Father had slipped away from her into an incomprehensible, mad world of schizophrenic thinking and impulse. She had tried to make sense of it for him, tried to help him, reassure him and look after him, and it had not worked. In fact I was suggesting that what had not worked for Jerry's father might work for Jerry.

These thoughts tie in with Hartmann's findings that nightmare-sufferers frequently see themselves as having been 'sensitive' children. One factor in this may have been the failure of their parents at the time to deal matter-of-factly with infantile terrors. These children seem to grow up with one 'skin' less of parental protection.

We have seen how dreams and nightmares are a way of dealing with, understanding and organizing into memory the experiences we encounter throughout life. The symbolic way in which dreams refer to people, places and events means that dreams can be a vivid illustration of thought processes. The story-telling of a dream punctuates an individual's life-history. We have seen how dreams can get hold of themes from the past and can express anticipatory thoughts about the future. Our dream thoughts underlie our conscious thoughts even in waking time. Perhaps with parents and infants, unconsciously so closely in touch with each other, dreams are a vehicle of communication about these intertwined thoughts.

CHAPTER SEVEN

THE DEVELOPMENT OF SEPARATENESS OF THE SELF

W E HAVE LOOKED AT how a baby develops physiologically, influenced by his parents' handling of him. Now we will turn to the normal emotional development of the baby, which is also influenced by the parents, at first principally the mother. We look briefly at the different ways various psychoanalytic writers have described this process; their theoretical languages are sometimes at odds with each other, but all have an interesting original way of adding to our picture of what happens between parents and babies.

This is a chapter about feelings, about how the baby's sense of self develops, how his sense of who he is on his own derives from who he is with his mother, and conversely how this depends also on his mother's picture of him. The process starts as early as pregnancy: one of the mother's first tasks is in thinking about her coming baby and herself in relationship to him. How she manages it can even affect the birth and the early weeks of life.

Mothers and babies establish intimacy and are then able to become more separate from each other. This is not an automatic development; rather it is a human drama, containing both pains and achievements. The mother of eight-month-old Dominic said to me, 'When he closes his eyes, I feel left out.' In one sense the problem for a mother in getting a baby to sleep is the basic act of putting the baby down, that is, of separating herself from the baby and the baby from her. It can be as difficult for the mother to do without the baby as it is the other way round.

Much of psychoanalytic and child development literature is occupied with showing us the process by which a baby starts from a state of dependence, physical and emotional, on its mother and gradually moves apart.

Donald Winnicott was a paediatrician and psychoanalyst who did a great deal of work with mothers and babies. He wrote on the subject for both professionals and general readers. A series of broadcasts for mothers, beautifully simple and evocative, was developed into his book *The Child, the Family and the Outside World* (1964). Although written from now outdated assumptions about the social context of the family, with mothers almost wholly responsible for a baby's care, while the father goes out to work as the sole breadwinner, the description of the depth of emotions that babies, their mothers and fathers feel for each other is still fresh and moving. 'There is no such thing as a baby', only 'a *baby* and *someone*' (1964), as Winnicott said with characteristic enthusiasm. The baby depends on his mother for survival and the mother is also for a while almost totally bound up with the baby. Winnicott called this 'primary maternal preoccupation'. The baby moves through various states to the separation and individuation we associate with maturity and the mother reciprocally pulls apart from the baby. This process and its vicissitudes have been described within various theoretical frameworks.

As we look at some of these ideas, we should hold in mind the question posed in Chapter 1, whether sleep is experienced as a disruption or as a continuation of the being together of mother and baby. We will also see how the ability to sleep, or sleep disturbance, may punctuate the various changing stages of the baby's development.

How do babies separate from their mothers and how do mothers separate from their babies? Paret (1983), in her research study on the connection between sleeping and the ability of babies to separate from their mothers, observed that in a sample of babies at the crawling stage the 'sleepers' were able to move significantly further away from their mothers than the 'wakers'. It seems that babies who sleep well are more secure and can put some distance between themselves and their mothers.

PREGNANCY

It is just as well that pregnancy, from conception to a full-term baby, is a process that takes nine months. Prospective (especially first-time) mothers need at least this time to deal with the enormous changes taking place in their bodies, their minds and their lives. Pregnancy is a preparation time, both physical and emotional. Incidentally it is no accident that pregnant mothers need a great deal of sleep, particularly in the first three months. One might think that the later stages, with a larger baby to carry inside, would make a mother even more tired. However, if we think of one of the functions of sleep as being to deal with the effects of change, we can see that both physically, with the body accepting the new foetus growing inside it, and emotionally, as the mother thinks over the consequences to herself and adjusts to the existence of a new life, this early stage will require much more sleep.

The theme of separation is present even in pregnancy. Raphael-Leff (1982) describes pregnancy as a process whereby the mother at first feels the baby is a part of herself and then gradually feels it to become separate. In the 'psychological tasks of pregnancy which serve as a rehearsal for motherhood' she says that there are three major tasks, which may be seen as: 'a) achievement of emotional fusion with the foetus in early pregnancy; b) gradual differentiation of foetus and self after the quickening; and c) progressive psychic separation of baby and mother, culminating in the physical separation at birth'. Her model of what happens before birth is based on Margaret Mahler's (1975) description of how mothers and babies interact after birth, which we will look at later in this chapter. Raphael-Leff points out that women who cannot make use of this preparatory period of pregnancy will tend to have corresponding difficulties in their relationship with their child and that failures in this process may also have repercussions on the manner of the birth itself and on the early months after the birth.

One part of the task of becoming a mother to her own baby for the mother-to-be is dealing with the feelings and memories stirred up about herself as a baby in relation to her own mother (Emde, 1988). Later on, in Chapter 10, we will see how the particular quality of the relationship a mother has had with her own mother colours her way of dealing with her baby, but here we are looking at more general and universal forces.

Dinora Pines (1982) shows how the ties to her own mother can make it difficult for the mother to separate herself in her mind from her baby: 'The inevitable regression occasioned by pregnancy and motherhood may be a painful and frightening experience' (p. 318). Confusingly, the mother may have opposing wishes to merge with her own mother and to pull away from her. Pregnancy thus throws a mother back into powerful links with her own mother and her attempts to extricate herself can get tangled up with her picture of how separate she is from her baby.

MOTHER'S AMBIVALENCE AND ANXIETY

Having conflicting feelings about being pregnant and giving birth is quite normal. In fact anyone who cannot let herself know about feelings of *not* wanting to have a baby, at the same time as also wanting to, may have a harder time either giving birth or adjusting to the new baby. Difficulties and adversities of all kinds in pregnancy may have a later effect, in various ways, on the baby itself, including on its sleep. Giorgis *et al.* (1987) have shown that one way in which this might happen is that the mother's anxiety during pregnancy can affect the rhythms that develop between her and the baby, thereby influencing its sleep. They also mention that the mother's ambivalence can have such an effect. Here I would add that it is the *unacknowledged* ambivalence of love and hate that is at issue. The mother's lack of self-knowledge about her own feelings carries over to a not-knowing about the range of her baby's feelings and rhythms. Giorgis *et al.* also crucially note that the effects of the mother's state of mind may be tempered by good support from the baby's father.

The ambivalence a mother may feel about the irreversible change in her own life is acutely expressed in 'Poem to my Daughter' by Anne Stevenson (1983).

> A woman's life is her own
> until it is taken away
> by a first particular cry.
> Then she is not alone
> but a part of the premises
> of everything there is.

THE EXPERIENCE OF BIRTH AND ITS DIFFICULTIES

We can see that a mother may be confused about whether the foetus inside her is a part of her body or something separate, and her reaction to the impending birth may include being afraid and unwilling to face the next stage of separation that birth implies.

There is evidence to show that difficult labours and birth have a deleterious effect which can include severe sleep problems (Blurton-Jones *et al.*, 1978). It is important here not to assume that separation or other psychological problems in the mother's own psyche are a cause of all birth difficulties. However, the *experience* of a difficult birth is described in such a way by some mothers. Birth experiences of course may affect either one or both mother and baby and physical and emotional causes and consequences may be separate or intertwined.

Moore and Ucko (1957) discovered that some infants who showed unexplained sleeping disturbances, together with general unpredictability and over-reactivity, had had some asphyxia at birth. They suggest that asphyxia might also lead to hyperactivity later on. Judith Trowell (1982) shows how unexpected Caesareans can affect the relationship between mother and baby. The mothers have had the 'distress, crisis and sense of failure produced by an emergency Caesarean section . . . their labours were longer and they had more medication before and after delivery and were unconscious at the time of delivery' (p. 87). Trowell shows how these factors can impede the sensitive early stages of mother and baby getting to know each other. At one year a group of mothers who had had Caesareans reported more problems with their babies than the control group. Crucially they reported leaving their babies to cry for up to five minutes before responding, the control group usually responding in two minutes.

We see from this that there may be later effects from a birth where the mother has been unconscious for some time after delivery and where she also needs to be preoccupied with her own state while recovering from an abdominal operation. She is less ready to respond to the baby's signals and it may take longer for mother and baby to feel closely in touch with each other. Trowell emphasizes the need for obstetric care which minimizes medication and allows the mother to participate as much as possible, both in giving birth and in the care of her baby afterwards.

We have already seen how the 'bonding' process between mother and infant starts immediately after birth and that the setting up of this closeness affects the way in which the mother is able to influence the baby's physiological sleep–wake rhythms. What follows is an illustration of how the experience of birth and shortly after can influence the bonding and therefore the separation process.

A CASE EXAMPLE

With Matthew and his mother it seemed clear that a difficult birth experience kept on getting in the way of Mother's picture of herself and her baby.

Matthew was nearly two and still breast-feeding; his mother was embarrassed by this, but could not let go of him. In the first session she cried as she told me about his birth. She had prepared herself well, but when the time came it was all unexpected, rapid, violent; midwives and doctors came and went, only her husband was there throughout. She spent ten days in hospital and began to recover. On the last night the hospital offered to baby-sit and she went out to dinner with her husband. She came back and found her baby apparently neglected – crying, hungry, in need of a nappy-change. She felt she should never have left him and that this experience must have damaged him permanently. Since then he had had problems in getting to sleep except when held at the breast, fed and allowed to go to sleep from there. He had never been able to lie in his cot and fall asleep on his own.

We talked about how the first 'letting go' of him, his birth, had gone so wrong and that she could not trust herself to let go of him without doing him damage. I questioned her assumption that bad experiences were the only significant ones. She had pinpointed the moment in hospital when Matthew had been left hungry, dirty and alone. I asked her to put this in the balance with all the times his needs *had* been attended to and suggested that his cumulative experience of this could be equally memorable. It was as though Matthew's mother felt that good experiences must be obliterated by bad ones – and that letting go or separations were the same as bad experiences. We talked about how Matthew might be able to enjoy a feed, let go of her, and she of him, and then lie in his cot, savouring the memory of his feed and digesting the experience along with the milk. We noted that emotional as well as physical growth comes from this.

Father had always been an enjoyable part of the bedtime routine, but had then handed Matthew over to Mother for the final feed. Mother now entrusted Father with sometimes putting Matthew in his cot. She left a bottle of milk and biscuits within reach and offered herself less quickly to Matthew in the night. The breast-feeding soon faded away and Matthew stopped waking up in the night. Mother then thought of the milk and biscuits as being too much of a direct substitute for her breast – she felt he would become someone always relying on food for comfort. She replaced the bottle with a musical toy, which Matthew loved and played to himself as he lay in the cot going to sleep and when he woke up in the morning. She made the leap herself, and presumably therefore enabled her son to do the same, of creating a symbol instead of a direct substitute for her breast.

I saw Matthew's mother over several weeks. She lost excess weight as she weaned him. In the last interview when she came to say goodbye, she had had a crisp new haircut. An outline that had seemed to merge with her child had regained definition as an individual.

Her relationship with her husband improved – two years of Matthew's night waking had left little time for their sexual life. She relaxed her tendency to exclude him from aspects of caring for Matthew through her idea that only the breast could send the baby to sleep. She became able to let Father help her with the weaning and, when Matthew was weaned, Father could be an equal partner in caring for his son.

The musical box served somewhat belatedly for Matthew as what Winnicott called a 'transitional object'. I often feel that what I am doing for mothers is providing them with something like a temporary transitional object through the medium of my words. I think with them about their position with the baby, then put into words what I feel is going on and leave them with these words to hold on to when they go back to their baby and renegotiate their relationship through the following nights. The words contain the combined thought of the mother and myself about the transition from one state to another.

INTIMACY AND SEPARATION

Matthew's mother equated separation with a 'bad' experience, but it is important to note that mothers may find it difficult to acknowledge the baby's separate existence for their own sakes, not just on behalf of their baby. Let us now look at the ordinary routes by which mothers and babies first establish intimacy and then achieve separation from each other. The clinical anecdote above serves as an introduction to more than one theoretical framework.

There is some disagreement among psychoanalytic writers as to whether the first experience of the baby is of a 'fusion' with the mother, as Mahler and Winnicott describe it, or whether, as Melanie Klein says, 'The new-born infant has an innate unconscious awareness of the existence of the mother' (1959, p. 248). From the detailed observations of babies carried out in recent years – both the psychoanalytically inspired ones initiated by Esther Bick ((1964), Martha Harris (1975) and most recently Miller *et al.* (1989)) and the research findings of developmental psychologists (some of which are summarized in Daniel Stern (1985)) – we see many examples of babies 'recognizing' their mother by sight, sound and touch. The inference from this is that the recognition of the mother includes an awareness of her as separate from the baby's own self. Probably the most accurate picture is in fact a combination of these two veins: the baby is able to recognize separateness at times and at other times lapses into a sensation of merging. As adults we may have fleeting recalls of such merging in both sensual or aesthetic experiences (Milner, 1936, 1950). Fred Pine (1986) has described graphically how the infant's body can 'melt' into the mother's body at times of falling asleep, while in a state of higher cognitive functioning there will be a clear sense of boundaries.

Melanie Klein was the first psychoanalyst to develop, seventy years ago, the therapy of little children, including two-year-olds. Her genius was to portray the feelings and imaginings within a little child's mind. According to Klein (1959) the baby

> not only expects food from her [the mother] but also desires love and understanding. In the earliest stages love and understanding are expressed through the mother's handling of her baby, and lead to a certain unconscious oneness that is based on the unconscious of the mother and child being in close relation to each other. The infant's resultant feeling of being understood underlies the first and fundamental relation in his life – the relation to the mother. At the same time frustration, discomfort and pain which . . . are experienced as persecution, enter as well into feelings about his mother, because in the first few months the whole of the external world, therefore both good and bad, come in his mind from her, and this leads to a twofold attitude toward the mother even under the best possible conditions. (p. 248)

From her unique viewpoint of sensitivity Klein describes how a little child can readily experience things in extremes, in black and white, all bad or all good, and can quickly switch from an experience of one to another; from all tears to all smiles. She stresses two very important processes in this, introjection and projection. Introjection is the process whereby an experience of something from the outside world modifies the child's sense of himself. Here the sense of self is changed, however minutely, in a long-term way. It is what happens in much emotional learning of course. Projection, on the other hand, occurs when something at first experienced as belonging to the self is then not acknowledged, or denied. The belongingness to the self is obliterated and the very same thing is felt as belonging to the outside.

Defining these processes, Klein says:

> introjection means that the outer world, its impact, the situations the infant lives through, and the objects he encounters are not only experienced as external, but are taken into the self, and become part of his inner life . . . Projection which goes on

simultaneously implies that there is a capacity in the child to attribute to other people around him feelings of various kinds, predominantly love and hate. (1959, p. 250)

We can see how Matthew's mother intuitively understood something of these processes of introjection and projection, though she saw it only as a malign process. She felt that the 'bad' experiences Matthew had undergone would influence him and become part of his internal world. In contrast to this Klein describes the way in which a mother's empathic understanding of the baby's 'bad' experience can mitigate its effect. But Matthew's mother was too convinced that he must have been damaged to help him in this way. Perhaps she herself felt too vulnerable and at the mercy of this 'damage' being projected back into herself.

The division into distinct good and bad experiences is referred to as 'splitting' and the maintenance of this splitting is important for an infant's being able to feel himself to be good and thus calmly at ease. He can feel purely good in the presence of pure good things, unmuddled by an awareness of 'bad' things. The process of 'emotional purification' is much assisted by projection, where badness is felt to be outside the self. This badness seems to have to go somewhere; mothers are usually on hand, so they often become the receptacle. If they do not do this easily, the external world and its figures can become increasingly 'bad' to the baby. Klein felt these processes epitomized the state of earliest infancy and because of the importance of splitting and projection she called this state the 'paranoid-schizoid position'. Many people have taken issue with her about such a state being centrally and crucially the one of earliest infancy. However this may be, her pointing out our human proneness to this way of dealing with extremes of feelings is of vital value.

If all goes well, the baby certainly seems to move from a predominantly egocentric position, when he sees his mother mainly in terms of *his* states of being, to perceiving her as a person with feelings of her own. He becomes aware of the effects of *his* actions *on her* and has some *concern* for her. Klein called this new state the 'depressive position'. A simple example is the baby at the breast who has produced his first teeth. His pleasure in his ability to bite, whether 'innocent' or 'sadistic', may be tempered by the realization that he is giving pain to the mother who feeds him. A delightful and frequently observed 'game' is where the baby 'feeds' his mother from the spoon he has just learnt to hold. Mothers perceive in this their baby's grateful wish to give something back for having been fed.

How does this connect with the ability to sleep or not? At an early stage of development the baby projects into his mother intense and passionate feelings of all kinds, including loving, hating and aggressive ones. To many mothers it is all in the day's work to 'receive' these feelings and 'give back' to the baby a sense of understanding and putting into perspective. However, a mother who, perhaps because of her own experiences, is frightened of what her baby is expressing, will not be able to reassure him. He will be left unsettled and maybe unable to sleep. If a mother is able to help the baby to deal with his feelings, repeated instances lead him to remember this and learn how to manage on his own.

What is the process by which a baby eventually learns to manage without having his mother actually with him? Edna O'Shaughnessy, a child psychotherapist and psychoanalyst who owes much to Klein and Bion, has one way of describing it. To understand her argument it is necessary to take both 'object' and 'breast' as ways of referring to aspects of the mother as a person.

She argues (1964) that at first the breast is experienced as 'good' when it is present and 'bad' when it is absent and needed. This is Klein's concept of splitting again. That is, a baby lying hungry and alone before a feed will feel that the breast that does not immediately come when he cries is leaving him to starve and must be bad. Gradually, as he has repeated memories that this breast does arrive to satisfy him, he will be able to look forward in its absence to a 'good' breast arriving. O'Shaughnessy, in asking how the absent object can cease to be a bad object, suggests that 'absence is a natural and essential condition of a relationship, which otherwise becomes a symbiosis detrimental to the separate identity of either person' (p. 42). Time away from the object is needed to get an emotional perspective on experience with the object. Appreciation too is sharpened in absence. Indeed the continuous presence of an object would be persecuting, the child would feel the object was intruding into his identity and he would also be burdened by guilt for claiming the object for himself.

O'Shaughnessy points out that

the absent object is a spur to the development of thought . . . there is a logical connection between thought and absence. You can be asked to think of something that is absent – a painting in a gallery (say), but you cannot be asked to think of a painting you are already looking at, perception shuts out thought, in this basic and simple sense. (1964, p. 34)

We can see how after the first few weeks a baby's capacity to sleep could be partly explained in terms of this concept of the absent object. We can think of an enraged, crying baby as one feeling neglected by the absent 'bad' breast and unable to sleep, while the peaceful one on his own remembers and anticipates the 'good' absent breast, his ability to *think* enhanced by the time apart, and he is able to slip from these thoughts into sleep. In 'On the sense of loneliness' (1963), Klein says, 'Memories of such happy experiences are a standby for the young child when he feels frustrated because they are bound up with the hope of further happy times' (p. 310).

Melanie Klein saw the mother as mitigating the baby's external experiences and above all the forces of his own internal drives. However, she had little experience of, and not so much interest in, what mothers and children really did with each other, as opposed to what was in the child's imaginings. Her unique vision came from spending time alone with children.

Winnicott, as a paediatrician, saw thousands of children on their mother's laps. His interest was in what really happens between mothers and children and he was fascinated by the interplay between them.

On the one hand Winnicott saw mothering as a hazardous process by which the mother could be the cause of the child's difficulties. On the other hand his descriptions of the 'ordinary devoted' or the 'good-enough' mother, who translates and transforms the external experience into one that the baby can manage and deal with, has caught the imagination widely: 'The good-enough mother (not necessarily the infant's own mother) is one who makes active adaptation to the infant's needs, an active adaptation that gradually lessens according to the infant's growing ability to account for failure of adaptation and to tolerate the results of frustration' (1971, p. 10). Like O'Shaughnessy Winnicott shows how 'if all goes well the infant can actually come to gain from the experience of frustration, since incomplete adaptation to need makes objects real, that is to say hated as well as loved' (1971, p. 11).

In this first satisfactory experience of having most of his needs met the baby has the illusion of being in magical control. The mother then has the task of gradually 'disillusioning' him and 'the stage is set for the frustrations that we gather together under the word "weaning"'.

Transitional objects are one way in which the baby gets through this stage of disillusion. I quote the following at some length, because Winnicott's ideas of transitional phenomena contain the essence of his unique idiosyncratic thinking about infants:

> There may emerge some thing or some phenomenon – perhaps a bundle of wool on the corner of a blanket or eiderdown, or a word or a tune, or a mannerism – that becomes vitally important to the infant for use at the time of going to sleep, and as a defence against anxiety, especially anxiety of the depressive type. Perhaps some soft object or other type of object has been found and used by the infant, and this then becomes what I am calling a transitional object. The object goes on being important. The parents get to know its value and carry it around when travelling. The mother lets it get dirty and even smelly, knowing that by washing it she introduces a break in continuity in the infant's experience, a break that may destroy the meaning and value of the object to the child. (1971, p. 4)

Winnicott lists some of the properties of the transitional object, including:

> The infant assumes rights over the object and we agree to this assumption.
> The object is affectionately cuddled as well as excitedly loved and mutilated.
> It must never change, unless changed by the infant. It comes from without from our point of view but not so from the point of view of the baby. Neither does it come from within, it is not a hallucination. Its fate is to be gradually decathected . . . it loses meaning . . . and this is because the transitional phenomena have become diffused. (1971, p. 5)

It is also vital to note that the essence of the transitional object is in allowing the baby to feel separate while still in contact with the parent. It in no way replaces the parent. In fact babies who have become separated from their parents lose interest in the transitional object, if they are not visited by their parents. The object loses its symbolic meaning, if this is not reinforced by a further connection with the parent.

In Matthew's case the use of a transitional object did not happen spontaneously. Only Mother herself would do for Matthew. Did his mother confirm his belief or was it unthinkable for her that he could manage without her? It is interesting that with my help in thinking it all through Mother was able to allow Matthew to have such objects and then was able to help him change the objects which stood for herself. The bottle and biscuits were replaced by a musical toy. The direct substitute gave place to a symbol. We are back to Bion's thinking in the absence of the object.

THE DEVELOPING SENSE OF SELF

Anna Freud is one of the major contributors to ideas about children's development, though her chief work was concerned with the period after infancy. She and her followers here and in America undertook detailed scientific observations of developmental processes in children. Her insights on sleep problems as developmental disturbances are clearly stated (1966) and I refer to these at various points in the book.

The American psychoanalyst Margaret Mahler was a disciple of Anna Freud. In her formulation of development she is crucially concerned with issues of separation. In *The Psychological Birth of the Human Infant* (1975) she describes how the biological and psychological births of the baby are not coincident in time.

Mahler uses many concepts she developed from Anna Freud, but she was more concerned with the period of infancy that also fascinated Klein. She and Klein have very different gifts in portraying the baby's development. Although Mahler is without Klein's brilliant insight into the individual baby's psychic processes, she thinks more about the developmental stages as being an interaction between mothers and babies. Further, despite some laborious 'jargon', she vividly portrays babies in action. We can see the baby depicted at a certain stage as a real baby, sitting up, crawling and walking. This is in contrast to Klein who, when at her most original theoretically, seems to have lost sight of actual, whole, real infants.

Mahler describes how the psychological birth of the individual is the result of a separation–individuation process from the mother or 'primary love object', which takes place over time. She defines an early symbiotic state as one before differentiation between self and mother has taken place. This state does not necessarily require the physical presence of the mother, but reflects the primitive images of oneself. Mahler suggests that the change from symbiosis to separation–individuation 'involves the child's achievement of separate functioning in the presence of, and with the emotional availability of, the mother'. We will see in Chapter 8 how Winnicott (1958) similarly traces the child's transition from 'I am' to 'I am alone' even in the presence of the mother.

Recent psychoanalytic and developmental observations show that an infant's recognition of his mother occurs very early on and this must mean that at least some of the time from soon after birth he is apparently seeing her as a separate being. This casts doubts on Mahler's conjecture of an early period where the baby's sense of self and mother is entirely 'fused'. Even so, we might guess that at some moments he feels himself to be so. Apart from these theoretical difficulties, Mahler gives us a very vivid picture of the baby's development. One of her particular gifts is her vivid, bodily illustrations of each stage of a baby's emotional development. For example, she says, 'We observed the holding behaviour of mothers with their infants and the moulding of infants with their mothers. We observed infants alternately moulding into, versus stiffening and stemming against, the mother's body' (1975, p. 24). Mahler shows how this physical alternating of closeness and pulling apart echoes the baby's emotional feelings in regard to distance from his mother. This process is intensified as the baby learns to crawl and then walk.

Mahler thinks of the separation–individuation process as occurring from the fifth month through the second and third years of life. From seven to eight months there is a pattern of 'checking back to mother' by the baby who is physically learning to move away from his mother, first by crawling and then by walking. Mahler movingly talks of the 'first tentative steps towards breaking away, in a bodily sense' from the mother. As the baby increasingly 'hatches out' into the world, there is the 'practising period' when his increased abilities in crawling, standing up and walking also represent a differentiation and moving away from his mother.

At this period, as many mothers know, the baby may suddenly become very intolerant of separations. A baby who can crawl out of the room away from his mother may be panic-stricken to turn around and find that *she* has moved out of *his* view. Some babies cannot let their mothers out of their sight even to go to the lavatory. Perhaps their own moving away makes them fear that Mother will vanish. In this stage, when mothers and babies start to feel increasingly separate, a mother may take it as a good time to go out alone or even return to work. She then may be surprised to find that although the baby can happily move away from her, he may panic if she moves away from him. It may be necessary to go through what Mahler calls a 'severe crisis of reunion' when mother and baby return to each other, where the baby cries inconsolably and may resist being put to sleep.

These stages defined by Mahler are useful for thinking about the origins of those sleep problems which start at this time. They are often attributable to the emotional anxieties caused by new independence of movement, which in our culture is often accompanied by weaning. Three different experiences may be coinciding: 1 the baby physically moving away from the mother as he crawls or walks away from her; 2 the physical and emotional separation of weaning; and 3 the mother physically moving away from the baby.

We can see how the 'separation' involved in being put down to sleep may re-evoke the panic or despair the baby has felt during the day at his mother's absence. Mahler suggests that such 'reaction to brief separations which is peculiarly specific to mother–infant reunions in the second half of the first year' might be understood in terms of a split (p. 67). The mother who went away became, as O'Shaughnessy (1964) described, a 'bad' mother. It takes time before she can be reintegrated with the 'good' mother who the baby feels would not go away. The baby has to be reconciled and 'forgive' her for having gone away before he can greet her easily.

As a psychoanalyst versed in developmental psychology, Daniel Stern (1985) provides another perspective on the processes of the first years of life. In *The Interpersonal World of the Infant* he has brilliantly combined the findings from both disciplines. He names four *senses* of self which develop in stages: the Emergent Self forms from birth to age two months, the Core Self forms between two and six months, the Subjective Self between seven and fifteen months and the Verbal Self forms after that. Once formed each sense of self remains active throughout life.

Stern suggests that even from birth there is an emergent sense of self, with no confusion between self and others. At each of the major shifts of self there is a forceful impression of change. 'One is suddenly dealing with an altered person.' For instance, when a few weeks old infant starts to smile responsively and gazes into the parents' eyes, a different social feel has been created. It is the altered sense of the infant's subjective experience lying behind these behavioural changes that makes the parent act and think about the infant differently. Further, Stern suggests that the change in the infant may partly come about through the adult interpreting the infant differently and acting accordingly.

In the forming of an organized sense of a core self, which

happens between the second and sixth month of life, infants are seen to have an integrated sense of themselves as distinct and coherent bodies, with control over their own actions, ownership of their feelings and a sense of continuity. They sense that they and their mother are separate physically, are separate agents, have distinct affective experiences and have separate histories. Between seven and nine months they 'discover that there are other minds out there as well as their own'.

Stern also distinguishes the sense of self *versus* other from the sense of self *with* other. He relates how the infant with an 'other' can make something happen that neither could do alone. For example, during a peek-a-boo game, 'the mutual interaction generates in the infant a self-experience of very high excitation, full of joy and suspense and perhaps tinged with a touch of fear' (1985, p. 102). This feeling state could not be achieved alone, it is a mutual creation. 'The infant is with an other who regulates the infant's own self-experience. In this sense the other is a *self-regulating other* for the infant' (p. 102, author's italics).

Stern shows how security and attachment are likewise mutually created experiences. He links the relevance of this to sleep. 'Others regulate the infant's experiences of somatic states . . . namely the gratification of hunger and the shift from wakeful fatigue to sleep. In all such regulations a dramatic shift in neurophysiological states is involved' (1985, p. 103). Thus, according to Stern, even though it is the infant's own self-state that is changed, such as from sleepiness to sleep, another person is involved in the 'physical mediation' of this self-state. So the processes of feeding, changing, rocking, of being put in the cot – all of which are part of the experience of going to sleep for an infant – are also experiences of the actions of this other person. Going to sleep is a social event.

We have seen from Klein and others that good experiences build up security and trust and that the infant's self-experience is altered and even created by being with someone else. Stern (1985) describes how repeated instances of a mutual experience build up into memories. For instance, a peek-a-boo game is never exactly the same each time it is played. The generalized memory of it is of a game that never happened in exactly that way, but is built up of the elements of what happened over many times. We can see how the memories of repeated bedtimes, with routines that are 'the same', but contain different conversations, games, actions and feelings every night, build up into these generalized memories.

Stern goes on to show how the person who helps the baby

regulate his own states becomes an 'evoked' companion who goes on being remembered, whether present or not. This is analogous to Klein's description of the internalized 'good' mother. Stern argues that this 'view of being almost continuously with real and evoked companions' is what leads to the infant feeling trustful and secure enough to be able to explore his surroundings. Like Klein he says that the memory of past experiences creates this trust. He makes the important point that for the baby being with this evoked companion is distinct from a 'we' experience; it is felt as an 'I' experience *with* another. The integrity of the core sense of self is not breached in the presence of the evoked companion. This is at the essence of the question so often pondered by parents: how does a baby acquire the ability to be on its own? Stern shows how the parent's presence contributes to the baby learning how to manage his own states for himself. The baby's ability to do this himself in the interested presence of his parent is different from the perception that it is the parent who regulates the baby's state. Penny's mother, whom we will meet in Chapter 9, had made this distinction when she said to herself of her baby, 'Why don't you *let* her go to sleep, not make her go to sleep?' The parents' reliable presence enables the baby to recall their support and continue with a feeling of having it, even in their absence.

As the baby develops the sense of a subjective self, from the seventh or ninth month, realizing that he has a mind and that other people do also, another of Stern's vital concepts, that of 'affect attunement', appears. We will see in various instances in the book how the satisfactory achievement of this, or failure of it, influences the baby's capacity to sleep.

Stern describes the importance of sharing affective states: 'What are the acts and processes that let other people know that you are feeling something very like what they are feeling?' (1985, p. 138). He shows how imitation is only a partial way of doing this. If a mother imitates a baby's facial expression, he can only tell from her face that she *perceived* what he was doing; she need not have *felt* the same as he did. For a real intersubjective exchange of affect, imitation alone won't do.

> First, the parents must be able to read the infant's feeling state from the infant's overt behaviour. Second, the parent must perform some behaviour that is not a strict imitation but none the less corresponds in some ways to the infant's overt behaviour. Third, the infant must be able to read this corresponding

parental response as having to do with the infant's own original feeling experience, and not just imitating the infant's behaviour. It is only in the presence of these three conditions that feeling states within one person can be knowable to another, and that they can both sense, without using language, that the transaction has occurred. (1985, p. 139)

Stern shows, charmingly, that parents do this by first imitating the baby and then adding a different mode of behaviour. For instance, if a baby is beating time with his hand on a toy, the parent may join in by singing to this beat or the parent may move her own body in time to the child's singing sound. 'Affect attunement then is the performance of behaviours that express the quality of feeling of a shared affect state without imitating the exact behavioural expression of the inner state' (p. 142). Its purpose is to show the baby that the parent knows how he feels. This new dimension, according to Stern, is added by mother when the infant is about nine months old and it is part of 'intuitive parental sense' to know when the infant has reached this state.

The concept of affect attunement is a crucial one for illustrating how human beings achieve a feeling of understanding each other deeply. From the point of view of our particular interest in sleep it has implications for the whole sequence of a baby's bedtime. The routines of bathing, stories, little games, in addition to the basic experience of feeding, provide opportunities for parent and baby to achieve this state of feeling attuned, which lasts beyond the excitements of the actual interchanges. The feeling of being in touch with each other's state of being is a major part of what can allow the baby to 'let go' into sleep. The various games of course have many other subtle functions, such as negotiating a transition phase or being a way of mastering fears. In Klein's view the baby's feeling of being understood by the mother is part of what enables it to withstand the vicissitudes of the night.

Stern's final sense, of a verbal self, takes us into the second year. He shows how language makes some parts of experience more sharable with other people and that 'It also finally permits the child to begin to construct a narrative of his own life' (1985). But, says Stern, language can be a double-edged sword – it can make some experience less sharable, creating a split in the self when experiences that are felt cannot be put into words. Parents and infants can find they have to live through a time when the infant's grasping for words almost creates a barrier of communication between them. The frustrations of this stage may lead to a state of tension in the infant which makes getting to sleep much harder.

As the infant's emotions develop, aggressive feelings become more complex and articulate. This can lead, as we saw when discussing Klein's ideas on the depressive position, to a growing concern for what these impulses might do to the parents and also to a fear of retaliation. All of this accounts for some of the anxieties underlying fears in the night, with sleep disturbances following on from them.

CONCLUSION

We have seen how parents and babies interact as the baby develops his sense of who he is. What happens next is that this process gradually allows the baby to venture out and be on his own.

The ideas on separation in this chapter are not to do with any ideal state of either fusion or individuation. They simply describe some of the ways in which each is experienced by parents and baby at various stages of emotional and physical development. Several central and fascinating questions follow from this look at separation. How much do mother and baby need to enjoy being together as a prelude to enjoying being apart? How much does being together enable future moving apart or how much does it prevent it? Is the disillusion that Winnicott talks of simply a failure by the mother to go on providing what the baby needs? He suggests that on the contrary she might be reading the baby's signals, saying that he now prefers managing on his own. There is also an important difference between genuinely having reached the stage of experiencing the self as a separate person and tolerating separation for a time, while still feeling the need to be with the parent.

I have attempted in this chapter to show that the ability to sleep is partially dependent on being able to feel safe, which includes feeling safe enough to be separate. So separateness needs to be experienced in relation to a protective and loving person, usually the parent. In order to achieve secure separation there must first be close, intimate contact with this loving, protective person. The intimacy gives the infant as he grows a feeling of self-worth and a feeling of being understood, which then lasts away from the presence of the parents and persists as he grows up. Physical closeness is one way in which this develops and so is a well-timed response to the baby's signals of his needs.

CHAPTER EIGHT

SEPARATION
AND ATTACHMENT PROBLEMS

I N THIS CHAPTER we will see how the baby starts to develop his own sense of a separate self and begins to move away from his mother. The security built up inside him, from the experience of the continuous and reliable presence of his mother, enables him to try doing things for himself. At first any moves away are quickly followed by a scuttle back into his mother's sight and presence.

The consequences of this stage are various. As the baby moves away from Mother, his bids for freedom and independence bring anxieties. We have already mentioned how sleep disturbances are one of the results of these. Moreover the degree of separation must be kept in perspective. At this period, that is, from the end of the first year, babies only start to manage to be independent; they need to practise this independence in the near presence of a parent or other who goes on being interested and available for much of the time. To put it at its simplest, a baby who crawls away from his mother into the next room needs, for quite a few of the first times he manages to do this, to find his mother still in the same room when he crawls back again. The first wanderings off are *in relation to* the parent. This has strong bearings on sleep problems, since one of my principal contentions in this book is that sleep problems are a form of separation problem.

To young children time can seem endless and, remembering Klein's idea that children see things in black and white, we can understand how at moments a separation might seem as though it is for ever. If Mother is not there, will she ever come back? How can a child be alone without also being lonely?

Babies and young children have difficulty enough in managing the stages of being on their own; surprisingly perhaps it can be even more difficult for their parents to manage it, both in terms of their own separation from their baby and in the sense of bearing the separation on behalf of the baby. While for some parents separation is a prized goal, for others it can be unbearable. For instance, it may symbolize bereavements and other intolerable losses that the parents have endured themselves. In such cases the ordinary repeated separations of bedtimes cannot be experienced in an ordinary way, each one contains echoes of previous traumatic separations or rejections.

Let us now look at how the separation process normally develops and at the important concept of the development of attachment between parents and baby.

ATTACHMENT

This is the name for a major system of theoretical ideas explaining some of what goes on between parents and babies. It originates from the thinking of John Bowlby, who is both a psychoanalyst and empirical scientist. Unlike most of his psychoanalytic colleagues Bowlby began to use ethological material to compare human behaviour with that of animals and his hypotheses about the reasons for infant behaviour always take serious account of evolutionary processes and survival mechanisms. He is deeply critical of other psychoanalytic theories that do not root themselves in biological realities. Bowlby's central theme is concerned with how instinctive behaviour constitutes patterns of attachment: 'Understanding of the response of a child in separation or loss of his mother-figure turns on an understanding of the bond that tied him to that figure' (1969, p. 221). Bowlby postulates that 'the child's tie to his mother is a product of a number of behavioural systems that have proximity to mother as a predictable outcome' (p. 223). He shows how at least five innately based instinctive patterns of response by the baby – sucking, clinging, following, crying and smiling – serve the function of binding the child to the mother and getting her care and protection in return; the result of this is that the child remains in proximity to the mother.

Bowlby describes how this behaviour, intended to keep the mother near to the baby, develops at each baby's own rate and increases as the baby himself becomes mobile. It shows most strongly in the second year, when babies are increasingly practising moving off on their own. As they move away they are at their most concerned about their mother's whereabouts. Either Mother's departure or anything frightening will activate alarm. The cure for the alarm is the 'sound, sight or touch of mother' (p. 223).

In a closely worked chapter on the 'Nature and function of attachment behaviour' (1969) Bowlby unravels the meaning of this behaviour, concluding with the delicately stated hypothesis, 'All in all, it is held, of the various suggestions advanced for the function of attachment behaviour, protection from predators seems by far the most likely' (p. 278). (It should be remembered that we spent four million years as hunter-gatherers during which this protection from predators was essential to our survival.) In building up this hypothesis, Bowlby argues that the by-products of attachment also shape human relationships. Infants and their parents are encouraged to stay in proximity to each other, originally for basic protection, but out of this grows love, intimacy and social relationships. He suggests that attachment does not derive from the feeding relationship itself, i.e. from the satisfaction of physiological need, but from the physical closeness which allows intimacy between mother and baby to develop while they are close to each other.

Security and the ability to explore confidently come from being in the presence of attachment figures. Citing Schaffer and Emerson (1964), Bowlby says that attachment develops to figures other than Mother, frequently Father and then often older children in the family. Crucially for theories about the child's need for his mother he says that Schaffer and Emerson 'found no evidence that attachment to mother was less intense when attachment behaviour was directed to other figures also; on the contrary, in the early months of attachment the greater the number of figures to whom a child was attached the more intense was his attachment to mother as his principal figure likely to be' (1969, p. 249). In thinking about children's need to make other wider and deeper relationships, we can see the benefits of an extended family or other network which a child can enjoy, while still having his mother as a base from which to get to know the other members. Attachment to Father is entirely separate and independent from that to Mother, that is, it may be secure with one and insecure with the other. Babies with no secure attachments develop symptoms of disturbance.

Attachment to parents continues throughout life in different forms. During adolescence other adults also become important and friendships and sexual attraction to peers may take precedence. In adults many of the attachment functions of the parents will be taken over by marriage partners. In old age when attachment behaviour can no longer be directed towards an older generation, it may be directed towards a younger one. Attachment in adult life is a continuation of such behaviour in childhood, so that in sickness, danger or disaster an individual will seek proximity to a known and trusted person and this behaviour is not a form of 'regression'. Even in adult life, Bowlby argues, we do not become totally self-reliant but need a companion to help us deal with difficult situations. Adult fears need not be rationally based and can be assuaged by company. 'How many of us, it may be asked, would relish entering a completely strange house in the dark, on our own? What a relief it would be were we to have a companion with us, or had a good light, or preferably both companion and light' (1979, p. 120).

A major facet of Bowlby's work is concerned with the effect of the *loss* of attachment figures and we will see later examples of this, such as hospital stays for children or the influence on a mother's parenting of the death of her own mother.

Bowlby describes what goes on when a child needs his mother. He cries, elicits her response and is satisfied by her reappearance and her touch. What happens, however, when this process goes wrong?

INFANT RESPONSE TO REJECTION OF PHYSICAL CONTACT WHEN ALARMED

Mary Main (1989), whose work stems from Bowlby's, describes one way in which an infant can be affected when parents are averse to physical contact with their babies. She shows the difference there can be in parents' responses to physical contact with their babies in situations where the infant is frightened and approaches the parents. 'Under these conditions a majority of parents adjust their bodies to an open posture and accept the infant in ventral–ventral contact. Others adjust their bodies so that the infant is barred from access, or turn the infant's body so that the infant's ventral surface does not touch that of the parent. Others simply push the infant away entirely' (1989).

When parents push their children away, a self-perpetuating conflict occurs. Main shows how a physical rebuff from the mother activates the attachment systems and when these are activated only physical contact with the attachment figure is able to terminate them. In other words a frightened baby calls for his mother; a rebuff from her causes him to be even more anxious; the rebuff in itself draws him to her for comfort, but again he is rejected. A baby in this situation becomes fearful and angry.

Here we can see the scene set for that angry confusion which builds up between some mothers and babies in the night. Such mothers are unable to offer physical comfort to their babies. The origin of this inability is often in their own experience of parenting. They go to their baby but are unable to satisfy him; moreover their presence is even a stimulant, causing the baby to want them even more. Mother and baby are thus in a continual state of activation without end. Possible solutions are that the baby may turn to the father or other relative or he may become more interested in toys, that is, in 'things' than in people.

The Strange Situation Test, designed by two of Bowlby's early co-workers, Ainsworth and Wittig (1969), is a brief laboratory examination of one-year-old children's reactions to reunion after a short separation. It has produced so much material that it is worth describing in some detail. Mother and infant are put together in a pleasant but unfamiliar room. The infant is then subject to a series of minor stresses in which a stranger enters the room and talks first to the mother and then the infant; the mother goes out and leaves the infant in the company of the stranger; the mother returns and the stranger departs; the mother goes out and leaves the infant alone; the stranger returns and Mother returns again for the final reunion. All this is carefully recorded. Each episode lasts three minutes unless the infant is very distressed. The test was intended to be no more disturbing than normal situations encountered by a baby.

The purpose of the test was not only to see how the infant dealt at the time with this sequence of brief separations from his mother in a strange place, but also how he behaved after he was reunited with her. In order that the infant can have time to mobilize a response to his parent at each session, the mother is told to pause in the doorway and greet the infant before going in to him. At the second reunion the parent picks the infant up (Ainsworth et al., 1978).

This Strange Situation Test has been used many times and increasingly sensitive material is being gathered about security and the nature of relationships from it. From test findings Ainsworth et al. classified the infant's attachment into three categories – secure, insecure (avoidant) and insecure (ambivalent). These are otherwise called Groups B, A and C. The classifications are based on the infant's response to reunion rather than on parental behaviour. Recent work has identified a further category (D) of babies with disorganized–disoriented responses (Main and Solomon, 1986).

The aim of attachment in terms of behaviour is proximity to the mother or other caretaking adult and in terms of integrative experience to produce a feeling of security. Ainsworth et al. (1978) found that about two-thirds of American babies in a healthy middle-class sample had *secure* attachments (Group B) to their mothers at age one year. This means that when distressed and alarmed they turn at once to their mother, express their anger and distress openly, are easily comforted by her and quickly resume an interest in play and exploration. Observation of these securely attached babies in their homes during their first year showed that they had mothers who were sensitive to their needs, emotionally available and ready to offer close physical comfort when the baby was distressed.

Of the babies with insecure attachments Group A (avoidant) represented about 20 percent of babies in Ainsworth *et al.*'s test sample. They actively avoid and ignore the parent during both reunion episodes, turning away from the parent and asking to be put down when picked up. They may show no distress during the parent's absence and continue to explore the room and toys. There is apparently an absence of fear, distress or anger. That is to say, they are already manifesting psychological defences and trying to be self-sufficient. Main *et al.* (1985) have shown that the mothers of avoidant babies tended not only to be insensitive to their babies' signals, but also to have marked difficulty in responding to them. Many of these mothers were found to be themselves averse to physical contact and also emotionally unavailable. Not surprisingly the origins of this inhibition have been found to spring frequently from the mother's own childhood.

Babies who have an ambivalent reaction, those in Group C, represent another 10 percent. They may be upset even before the first separation and are often fearful of the 'stranger'. They express extreme anger with the mother, are also distressed, clinging and not easily comforted. Their mothers are found to be very inconsistent and insensitive and often intrusive. In terms of the likelihood of babies having sleep problems these ambivalent babies are obvious candidates. The avoidant ones might include some excellent sleepers as a result of their ability to shut out distress. The secure babies, as we will see later, are often able to sleep well, knowing that their mothers are available and responsive if needed.

A CASE EXAMPLE

Let us turn to an exchange between a mother and an eight-month-old baby girl recorded by a health visitor during a home visit. We see what happens when a mother does not at once offer physical contact to a baby who is asking for it. This is not, however, a baby in a state of alarm.

The baby sat crying in her chair as Mother ironed with her back to the baby. She quietened as I spoke to her. Mother continued to iron in silence and then asked the baby, 'Have you stopped crying?' Immediately the baby started crying strongly again. She dropped the toy she was holding and arched her back. She looked at her mother, who continued doing the ironing, and persisted in crying. Mother said the baby was crying a lot these days, as she is teething. The baby was still crying, with her arms now outstretched towards Mother. Mother bent down near her and asked, 'How many teeth? One, two, three . . .' She smiled at the baby, and returned to the ironing. The baby was calmer, but still crying. Her attempts to leave the chair left her in an uncomfortable position. Mother finished the ironing and sat baby in a more comfortable position with her back upright. As she moved her, the baby looked up at Mum and became very excited, stretching her arms towards her as if expecting to be held by Mother. As it was not so she protested and began crying again, but stopped when mother gave her a biscuit. She grasped the biscuit with her right hand and brought it to her mouth, took a bite and sucked on it. She now had three pieces of the biscuit, a bit in her right hand, another bit in her mouth, which she was chewing, biting and sucking, and one which had fallen on her bib which she looked at several times. Mother came and sat in front of her, smiling at her and saying she was doing it very well. The baby looked pleased, took a piece of biscuit out of her mouth, offered it to Mother, smiling. Mother took the biscuit and put it back in baby's mouth. The baby ate it, looked happy, and then ate the piece still on her bib.

In this sequence there are two occasions when the mother approaches the crying baby and by doing so seems to increase the baby's wish for physical contact with her. Because she moves away again without having held her, the baby is left more unsatisfied and continues to cry. However, in the moment when the baby hands the piece of biscuit to Mother, and is given it back, it seems as though a symbolic interchange takes place which is enough to content the baby. It is not of course possible to say what the outcome would have been had Mother picked up and held the baby at the time when she stretched out her arms. The health visitor felt that the baby would have stopped crying. The mother may have feared that picking up the baby would have meant having to go on holding her and not being able to finish her household chores. The differentiation between the need of the baby to be picked up and held and whether or not the baby then needs to *continue* to be held is important. It is interesting to consider whether the emphasis of this account is that the mother was failing to respond at once to her baby's signals or that she was very sensibly getting her housework done while she could.

Some parents worry that it is 'inconsistent' to pick a baby up and then put him down. Some solve it by picking up the baby and then *not* putting him down again if this leads to crying. Others may solve it by not picking up the baby in the first place. While they may be worrying about 'consistency', these parents may be the ones struggling with their own problems of aversion to physical contact. In fact offering physical holding to a baby, while disliking it, can lead to a very confused experience for the baby. In our illustration, when Mother and baby had an exchange via the biscuit, this seemed to be a solution for both of them and of course it is important that this baby seemed to be cross about not being picked up rather than in distress. Whatever was going on between Mother and baby, both were able to deflect what the baby needed into the 'holding' of the biscuit.

CRYING

Crying is one of the main ways by which babies signal their needs to their parents and parents with varying degrees of success respond to the signal. Bell and Ainsworth (1972) show that responding to crying in early infancy has a satisfying effect that enables babies to cry less. They say that 'by the fourth quarter infants whose mothers had responded promptly and appropriately to their crying early on now cried less.' They also show that maternal sensitivity to infant signals during feeding, play and episodes of close bodily contact in the course of the first three months also turns out to be correlated to the infant's behaviour at twelve months; babies who had been sensitively responded to early on had fewer problems later on.

However, it is relevant to note that babies in residential nurseries cried *less* with the nurses who responded less quickly to them and more with the nurses who responded more quickly. Their expectations of whether they would be responded to presumably coloured their expression of need and would also affect their future hopes of being listened to when in need. The opposite reasoning may also pertain: a baby who has been responded to may seldom cry because he feels secure, while a baby who has not been responded to may cry to voice his hopeless feeling about being attended to. Crying can have many meanings and so also can not-crying.

It is also important that babies in some institutions sleep for unusually long periods. I would surmise that such a baby is escaping into an internal world, a sort of self-consoling situation, or into a state of despair when there is no adult who looks forward to the baby being awake in order to be able to feed, play with and cuddle him, in the way that parents usually do. If there is no one who actively delights in a baby's company, there is nothing much for him to wake up for. Foster-mothers taking babies from some institutional settings report that they sleep excessively at first and then begin to sleep for fewer hours in response to the individual care from the foster-mother (Provence and Lipton, 1962).

LEAVING A BABY TO CRY

Bell and Ainsworth (1972) stress the importance of responding *appropriately* to a baby's cries. This need not mean always picking up a baby who cries. It also need not mean that a baby who cries for a few moments when put down after being attended to should always be picked up again.

Parents who are unable ever to put a baby down and leave him to protest may be ostensibly worried about the baby's feeling of being left. It could also be that they are upset by the way his cries express a difference of opinion. Turning this around somewhat, parents who can never tolerate their baby crying about being put down may be practising very heavy emotional 'blackmail'. In such a case picking the baby up every time he cries may be a way of insisting that he should have the same view as themselves about being put to sleep, that is, that they are 'kind' in not putting him to bed, but it actually means that no mixed feelings or protest can be tolerated. Parents of course have to be sensitive to what a baby's crying means and to the real needs that he may be expressing. Allowing a baby to be separate includes allowing the baby to be angry and to express this anger.

Unadmitted anger can underlie extreme fears of separation, particularly, as we will see in this chapter, fears whose logical conclusion is that the baby will not survive the separation. Bound up with this may be the apparent opposite, Mother's anger at *not* being able to separate from her baby and her over-reactive response of keeping the baby too close may be to protect him from her wish to be off and away. Many mothers who cannot leave their babies say, half jokingly, 'If I went away from him I'd never come back.'

Others cannot think what they would do if they regularly left the baby with a friend or family for half a day and had some free time. This inability to think of what to do separately from the baby may be partly a slight over-indulgence in 'primary maternal preoccupation'. In other cases the mother may feel unadmitted anger at having to plan for such limited precious freedom.

Other mothers may be suffering from some degree of postnatal depression. They may feel depressed much of the time, with or without the baby, but have some sense of purpose while with the baby which disappears away from the baby. Such a mother may have no sense of self when the baby is out of sight. In extreme cases we can see how the origins of agoraphobia in mothers, and school phobia in children, may be foreshadowed or stirred up by these early difficulties in separating between mothers and babies.

DEATH WISHES AND DEATH FEARS

Conflicts about 'holding' a baby or putting the baby down can represent deep-seated conflicts about having a baby at all. Some parents have great difficulty in preparing themselves during pregnancy for the arrival of the baby. One such pair of parents described the idea of buying equipment for the baby as being conventional and 'consumerist'. Instead of a cot or cradle they would put the baby in a drawer. Their doctor, telling me of this added, 'and shut it away'.

These feelings can persist after the baby's birth, sometimes as the predominant feeling about the baby, sometimes just as a fleeting thought about a baby who is crying and refusing to go to sleep. Negative and hostile thoughts about a baby can come either from the parent's own emotional lack of readiness to have a baby or they can equally come from a situation where matters have gone wrong in the immediate present between parent and baby. When a baby cries and cannot be consoled, the parent is, quite naturally, likely both consciously and unconsciously to wish to be able to put the baby down and walk away from it. Parents who are conscious of such wishes and can 'own' their angry feelings towards the baby are those in the best position to deal with these feelings, to moderate them and go on working out how to attend to the baby. When, on the contrary, parents in this or other situations do not acknowledge their own feelings, when in Klein's term they 'project' them, that is, attribute them to others or get rid of them in some other way, they lose the power to confront and change the feelings in themselves. Parents who are shocked by their own wish may go on holding the baby excessively as a counter-reaction to it. The extreme logical extension of putting a baby down and getting rid of it is in fact for the baby to die. Fleeting thoughts like this may underlie tensions and hostilities in all relationships. Usually they disappear into the jumble of strong emotions that characterize family life and are counterbalanced by equally strong loving feelings. When things are not going right emotionally, these hostile feelings, especially unacknowledged ones, can get fixed as 'death wishes' which themselves can get translated into death fears.

All parents have such fears at moments about their babies. They are indeed rationally part of the background to making things safe for a baby. However, when these fears persist and have an obsessional quality to them, then something is going wrong between parents and baby. When straightforward channels for communicating feelings, especially angry ones, between parent and baby have gone awry, parents are perhaps obliquely expressing such feelings through their fears. They will also be rejecting in their behaviour to the baby, who will turn away from the unacknowledged impact of the rebuff.

TRANSITIONS

Where death fears exist they may also colour the parents' picture of what going to sleep entails and of the transition from wakefulness to sleep.

Going to sleep is in itself a transition. Managing this state of change depends partly on the picture, the anticipation, of what the new state will be like. Is 'sleep' a place of safety or a place of danger? Each individual has their own, albeit fluctuating, picture of it. The parents' picture has some bearing on their child's ability to fall asleep. Not only is there the problem of achieving the new state of sleep, it is also necessary to manage being in transition.

A seven-year-old girl in therapy had great difficulty in getting to sleep. Her mother had similar problems. The girl said to her therapist, 'What will I do if I can't get to sleep?' This poignant question seems to be not about lack of sleep, but of *where to be* during the fruitless transition period. In the extended family of this little girl a baby had recently died and perhaps there did not seem to be a safe place for her to be, either in her own mind or in her mother's.

All cultures have ways of dealing with the passing from one stage of life to another; we call them rites of passage. Rituals are likewise used in helping to pass from wakefulness to sleep. We have seen from Winnicott how transitional objects can help infants deal with being away from their mothers, how the object can represent the relationship. What these objects can also represent is the ambivalence that mother and baby have about each other. The object is fated, Winnicott (1971, p. 5) says, to be hated as well as loved and this derives from the hatred the baby feels for the mother who has dared to put him to bed. Part of the function of the object which is cuddled and mauled is to *survive* this love and hatred.

Klein (1932) suggests another function of the toys that a small child takes to bed. Her patient Rita, aged two, had an elaborate ritual to go through before dropping off to sleep. She had to be tightly tucked up in bed and her doll had to be tucked up beside her. This doll represented the 'super-ego' or 'conscience' and was there to ensure that the little girl did not get up in the night and disturb her parents' time together. Fraiberg (1950) shows how a little girl Kathie, aged eighteen months, suffering from a sleep disturbance, was in a state of conflict about her own impulses and about her relationships. She particularly had mixed feelings about being toilet-trained. Kathie began to take two toys to bed with her – one, a teddy, was cuddled and offered endearments; the other, a doll, was battered unmercifully, flung about and scolded. We can see how two sets of feelings about herself as well as about parents or others were expressed through her treatment of the two toys. As she played this out, her sleep started to improve.

Winnicott has described how the infant deals with intermediate experiences. In theoretical formulations, and also in poetry, the intermediate state of going to sleep is variously described: from the somewhat coy 'into the arms of Morpheus' to the powerful image of Dylan Thomas's, 'Do not go gentle into that good night', often recited at funerals. With the symmetrizing logic (see Matte-Blanco, 1975; Rayner, 1981) typical of them, sleep and the unconscious know no gradations, no similarities between things, only sameness. At such levels of imagination death is sleep and sleep is death. So fear of going to sleep may include a fear of dying and for a parent this may extend to death fears for their baby.

When parents recount these fears to me, I am shaken each time by the genuine life and death quality of the story I am told. There may indeed be some external cause for anxiety – difficulties in birth, such as Matthew's mother experienced (see Chapter 7), or other problems in the early weeks that the mother has not recovered from and not properly absorbed. Even without such personal experience these fears can be based on reality in that

131

everyone knows or has heard of tragic deaths of babies. Similarly mothers, even in these relatively advanced days, may fear the possibility of death for themselves when they go into labour. The risks are very small, but they exist. Looking at the possible real bases for these fears does not, however, take us very far in understanding them. To use an analogy, all forms of transport have their risks of death, but we still think of someone unable to travel as having some particular unrealistic difficulty or being phobic. We might also expect that, usually, the thrust of life-forces involved in the process of giving birth has an overriding effect that allows a mother to set aside such fears.

For each mother the actual experience of herself and baby surviving may or may not have a degree of reassurance that all will continue to go well. For vulnerable mothers talking through these fears and experiences may make them more manageable. In working with such mothers I often also feel that what I am doing for them is directly containing their anxiety, so that they can go back to the baby and contain the baby's feelings. When a mother then meets her baby's anxiety in the night, it no longer connects with her own infinite experience and she can respond to it appropriately. Some mothers also, poignantly, feel they have never had a 'blessing' bestowed on them with their babies. Their right to have a live baby has not been confirmed either by their own mother or by another significant person. This idea is developed in Chapter 10 on parents' own childhood experiences.

A CASE EXAMPLE

Peter's mother had fears with a life and death flavour. When I first met Peter and his family, they were all in a desperate state of sleeplessness and mutual fury. Peter was almost a year old, woke up repeatedly during the night and had to be breast-fed each time by Mother. He cried so persistently that the family were all disturbed; Father often escaped to sleep in a room downstairs; Mother rushed to attend to Peter before he woke his three-year-old sister, Sophie.

Two powerful themes arose in our work together: firstly, the fear that these parents had that there must be something wrong with their baby, so that he had to be attended to at once and could not be asked to wait; and secondly, a difficulty in dealing with his anger and their own.

Both of these themes were vividly represented in the meetings between the parents and myself. In the early sessions they angrily recounted the endless wakings of Peter in the night and the moves in and out of beds and rooms. I could not understand or make any pattern of it in my mind, although I was aware of the parents' angry disappointment with my inability to share their experience or to help. In one early meeting Father stormed out of the room, taking one of the children who was somewhat restless out with him; after a brief walk he came back in a friendlier mood.

In spite of my perplexity as to what was going on I encouraged Mother to start to wean Peter and she did so with Father's support. It seemed as though this helped both Mother and baby to feel more separate in the night and Peter woke fewer times. I then realized that the parents, and particularly Mother who came to some appointments on her own, were usually late. They also often left early, apparently because both had very tight working schedules. One morning while I was waiting for mother's late arrival, her health visitor told me that the family had called the doctor three times the previous weekend for advice because of an ear infection that Peter had. As I waited, I started to put all this together.

When Mother arrived, I told her of the conversation her lateness had provoked. She took this in good part and seriously examined the implications of the information with me. I compared her inability to wait to talk to the doctor in surgery hours with her inability to make Peter wait until morning for a feed. I asked her if she could remember the feeling of 'waiting' herself when she was a child. She immediately thought of what long hours with a house-keeper felt like while her own mother was out at work. I connected this also with her lateness in coming to see me; perhaps she wanted me to know what it felt like to wait. But more vitally I pointed out she was communicating to me that she was never seen when she needed to be, the times that I saved for her did not fit with the times she really needed help. The times she really needed from me were when she felt desperate in the night.

We also thought about what happened to her own judgement of how bad her son's ailments actually were; on the visit from the doctor and the subsequent telephone conversations with him at the weekend little actual 'medical' interventions were either needed or given. We thought about her inability to act on her own experience – Peter is her second child and although her confidence was much greater than when her first child was born it tended to evaporate at times of illness. It seemed to Mother, thinking about all this, that her lack of confidence now was a legacy from the feeling as a little girl that her own mother's interest and excitement were directed mainly towards her work. As a little girl she had felt that she wasn't really worth talking to and spending time with.

Peter's mother was then able to put my comments on her time-keeping into immediate effect. She came on time to future appointments, humorously wondering if this was a compliance, being 'good' to please me. More importantly she was able to think about helping Peter to use her at the 'right' time, that is, during the day. This was complicated, as she was away at work for much of the day. However, she was trying to face up to the fact that she was doing with her children what she had so much resented in her own mother. Her seeking to attend to Peter in the night was partly a well-meant wish to make up to him for her absence. But this continued a kind of chain of reproach passed on from one generation to another and in a way left Peter no more satisfied than she had been herself as a child. However, as she became less eager to meet his needs at night, he woke up less.

Father meanwhile was thinking hard about his role in all this – he had tried to help Mother cope with a very demanding baby who could not be kept waiting; he also had felt the brunt of Mother's feeling of being kept waiting for him to come back from work and help out. Now he too started to think about how to help Mother question the baby's demands and how also to help Mother feel his support and confidence in her ability to cope when he wasn't there.

As Peter's parents came to know and trust me, we were able to look more clearly at their anger. I suggested that this inability to be ordinarily firm with Peter might connect with a worry about going too far. If they started to get angry with him, would they know how to stop?

A crucial problem for many parents is dealing with a baby's anger in the night, while at the same time feeling their own anger at not being allowed to sleep. Many parents are particularly afraid of battering their baby in the night. The fears of going too far may stop them from being reasonably firm. Experiencing anger within bounds may be as much a relief to the baby as to the parents. Babies who go on crying in the night undermine parents' belief in the quality of their parenting and in their judgement.

With Peter's parents we had an intense version of this problem. They were now able to confide in me examples of their worries about their own aggressiveness. Father told me how nervous he sometimes felt when he was driving – he felt he might kill someone. This was a chance for us to talk about the problem of keeping anger and aggression in check when dealing with a vulnerable small baby. This in turn enabled us to turn our attention to Mother's problem of never being sure how ill her children were: each time they had a high temperature she thought they might die; that was why she had to keep calling the doctor. We started to understand how unsure she was of herself as a mother and unsure of her own judgement, so that it felt to her that she was unsure of her ability to keep her children alive.

To both these parents it came as a great relief to share their fears with me and with each other. Putting their fears into words and making connections with their own childhood emotions made them begin to seem manageable. You could say that they started to like themselves better and, as this happened, their natural humour appeared. Peter seemed relieved at his parents' new assurance, he slept better, and the parents started talking with me about their marital relationship. I continued for a time working with them on family problems and then referred them on for more intensive marital work, though there was a long delay in this being available.

At this point I thought back to the way that these parents had, for several weeks when they felt most desperate, dosed Peter almost nightly with sedatives of various kinds. I then realized the incompleteness of my work with them. At the point where Mother had been able to tell me about her extreme lack of assurance of her ability to keep the children alive I had let the subject slide, believing that we had 'aired' her fears sufficiently. I had not, however, really helped her look at the implications of what she was owning to. This mother's fear was of a 'sin of omission', not of actively doing something to kill her baby, but of failing to do something to keep him alive. By forgetting him, she would bring about what lurks ambivalently in nearly every mother's mind, the wish to get a troublesome baby out of the way. Other mothers have similarly told me of sterilizing their baby's bottles more than once because of their fear of not getting it right and inadvertently allowing the baby to be poisoned by the 'germs' in the bottle. By calling so frequently on the doctors, the mother was in a sense making a valiant and sincere effort to counteract this unconscious wish to 'forget' her baby and sedate him. Instead of trying to understand the cause of the sleep problem, she was perhaps trying to alert the doctor, and myself, to this conflict in herself about wanting to 'get him out of the way'. *Our* sin of omission was in not properly noticing this.

These two parents had told me, very movingly, of a range of fears that their kind of parenting was harmful to their children. My belief, from thinking retrospectively about what they told me, is that *not* taking up the implication of this sufficiently was a failure on my part. This belief in itself requires an examination of what good it does to discover deep fears, such as these parents possessed. Sharing these fears should make it easier for parents not to act them out towards their children, though as professionals we often worry about whether bringing them to consciousness might make it more likely for parents to act on them. With Peter's parents I felt that only partially discovering their fears left them in a state of perpetuating the problem.

Selma Fraiberg (1980) has described the inherent difficulty when patients, afraid of abusing their own children, start to connect this in therapy with what happened to themselves as children. In the chapter 'Ghosts in the nursery' she says of a patient:

> She remembered factually the experience of childhood abuse. What she did not remember was her suffering. Would the liberation of affect in therapy increase the likelihood of acting out towards the baby, or would it decrease the risks? . . . It is the parent who cannot remember his childhood feelings of pain and anxiety who will need to inflict his pain upon his child. And then I thought, 'But what if I am wrong?' (1980, p. 182)

Looking back at Peter's family's problem, what stands out is Mother's experience of neglect by her own mother. This feeling may or may not have been based on reality. Like her mother she also went out to work and of course for many mothers with a year-old child this is not a problem. This mother, however, was doing to her child what she had not been able to bear for herself as a child. Her flustered attentions to Peter in the night stemmed from this dilemma.

She seems to have felt that her mother did not take responsibility for her, either when present or not. We do not of course know whether her mother was in fact unduly absent, or whether she was unable to bear what could be thought to be quite reasonable absences. In either case the feeling got passed on, that she as a mother did not know how to be responsible for her children. Keeping them alive is the ultimate way of describing what this responsibility entailed. Her repeated frantic calls to the doctor, and her use at times of me, were perhaps part of an attempt to get someone else to take over this responsibility. In conclusion perhaps no one, neither her mother nor any other person, had let her know that she really *deserved* to have live, healthy children.

SLEEPING TOGETHER OR ALONE

I change direction here to look at another facet of separation: the question of children sleeping alone or with their parents. This may be an issue determined within a family or it may have cultural meaning. In the previous chapter we thought about separation and individuation and two questions come to mind about this: firstly, how much is 'separation' prized in a cultural context only and secondly, how much is it necessary to be alone to feel oneself to be a separate individual?

Lozoff *et al.* (1984) have looked at co-sleeping, that is, parents and babies sharing a bed, within a cultural subdivision, by means of samples of US black families and white families. They make a differentiation in their study between the black families, where 70 percent reported sleeping with their children under four as a normal family practice, and the 35 percent of white families who reported sleeping together, where it appeared to correlate with some family stress. They found that in white families co-sleeping happened mainly with 'toddlers' beginning to walk, whereas among black families it was a customary parenting approach with young infants.

Sleeping together was thus associated with stress in white families, but not in black ones. Furthermore sleep problems were more common in co-sleeping white children (i.e. more common than in black children and also than in white children who did not sleep with their parents). Highly pertinent for the arguments in this chapter Lozoff says that in the white sample co-sleeping was associated with a more ambivalent maternal attitude towards the child, whereas among black children there was no association between co-sleeping and stress, maternal ambivalence or sleep problems.

Whose needs are being met by taking the child into the parents' bed? Lozoff *et al.* (1985) point to the complexity: 'Sleeping with parents may occur in reaction to the child's sleep problem and/or to the mother's awareness of her partial emotional withdrawal from the child. Such bedsharing may be one avenue via which an ambivalent, stressed mother expresses both her positive feelings towards her child, and her own needfulness' (p. 482).

Putting all this together, it appears that co-sleeping as a normal cultural practice is independent of stress; but where it goes against the cultural norm it indicates, by definition, that family functioning is out of the ordinary. From the point of view of the individual child with a sleep problem, Lozoff *et al.* (1985) imply that co-sleeping may postpone grappling with the problem and that the proximity itself may prolong the problem. Conversely it may sufficiently answer a need in both mother and child to allow the child to sleep.

What is *not* addressed by Lozoff *et al.*'s study is the wider issue of separation. We see the effect that sleeping with parents has, adversely or not, on children's ability to sleep. We do not see the effect it has on their ability to be on their own.

In the black families we see an assumption that it is normal for parents and children to sleep together. Within this assumption the children usually sleep well. The white families usually assume that sleeping should be separate. Therefore when white parents allow their children into their bed, one reason may be because the child is already sleeping badly and this is a response to the problem. In other cases the reason may be that these are parents who go against the grain of normal social practice among whites. It seems also that their nonconformity does not serve them well, at least in the sense that their children tend not to sleep so well. Perhaps these parents are themselves protesting against children and parents being kept apart in the night. Without knowing the personal details of any of these families we might still guess that some of these parents have unresolved problems with their own parents about being kept separate in the night. Since their children do not sleep even when they are allowed to be with the parents, perhaps what is communicated to the children is not so much that a gratification of a need is being offered, but rather that the issues of separation in the night are complex and insoluble.

We are still left with the problem of how parents and babies ultimately achieve a state of separation necessary for adulthood. Lozoff *et al.*'s study vividly shows us the differing basic assumptions that the black and white families had of what degree of separation there should be at night between parents and babies. These assumptions contain two kinds of ideas, one about how to help children sleep well, the other about whether separation at night in itself is seen as a desirable practice. This leads on to more far-reaching questions about how much individuation in adults is prized and how to achieve whatever a particular family or culture's goal of individuation is. One aspect of this is how do co-sleeping children, in whatever culture they may be, eventually move *out* of their parents' bed?

Lozoff *et al.* (1984) studied babies and young children sleeping in the same bed, not just the same room as the parents. An essential factor here is therefore the bodily contact between parents and children and not simply being present in the same room as each other.

McKenna (1986) is particularly concerned with the importance of this bodily contact. As we saw in Chapter 5, he argues that sleeping apart from parents is a sensory deprivation for a young infant, who is indeed not at first physiologically independent from them. For example, he says that parents and infants respond to each other's breathing sounds to the extent that vulnerable infants can be 'reminded' to breathe through the sound of the rhythmic movement of the parents' breathing against their own body.

There is a dilemma in putting this together with our Western ideal of individuality, of the importance of differentiation and of individually recognized achievements. The baby who is given his own cot, his own specially decorated room, which is recognized as his own space, is the inheritor both of material 'progress', but also, if McKenna is right, of a certain poverty in this philosophy.

It is essential always to differentiate the needs of babies at different ages. Perhaps there is a *universal* need for parents and babies to be in close contact in the first days or weeks. Perhaps the time to separate then depends on the concept of separation and individuation that obtains in each family or culture. McKenna's argument, empirically based though it is, that nocturnal separation can in some circumstances be one of the converging factors leading to cot deaths, also connects with the pathological phobic perceptions of some parents that their offspring will die out of their sight. It is not easy to work out where realistic anxiety in parenting and phobic concern begin and end. Parents teaching their child to cross the road alone know this only too well.

Winnicott is helpful in describing the psychological processes involved in separating. In 'The capacity to be alone' (1958), he shows how the infant's first experience of being alone is in fact 'in the presence of the mother'. The infant achieves the awareness of 'I am' protected by a mother who is preoccupied with him and with his needs. She is also able to identify with his being ready to change. Following 'I am' comes the thought 'I am alone'. Winnicott tells us that 'I am alone' is a development from 'I am', dependent on the infant's awareness of the continual existence of a reliable mother whose reliability makes it possible for the infant to be alone, and to enjoy being alone, for a limited period (1958, p. 33).

Winnicott, following Melanie Klein, says that the capacity to be alone depends on the existence of a good object in the person's psychic reality. This belief comes from a repeated experience of having instinctual needs met. Infants first need their mother's reliable presence before they can have an internal picture of her which can remain enjoyably with them in her absence.

THE PARENTS' RELATIONSHIP

How does the parents' own relationship fit into this? Winnicott points out that

> an individual's capacity to be alone depends on his ability to deal with the feelings aroused by the primal scene. In the primal scene an excited relationship between the parents is perceived or imagined and this is accepted by the child who is healthy and who is able to master the hate and to gather it into the service of masturbation. (1958, p. 31)

Winnicott is here implying that a healthy child will have an imagined idea of intercourse, whether actually having perceived it or not, and will find a way of dealing with the jealous feelings stirred up by it. Joyce McDougall (1974) looks at it from another point of view – a mother not invested sufficiently in her own love-life will be over-involved with her child.

Other writers have described the effect that children in the parents' bed have on parents' intercourse. Lozoff *et al.* (1984) comment on a Japanese study (Caudill and Plath, 1966) where co-sleeping and letting the child fall asleep not in his bed and in adult company 'reflect an emphasis on nurturance in family life, rather than on the relationship between father and mother' (p. 180). Are babies in the bed a bar to sexual intercourse? A survey in a women's magazine showed that many parents use the living-room to have intercourse. Ralph Glasser, recalling his childhood in Glasgow in *Growing Up in the Gorbals* (1986), describes memories of being lifted out of the parental bed and then put back in. However, these experiences still imply that the family/parental relationships take precedence over the marital one. The child is reared 'in the bosom of his family'. Families with limited accommodation may feel distraught at the lack of privacy or be quite tolerant of the situation. But what different view will a child sleeping in the same bed as his parents have of them, and of himself, from the child sleeping alone in his own bed or in his own room?

Parents who come to discuss their children's sleep problems sometimes report 'success' in dealing with the problem as getting the child out of sleeping in the parents' bed to sleeping in another bed in the same room. In some of these cases it would seem as though a child in the parents' bed is experienced as breaking up the parents' relationship. As we will see in Chapter 11 on parents' marriage, a toddler who gets into the parents' bed and then either keeps the parents awake by kicking or actually ousts one parent is acting out his dissatisfaction about how he fits in with the parents' relationship. A child in the same room, but not in the same bed, may be needing some security of being in the parents' presence, but expressing this in the context of accepting the parents' relationship with each other and feeling protected within it.

DISTANCE FROM MOTHER

Separation has to happen in some form when a baby falls asleep; it is *his* organism that changes its state, however close he might be lying to his parents.

Paret (1983), as I have mentioned earlier, looks at the connection between sleep problems and the distance the baby keeps from his mother. Citing the rise in frequency of sleep problems in the second half of the first year, she reminds us of Anna Freud's concept, that sleep disturbances are transitory difficulties due to both the external and internal stresses of this developmental phase. As 'attachment' to his mother increases during the first year, this can then interfere with the baby's ease in falling asleep. Paret describes how the anxiety produced by awareness of his attachment and his new ability to move away from his mother may produce stress. 'During the daytime we see that the nine-month-old baby cannot venture too far or for too long without checking back and "refuelling" (Mahler) and reading his mother's signals in order to feel safe (Emde, 1984).'

Using video recordings Paret studied a group of thirty-four babies and found among these eleven 'night wakers' and twenty-three 'night sleepers'. The wakers slept an average of seven hours, 18 minutes and the sleepers nine hours, 19 minutes. Of the sleepers none woke more than twice during the whole night; of the wakers eight woke between three and six times and not one woke only once.

In looking at the differences between these groups, Paret found that the 'sleeping' babies were further along with weaning and that they did not need to be moved or rocked to get to sleep. She also discovered that more of the sleepers used transitional objects or sucked their thumbs. She suggested that although these babies may wake up at night, they are able to *put themselves* to sleep again, whereas those in the waking group will require the physical presence or even the breast of the mother.

Paret speculates upon what in the interaction of a mother with a 'sleeping' baby encouraged the capacity of the baby to comfort himself, put himself back to sleep and create a transitional object. She then tried to correlate a measure of how well the child slept through the night with a measure of the child's physical distance from the mother during the period of observation in the day. She noticed that 'wakers' stayed close to their mothers and were more likely to be held on their mothers' laps and to be touched by their mothers. Good sleepers showed a tendency to travel away from the mother earlier in the observation, to go further and to look at the interviewer more. The babies who maintained the greatest mean distance from their mothers also sucked their thumbs more. Their mothers showed a tendency, though not statistically significant, to interact with them by looking at and talking to them during the interview. A really striking connection arises from this: 'These babies, the thumbsuckers who played at the greatest distance from the mother, were the babies who slept through the night' (p. 175).

Paret conjectures that some of the babies had reached a developmental stage which then allowed them to sleep well.

As we observed on the videotapes all the babies woke up but all of them did not disturb their mothers. Perhaps the so-called good sleeper does not demand the presence of his mother during the night because he has already taken qualitative different steps in ego development, he has the capacity to reduce tension and comfort himself, to enjoy exploring and mastering the new environment on the floor, to assert comfortable control over the physical distance between himself and his mother while still maintaining contact with eyes and ears. The baby's mother is able to tolerate – perhaps one can say encourage – such developments by her willingness to reduce his dependence on her (weaning), permit gratification (thumb sucking, transitional objects, other than those she personally provides (Anna Freud, 1953)), enjoying his distancing of himself and his interest in new things and people and respond to rising tension in her nine-month-old baby by reassuring with looks, smiles and gestures in addition to holding or feeding. (1983, p. 176)

From this we can see that the sleeping babies who can travel from their mothers are not, however, also emotionally distant from their mothers. For these babies independence seems to be based on having a secure idea of a relationship with their mother. According to Paret's observations mothers and sleeping babies stay in contact with each other through looking and talking. (This is very different from Mary Main's category of 'avoidant' babies, who after a short separation are unable to greet their mothers and turn away and occupy themselves with toys, seemingly *in place of their mother* and not in addition to her.)

Mike Tomson (1989) made a similar discovery to Paret's about the connection between the distance babies are able to travel from their mother and the ability to sleep well. He and a health visitor colleague worked with a group of four mothers and infants with sleep problems aged between nine and twenty-two months. All these babies fell asleep at night only in their mother's arms. They noted that during the first group meeting *all* the babies sat on their mothers' laps. As the group went on in later weeks, the babies began to sleep better at night. At the same time they became able to separate from their mothers and to move away from them across the room when the group met. As their babies started to sleep, the mothers' clothes became smarter and they also used more make-up. It seemed as though the mothers' sexual identity was able to come back into focus, as their closeness to their babies lessened.

The babies who can best manage separations from parents are perhaps those whose parents are known to be reliably available when needed and also those who signal their comings and goings. One important route for the mastering of separations is learning to say 'goodbye' and, following from this, playing games about separation.

Freud (1920), in a famous, and for him rare, observation of a child's play, observed his grandson aged eighteen months playing a game with a cotton-reel on a string. In this game the child held the reel by the string, threw it into his cot, so that it disappeared into it, and uttered the sound 'o-o-o-o'. This was his favourite expressive sound, which his mother thought represented the German word 'fort' (gone). In the game the little boy pulled the reel out of the cot again by the string, with a joyful 'da' (there). Freud interprets this game as being the child's way of dealing with his mother's absences. By himself staging the disappearance and return of the objects within his reach, he was taking an active role, rather than being a passive recipient of her absences. The implication is both that the little boy, instead of being helplessly left, could feel as though he was in control of his mother's goings and comings and also that the completed game would *ensure* that she did return after each leaving.

I saw a similar game, when looking after a friend's child of the same age while she went shopping. This child, lying on my lap, cried desperately for a few minutes after his mother left. Then he quietened, climbed down, took a wheeled toy and pushed it to and fro away from him and back towards him, over and over again for several minutes. Unlike the child Freud observed, he at first played in dogged silence. After a while he allowed me to make a verbal game of 'gone' and 'come back' and then went on from this to play a more varied game of moving little cars around. Here we see equally vividly this child's recovery from the desolation of his mother's having left him by a game where *he* makes something 'go' and 'come back'. It is also crucial that he could express anger and despair *first*, before marshalling his resources to deal with the separation. If I had tried to jolly him into such a game as soon as his mother left, it would have had much less meaning for him (or if his mother had slipped away unnoticed).

Similarly Selma Fraiberg (1959) recounts teaching a baby who was waking in the night to play the game of peek-a-boo. By playing this game of disappearance and reappearance, the baby got some control over the idea of her mother 'disappearing' in the night. The peek-a-boo game was a way of playing with ideas about separations and thus becoming less vulnerable to them. In my work with parents and children on these problems perhaps the parents and I also play with these ideas about separation, so that the parents get some mastery over the ideas.

CONCLUSION

The underlying theme of this chapter has been of communication between parents and babies about signals given out and then picked up or missed, of the needs of the baby being responded to or not heard, of shared states of understanding or of misunderstandings. One of the vital communications is about changing needs and the baby's need to be looked after differently as he matures, and separates out from his parents.

We have seen how separation is about moving apart and becoming reunited again. It does not necessitate feeling emotionally distant, in fact the opposite applies. Intimacy between two people, parent and child, depends on being separated out in order that a relationship between the individuals can happen. When the separations of the night seem really impossible, we guess that the difficulty is as much for the parent as for the child and that this ordinary parting is coloured by unbearable bereavements or losses of some kind. Similarly for working parents the separation from their baby during the day can leave too much painful residue to allow peaceful partings at night-time (as happened for Peter's parents). We have also seen how children with insecure attachments do not feel the protection of their parents through the night and cannot settle to sleep. Throughout the book these themes recur.

Part III

CHAPTER NINE

THE CONNECTIONS OF
SLEEP PROBLEMS
WITH FEEDING AND WEANING

F EEDING AND SLEEPING are closely linked. In the first few days and weeks babies sleep much of the time and wake mainly for feeding. The setting up of the timing and rhythm of both feeds and sleep are thus really a part of the same process.

New-born babies often fall asleep at the breast so that the end of a feed and going into sleep can be almost the same experience. In such a case neither the end of the feed nor going to sleep are experienced as a separation from the mother. If this continues after the first few weeks, then the baby actually misses out on what could be thought of as an emotionally maturing experience, that of at least sometimes digesting a feed while awake and away from his mother's arms. If a baby only goes to sleep while being held by a parent, then if he wakes later on alone in his cot, he may feel that only the parent can help him back to sleep. Furthermore if going to sleep is associated only with breast-feeding, he may demand a breast-feed to help him deal with each arousal. When babies have only been able to fall asleep directly from a breast-feed, weaning can feel like a desperate problem for a mother and baby about to lose their known way of the baby getting to sleep. With bottle-feeding some of these issues also apply, though the fact that fathers or others can also give the baby a bottle may help to disperse problems that might have arisen specifically with a mother and baby couple.

Difficulties in weaning may highlight unresolved problems in the feeding relationship and there is an interesting connection at this stage where success in weaning can correlate with ability to sleep. Playing at the breast, during or after a feed, also connects with good sleeping. This leads us to think about the need for mothers and babies to play with ideas about their relationship in order to enjoy and manage feeding, transitions and separations.

Leaving the Clinic after our first meeting, six-month-old Penny's mother went into a shop, bought a packet of chocolate biscuits, put them on top of the pram and ate her way through them on the way home. Surprised at herself, normally a sparing eater, she thought, 'Food for comfort'. It seemed as though the consultation with me had been hard going!

Penny's mother was dramatizing the theme of our talk together. She had told me that Penny needed feeding on and off throughout the day and also the night. She could not take solid foods and was solely dependent on the breast. We had talked about Mother's assumption that Penny *had* to be fed every time she woke and cried. Penny had in fact lain asleep in her pram during this first meeting and woke near the end. Mother held her up to me and I met Penny's steady, dignified gaze.

Next week Mother came back beaming and showed me a chart of Penny's waking and feedings during the night, now strikingly fewer in number. She told me the anecdote of the chocolate biscuits as a way of introducing the theme of her thoughts during the week about herself and Penny. 'Food for comfort' was her interpretation of her own chocolate biscuits. She had then reflected that she did not have much imagination about how to comfort her daughter – it had to be the breast each time.

We discussed whether the breast really was always needed to comfort Penny and indeed whether the source of comfort had to come from Mother. It was also relevant that in spite of a very difficult birth, Penny had slept well in her first few weeks – the traumatic wakings had started after a trip abroad and Mother and I discussed the possible stresses contained in this visit.

Somehow Mother and baby had become hopelessly enmeshed. In this week of reflection Mother had said to herself, 'Why don't you *let* her go to sleep, not make her go to sleep?' As we talked, Penny woke up. Mother picked her up and, in order to prove to me the progress the week had brought, did not immediately start to feed Penny. I was able to see for myself how painful it was for this mother and baby not to have their instant reunion at the breast. How could they be together and at the same time separate? Mother told me that she now wears night-clothes, so as not to stimulate Penny with her naked breasts when she picks her up in the night. She felt this was a large factor in helping them both cut down the night feeds. Penny fussed and Mother said, 'You're sleepy, go to sleep by yourself.' She handed her teething rings, which Penny first pushed away and then took hold of. Penny cried fussily again. Mother noticed that she had been holding Penny close and in the position for breast-feeding and remarked that this was not fair to her. She put her back in the pram. Penny kept up a low wailing sound and Mother tried to ignore it. I suggested, perhaps fancifully, that the noise was Penny's way of keeping a connection going between herself and Mother with her mouth and voice, keeping the link to replace her mouth on Mother's nipple. Right or not, my comment helped Mother listen to the noise for a while without feeling obliged to *do* anything.

For Penny and her mother the feeding had got out of proportion as an aspect of their relationship. Let us now look at the way in which feeding usually gets established between mother and baby.

FEEDING AND CLOSENESS

Feeding and sleeping have a major factor in common. Both are somatic states involving a change in neurophysiology which, as Stern (1985) points out, 'require the physical mediation of an other'. Achieving a rhythm and pattern for both these basic physiological needs is the main preoccupation for mothers and babies in the early weeks – working out the realities of the baby's own needs and rhythms and finding a pattern that is understandable by both mother and baby. The negotiating of this, as much as the achieving of it, influences future relationships. Many writers have also noticed that problems in one area may well go with those in another.

Winnicott (1947, p.90) describes the setting up of breast-feeding in poetic terms (I am indebted to Madeleine Davis and David Wallbridge's very clear presentation of Winnicott's thinking):

Imagine a baby who has never had a feed. Hunger turns up, and the baby is ready to conceive of something; out of need the baby is ready to create a source of satisfaction, but there is no previous experience to show the baby what to expect. If at this moment the mother places her breast where the baby is ready to expect something, and if plenty of time is allowed for the infant to feel round, with mouth and hands, and perhaps with a sense of smell, the baby 'creates' just what is there to be found. The baby eventually gets the illusion that this real breast is exactly the thing that was created out of need, greed, and the first impulse of primitive loving. Sight, smell and taste register somewhere, and after a while the baby may be creating something like the very breast that the mother has to offer. A thousand times before weaning the baby may be given just this particular introduction to external reality by one woman, the mother. A thousand times the feeling has existed that what was wanted was created, and found to be there. From this develops a belief that the world can contain what is wanted and needed, with the result that the baby has hope that there is a live relationship between inner reality and external reality, between innate primary creativity and the world at large which is shared by all. (1981, p. 44)

We see from this account how the physical and mental experience of feeding produces much more than satisfaction of hunger. Winnicott is ascribing to it the basis for optimism and the freeing of creative thinking in the present and in later life. Also engendered by a reliable feeding relationship is the building up of trust and of intimacy between the feeding baby and mother.

Winnicott has described this building up of trust and intimacy in terms of breast-feeding, but bottle-feeding can also be close, intimate and satisfying for both mother and baby. Breast-feeding is an efficient way of promoting intimacy, as mothers and babies have to be physically close during the feeding. Many settle easily into this intimacy; for other mother–baby couples who have had an uneasy start intimacy may at first seem daunting, but the task of feeding may be a route for learning to manage it; for some other couples breast-feeding never seems to work properly, with mother and baby not being able to find a mutually satisfactory position, rhythm or pace. Bottle-feeding can equally be carried out either as an intimate physical closeness between mother and baby or in a way that illustrates an inability to be close.

It is not therefore the method of feeding that determines the relationship that grows between mother and baby, but that the use of the opportunity for intimacy develops from the feeding. Perhaps, however, an intensity and range of feelings can be expressed more easily in breast-feeding than in bottle-feeding. The excitement of the experience and the expression of loving and aggressive feelings can be witnessed more openly when the baby is dealing directly with the mother, without the intermediary of the bottle. Winnicott says 'the survival of the mother is more of a miracle' in breast- than in bottle-feeding.

Bowlby (1969) suggests that it is not even the physiological process of feeding which is the essential basis for the relationship, but the comfort given by the contact with the mother. He quotes Harlow's (1961) experiments on rhesus monkeys, which enable a differentiation to be made between the effects of contact comfort and of actual feeding. In these experiments infant monkeys were removed from their mothers at birth and provided with model mothers, consisting either of a cylinder made of wire or of one covered by soft cloth. Feeding was from a bottle on both models.

> In one experiment eight infant monkeys were raised with the choice of a cloth model and a wire model. Four infants were fed (on demand) from the cloth model and four from the wire model and the time the infants spent on each model was measured. The results showed that irrespective of which model provided the food, the infants came rapidly to spend most of their time on the cloth model. Whereas infants of both groups spent an average of fifteen hours a day clinging to the cloth model, no infants of either group spent more than an hour or two out of the twenty-four with the wire model. Some infants whose food came from the wire model managed to lean over and suck the teat whilst maintaining a grip of the cloth model. (Bowlby, 1969, p. 262)

Harlow and Zimmermann (1959) use this work to show the 'critical importance of contact comfort in the development of affectional responsiveness to the surrogate mother' (p. 262). We can infer from this that in normal mother–child relationships being held closely and regularly by the mother is an important experience in itself and not just part of the background of feeding.

A study reported in the *Lancet* (Cunningham *et al.*, 1987) showed how carrying a baby close had more effect on mother–infant attachment than the method of feeding. The researchers started from an assumption that mothers carrying their infants close to their bodies in the first few months would become more responsive to their infants than mothers who did not and the 'cuddled' infants as a result would develop secure relationships with their mothers. Next they randomly gave either soft baby-carriers or plastic infant seats to a group of low-income mothers directly after birth and asked the mothers to use them regularly, which they did. Twenty-three mothers were in the group which used the 'snuggle' carriers; there were twenty-six in the control group. The method of feeding between the two groups was by chance almost equally breast- and bottle-feeding. The researchers then examined the quality of attachment between mother and baby at thirteen months (using the Ainsworth Strange Situation Test) so as to assess the effects of the methods of carrying and feeding upon security of

153

attachment. They found that 83 percent of the carried infants were securely attached, compared with 38 percent of the infants whose mothers were given infant seats, and that these results were almost identical for the breast- and bottle-fed babies.

Their conclusion is that 'carrying a baby close to the body in the first few months of life has a more positive effect on the mother–infant relationship than does breast-feeding' (p. 379). They also link this with Hunziker and Barr's (1986) finding of reduced crying and fussing in infants given extra carrying in the early months.

These results tell us that secure attachment is promoted by mothers and babies being close to each other for long periods and thus having the chance to respond to each other. We can see that for mothers and babies the opportunity for mutual exchanges creates an emotional climate. Presumably the babies in the plastic seats could be walked away from, have backs turned on them, be momentarily forgotten, so that chances to exchange signals would be lost. As we saw in Chapter 8, we would expect that closeness would in time allow the development of independence in the baby.

The findings in Cunningham *et al.*'s study allow mothers to speculate on the different elements there are in their baby's need for them. Penny's mother realized she had become stuck on the idea of 'food for comfort' and that she could have other ways of comforting her baby. What this study, looking at security of attachment, cannot encompass is seeing whether direct expression of feelings is facilitated more in breast-feeding than in bottle-feeding. It may also be that the proximity to the mother of a baby in the snuggle carrier likewise promotes this and overrides the different feeding experiences.

OVER-FEEDING AND SLEEP PROBLEMS

Working out the baby's physiological needs is one of the main tasks for mothers in the early weeks.

Richards and Bernal, writing in 1974 when bottle-feeding predominated, show that breast-fed babies need to be fed more often than do bottle-fed babies; since human milk contains less proteins and calories than commercially produced milk, the bottle-fed baby will get more food per feed and be likely to sleep longer. They argue that advice given on duration between feeds is geared mainly to bottle-feeding, so that breast-feeding mothers think that their babies' 'short' sleeps are a failure on their part to provide enough milk, rather than being a reason for giving more frequent feeds. Richards and Bernal suggest that with the right information mothers will tolerate more frequent feeds and shorter sleeps will cease to be seen as a problem.

Klaus and Kennell (1976) put this case more strongly:

> Among mammals one can predict the frequency of feeding for any species from the ratio of fat, protein and carbohydrates in the milk. On the basis of the composition of human milk, human new-borns should be fed every twenty to thirty minutes, as was once the custom, rather than every three or four hours, as is present practice. (quoted in Stern, 1985, p. 237)

These findings are somewhat extreme and do not fit in with the observations of most mothers, even of new-borns, of their baby's needs. I have not found any evidence of adverse effects from longer feeds with lengthier intervals between them. In any case, however frequent the new-born's feeds may be, the older baby increasingly can go for longer periods between feeds, with the consequence that he can also sleep longer.

Feeding and sleeping go closely together and the baby's ability to sleep may be heavily influenced by his mother's beliefs as to how often he needs to be fed. Ferber (1987) summarizes how the mother's misunderstanding of what the child needs can actually cause or perpetuate a problem:

> Thus although an infant at six months of age certainly has the ability to obtain satisfactory nutrition during the daylight hours and to sleep through the night without sensations of hunger, repeated feedings during the night only condition the child to become hungry at these times. Therefore it is likely that some of the extra wakings are actually triggered on this basis. Some wakings may also be in response to the unusually wet diapers. Finally the intake of liquid nutriments during the night prevents the appearance of a more mature circadian pattern. The child's sleep and hunger feeding patterns remain infantile. Instead of the digestive/endocrine–sleep/wake rhythms adjusting to a day/night cycle with consolidated sleep and no feedings during the nocturnal period, they remain 'set' for recurrent interruption and intake. Consolidation of night-time sleep is prevented and frequent wakings persist. (p. 152)

We see here how feeding the baby in itself causes the baby to wake to seek food. Often parents and babies have got into such a tangle for reasons to do with the emotional issues going on between them. In such cases mothers and babies may find that they have to sort the problems out first during the day and that the sense made of feeding patterns then carries over to a more comprehensible situation in the night.

One baby, Agnes, whom I saw at fifteen months, had a physical origin for her night-time feedings. She had been severely jaundiced at birth, following a very difficult pregnancy. Mother was instructed to give her fluids three hourly, day and night. This was obviously a necessary procedure medically, but one consequence was that it restrained the baby from settling into longer sleep periods. It also of course kept the mother on the alert through the night, waking herself to the alarm clock, not even to her baby's cries. In addition the mother had been justifiably anxious for her baby's survival during the pregnancy and in the first few weeks. Having lost their chance of working out the baby's sleep rhythms early on, a year later both Mother and Agnes were still jumpily unable to settle into long and deep periods of sleep.

One worry for many parents, including Barnaby and Clare's parents (see Chapter 2), is whether what they have given their baby is good enough. Health visitors and doctors see innumerable mothers who wonder whether their milk is 'good' (Kahn and Wright, 1980). Such a mother may find it very hard to let a baby know clearly that she believes he has had enough food and care and can manage on his own in the night. When he cries, is he reproaching her for not giving him enough 'good' nourishment? Many mothers' uncertainty at night seems to be a continuation of this unsureness about feeds.

The example of Luke and his mother shows how issues in the mother–baby relationship can get in the way of sorting out feeding. Luke was six months old and his mother came in a panic about having to wean him in two months time, because she was going back to work. She was feeding him constantly, night and day. We looked at how her grief at the coming separation, which felt like a forced one to her, had left her unable to discriminate between when Luke needed her and her breast and when he needed to be away from her. He fed often and was often sick. She muttered that her milk was poisoning him. I asked about her own upbringing and she told me about her mother's uncertainties in her marriage and in her sense of herself as a mother. Returning to herself with Luke, it seemed that her sense that she and her milk might be really 'bad' for Luke, together with the parting to come, were interfering with her ability to see how he was really using her. Luke meanwhile played in my room, bringing toys to his mouth and then blowing bubbles and uttering little 'talking' sounds. I showed Mother how the use of his mouth and the pleasures he could get from it were developing and that we could hear the beginning of speech from Luke's use of his mouth to communicate at a distance from her. None of this happened when just clamped on to her breast.

Next week Mother came back to say that Luke had slept right through the previous night. At first she could not remember whether anything different had happened that day; then she recollected that she had not breast-fed him during the day – she had stayed out with him in his buggy as long as possible and kept moving. She had fed him once in the morning and once at night. As she talked, Luke pulled himself up and bit at the straps of his buggy. Mother said she had just realized he had a tooth when he had bitten her breast. We speculated that by not being allowed at the breast on and off all day, Luke had calmed down from a continual state of excited arousal. He was free to use his toys and experiment with his aggressive feelings without worrying about hurting his mother. His sense of self could develop both emotionally and cognitively. Similarly Mother was free to own more of her feelings towards her baby – it occurred to her that the separation to come had masked her natural feelings of *not* wanting to be with her baby all the time. We saw Mother's dream about this in Chapter 6.

What the examples of Penny and Luke show vividly are the problems for mothers who firstly, always interpret their babies' wakefulness in the night as the need for a feed and secondly, who have always allowed the baby to go to sleep at the breast. Neither of these babies had experienced being put into their cot while still awake and being able, while semi-alone, to digest sleepily the emotional experience of the feed along with the milk. (In Chapter 8 we looked at the question of how much emotional maturity depends on experiencing separation.) A specific consequence of this situation can be that after the baby wakes in the night he has then no experience of how to get himself back to sleep. As far as he knows, only Mother and the breast can do it. Ferber's (1985a) chapter, 'What your child associates with falling asleep', is useful in this connection.

Several families with this particular problem of night-time feedings have referred themselves for help at a point when Mother is thinking of weaning the baby. It seems impossible to lose the only known way of getting the baby to sleep.

Simon's parents came, shortly before his first birthday, in this dilemma. The parents were young, lively and good-looking, each working part-time and sharing in Simon's care. Simon had recently started at a morning nursery and both parents were worried about making a change like weaning while he was getting used to the nursery. They had in fact taken him away from another play-group where he seemed to be unhappy.

Mother's pregnancy and Simon's birth had both been easy, but the first few months were miserable. They were isolated in a district where Mother knew no one, the local health visitor was herself on maternity leave, Mother had a difficult relationship with her own parents and felt herself to have no support. She had suffered from eczema as a child, brought on initially as a milk allergy. Stress, however, could also activate the eczema and did so now. In later meetings she increasingly attributed the onset of her eczema to the fraught relationship with her mother. When her eczema was bad, holding Simon was difficult. Perhaps when the eczema subsided, she made up for it by holding him 'too much'. In any case the pattern of holding was not consistent from Simon's point of view.

The problem that brought the parents to me was that Simon woke repeatedly in the night, cried, was fed by Mother and took sometimes an hour to get back to sleep. While she told me all this over two or three weeks, she and her husband worked out together at home how to change things to help Simon. They thought he was frightened of the bars of his cot and bought him a bed. At first he was delighted, but soon found it as hard to stay alone in this as in his cot. He cried for his parents or came into their bed, but still disturbed them when he got in with them.

They decided that Mother would wean Simon, so that both parents could equally attend to him if he woke in the night. This was a courageous step, as they were losing the means by which he and Mother dealt with his waking. However, he took easily to the bottle. The day after this weaning was completed Simon, sitting in the back of the car, said clearly for the first time, 'Mummy' and 'Daddy'. Simon's parents realized that this step of separation from Mother had given a boost to Simon's rudimentary ability to conceptualize and to relate to both parents through this new medium of talking. Even so, Simon was still waking up repeatedly; his parents felt I was not being useful and we stopped meeting.

We resumed, however, a few weeks later, with new energy and significantly Father agreed to attend whenever work permitted. Now a new theme emerged – how people could be angry with each other. Mother came one week to tell me she had felt angry with me the previous week, when I had asked her to define her ideas of what her child should or should not be allowed to do. We had seemed caught in a nebulous misunderstanding of where we were aiming for with Simon and I had asked her to clarify her thoughts. As Mother talked about *her* anger, Simon, for his part, cried angrily all the time. Mother held him, unsure of what to do. I said I thought he was listening to what we were saying and was showing *his* anger about us trying to change what happened at night. The next week both parents came. As we talked, Simon brought me toys and then hit me. Again it seemed a justifiable comment on our conversation, as Simon was listening to the three of us discuss plans to keep him in his bed! Simon was still unable to get to sleep on his own. Since his weaning, Mother or Father had to sit by him, stroke him or hold his hand, till he fell asleep. Each time he woke the process had to be repeated.

I suggested that his parents sit by him, stroke him for a while and then go out for a few minutes, telling him they would come back soon, and to be sure to come back, whether he cried or not. They did this and to our joint astonishment found that Simon was sleeping several nights a week through the night, though he still kept getting out of bed during the first settling period. I suggested that they let themselves be angry with Simon and tell him not to get out of bed; the parents were politely incredulous that this could have any effect. I spent the next week pondering to myself how anyone ever got anyone else to do what they were told! They came next week and again surprised me by saying Simon was staying in his bed when told to. The parents would go out and come back as promised. Mother had started with a promise that she would 'come back to see if you're all right'. After a few days she changed this to a promise to 'come back to see if you're asleep' and Simon was managing to fall asleep in her absence. Father realized that his method was less confident than Mother's and each voiced criticism of the other. As his parents cleared the air by coming out with their conflicting opinions, Simon illustrated the mood of the conversation by banging his toys. Simon had a special teddy that he took to bed. During the day he played at putting Teddy to bed and sometimes told him he was 'naughty'. It looked as though he was mastering his own situation as he played with Teddy.

The theme of all this seemed to me to be the evasion of direct conflict. Mother and her own mother had never been able to have things out together. As I shall suggest in Chapter 13, perhaps

Mother's own eczema was the physiological expression of her dilemma. In any case she and Simon had to go on with breast-feeding when it did not really suit either of them any more until both parents' combined firmness released Mother and baby from an impasse. Like Luke, Simon was also freed to speak and to play symbolically.

COLIC

Colic is an interesting symptom which bridges physiological and psychological thinking. Weissbluth (1987a) reports that it affects a fifth of all infants. He quotes Illingworth's (1954) definition of colic as 'violent and rhythmical screaming attacks which did not stop when the infants were picked up and for which no cause, such as underfeeding, could be found' (p. 129). These unexplained screaming attacks start at about two weeks, with infants crying for about three hours per day, usually at a regular time. The attacks disappear in most infants by two to three months.

Weissbluth suggests that 'colicky crying appears to represent an extreme form or excessive amount of normally occurring unexplained fussiness present in all healthy infants' (1987a, p. 131). However, he says that colic is more than crying. Colicky babies tend to have a difficult temperament and cry and fuss in many situations. They also have irregular sleep patterns with frequent wakings. They have brief and irregular daytime sleeps and tend to miss periods of quiet sleep during the characteristic evening crying. From three to eight months infants who cry frequently during the day or night are more likely also to cry during sleep/wake transitions.

In his book *Sleep Well* (1987b) Weissbluth sums up one aspect of thinking on the definition and causes of colic. He says the crying spells may be set off by 'physiological disturbance such as disordered breathing during sleep, sleeping patterns that are out of synchrony with other body rhythms, or abnormal levels of naturally occurring substances (like prostaglandin or progesterone) . . . it is most likely that colic is related to those physiological factors as well as a baby's measurable temperament characteristics.'

Weissbluth vividly describes the uninhibited motor activity which occurs during the colicky crying spell, such as stiffening of the body, with fists tightly clenched, legs flexed rigidly over the abdomen, twisting or jerky movements. He says that 'facial grimacing coupled with the crying suggests to the parents that the intensely energetic, excitable wound-up infant is in severe pain' (1987a, p. 131).

In the past colic was thought of mainly as a gastro-intestinal problem caused by, for instance, allergy to cow's milk in bottle-fed babies or wind in the mother's milk, due to her diet, in breast-fed babies. Many parents describe the condition as being due to their baby's failure to bring up wind and surmise at pain in the abdomen, when the baby draws up his knees.

Recent thinking is that this pain is the *result* of taking in wind during the crying, not the initial *cause* of the crying. This is a useful idea, but it seems to me that this begs the questions that too much wind could be produced by the manner in which some babies feed and that uncomfortable relationships between mother and baby lead to uncomfortable positions for feeding. Some such feeds could be experienced as 'indigestible'. Taking in wind while feeding at breast or bottle might be a consequence of an uneasiness or awkwardness in the way the baby is sucking. Perhaps an anxious baby gulps too quickly or strains away from the mother's body as he sucks.

It is also highly interesting that babies in institutions may have less colic. In a five-year period of investigation of babies in one institution no baby had colic during that time (Provence and Lipton, 1962). This would seem to support the hypothesis that colic is an aspect of something going wrong in the relationship between parents and baby. Where there is no relationship, there is no colic!

Colicky babies often appear to be 'inconsolable'. John Kirkland (1985) writes of the varied ways in which parents hear a baby's cry. He says of the cry: 'not much of it is needed to serve as a reminder of previous horrors'. The implication is that parents' panic does not help the baby in settling his mood and continual crying in any case can make colic worse. The irritated feeling in the baby's body is illustrated by an irritating cry, which makes the parents feel full of an irritating or persecuting pain.

All this is not intended to make parents feel even worse, but to help them locate where to start to make things better. The old wives' remedy of holding the baby upright, tightly against the parent's body, sometimes works. The baby may feel held together both physiologically and psychologically by this. He may also feel that what he is going through in his body can be felt in the body of the parent holding him. It is crucial here for the parent to hang on to the knowledge that this is the baby's pain, that he needs help for it within himself; it need not be experienced by the parent as though it was his own pain. A baby who is kicking and thrashing about all over the place may be relieved by firm holding, although some babies may not be able to bear it.

It is also crucial to keep in mind another way of describing the baby's experience. In psychoanalytic terms the force of unconscious processes may at times lead a baby to feel as though he is psychologically 'falling apart'. Crying may be an expression of this feeling and a need to be held physically would follow. Sucking is another way a crying baby can comfort itself and again we can see the psychological parallel to a neurological process. The baby who feels emotionally fragmented gathers himself together through the focus of his sucking mouth.

SOME CASE EXAMPLES

Justine was a baby who cried, it seemed, endlessly. Justine's mother had given birth to her on a date very near the first anniversary of her own mother's death in an accident. In one visit to me Mother walked around with her and suddenly handed me the baby. I very rarely hold babies while doing this work, seeing my job as being concerned with a mother holding her own baby and showing me the difficulties and pleasures. As I held Justine, I was taken aback by the absolutely rigid feel of her body, particularly the 'knotted-up' feel of her little stomach. It seemed to me that there was a connection between Mother's bereavement, reinforced by the near coincidence of dates, that had not yet been absorbed and her inability to absorb and receive the 'pain' her baby experienced. Justine's rigid body might also have been like her experience of a rigid, unyielding mother, too full of grief to take in the ordinary needs and pains of her baby; perhaps in this way the baby was also suffering some of her mother's pain.

When I started to put some of this into words, Mother took Justine from me and stood with her back to me as she listened. I graphically felt how unbearable this whole subject was. However, it seemed as though something in all this worked. Mother reported next week that Justine cried much less. Perhaps my brief holding of Justine, followed by my trying to understand the significance of her rigid body, felt to Mother like some of the 'maternal holding' that she herself had lost with her mother's premature death. Babies who cry inconsolably may be expressing some grief of their mother's. Perhaps by talking to me about her mother's death, this mother's unresolved mourning was able to shift, freeing Justine as well as herself.

Patrick was a baby with colic. Perhaps he was physiologically vulnerable in some way, but the repercussions on the relationship between him and his parents were devastating.

Patrick's mother brought him to see me at three months. After an easy birth he had always slept badly, with long spells of frantic crying from the beginning. He frequently had very explosive bowel motions and Mother was sure that his crying stemmed from a build-up of wind, only released through his bowels. As I mentioned in Chapter 2, Patrick's mother came in to the first visit angry, suspicious of anything I said and critical of all the help doctors and health visitors had given her in the previous weeks.

It seemed to me that the pain in Patrick's belly was experienced as overwhelming by his mother. When he had the pain, so in a way did she. Not only could she not help him deal with it, she was equally at its mercy and when she frantically went to the doctor she, so to speak, took it with her. This pain was perhaps also an 'accusing' one – she felt 'accused' by her baby of causing it or at the very least, not making it better. From this point of disadvantage whatever 'advice' she was given by professionals felt like yet another 'accusation' that she had again not got it right.

I put some of my thoughts about this process into words and Patrick's mother was at first full of fury at what I was saying; gradually she became intrigued and leant towards me as I spoke. She started to confide both the details of Patrick's birth and the agonizing unsuccessful attempt she had made to leave him and return to work when he was six weeks old. It was likely that there was a connection between the prospect of this premature separation and the troubles between them, but to make too quick a formulation would have been in itself premature.

Next week Mother told me that Patrick had been sleeping through much of the night. She had gone to the chemist and bought some medication which had cured his wind. A medical colleague later authoritatively told me that this preparation 'doesn't work'. But something *had* made a difference. I felt that my descriptions to Mother of the effect Patrick's pain had on her released her from some of its consequences. She had felt like a mother who could not cure her child's pain. Each time she sought advice she had in a way reproduced this situation; she had taken an insoluble problem to each professional. By describing this I had broken the chain. In particular I had *believed* Mother's description that unbearable pain existed. She began to have some confidence in her own judgement and then in her capacity to do something for her baby. I think that she went to the chemist in the belief that something she did for her baby could make him better. In this spirit she gave him the medicine and it cured his discomfort.

The following week when I said some of this to Mother, she was dismissive of such thoughts. She said talking did not make a difference, the medicine had cured Patrick. I ingenuously asked why in that case she had not given it to him long ago. It again took a confirmation by me that I thought Patrick was a very difficult baby, before she could trust me to know a bit more about what she and he had been going through. She started to think about why Patrick had had so much wind. She described a very easygoing pregnancy when, unlike her usual self, she had had no anxieties. The shock of Patrick's birth and his frantic crying since had been tremendous. I thought that here was a real clue – that in this 'easygoing' pregnancy this relatively elderly (in her mid-thirties), first-time mother had not been psychically preparing herself for the birth and the impact of a baby. Mother then confided in me the disturbing dreams she had had in the early weeks after Patrick's birth about breast-feeding. In these dreams babies, animals and parts of the body were all shockingly interchanged. It appeared that breast-feeding was not pleasurable and was a 'shocking' new experience to absorb. As Mother told me of this, she herself started to wonder how much of this had got through to her baby. Maybe, she suggested, her awkwardness about all the images stored up in her mind by breast-feeding had actually affected how she held him during feeding. As she thought about this, Patrick cooed and smiled at Mother from his pram; she smiled and talked back to him.

Patrick's mother told me all this against a background of another impending separation – at four months she would have to leave him to return to work. It occurred to her that it made her feel as though she never really had had him as *her* baby. She then recalled with some bitterness all the family visitors who had come to see the new baby in the first few weeks. Instead of finding the visits gratifying, it seemed as though she felt their visits had claimed him as the family baby, not as hers.

Patrick's mother postponed her return to work and, with a long waiting-list, I changed our meetings from weekly to fortnightly. After the first longer gap I was also five minutes late in starting the session. Mother told me that Patrick had slept through every night until last night, when he had woken up often. I half jokingly said it sounded as though he could not last out the whole fortnight. I said

I thought she had perhaps also felt like that when she had to wait five minutes to see me, after waiting for two whole weeks. Mother looked surprised, then laughed and said, 'I've always felt I want it now!' She then told me again something she had told me in an earlier session, that she had been a voracious eater as a child, but had remained very thin. Until she was sixteen her mother had left sandwiches and a drink for her to have in the night. I said that it sounded as though *her* mother had not been able to believe she could last the night without food. It was no wonder she could not believe that Patrick could manage either. Mother thoughtfully considered this. Patrick's problems were of two kinds: his colicky pain and his inability to sleep for long stretches in the night. Both were connected with the feeding relationship with his mother. The colicky pain, Mother felt, was due to her way of feeding him and it took the sorting out of both Mother's own disturbing experience of breast-feeding and her processing of her baby's pain, before he was released from that.

The sleepless nights were also related to feeding. When Patrick woke in the night, Mother was irrationally sure he was hungry and immediately fed him. We have seen how as a child she herself had not been able to conceive of waiting till morning for food. One night while suffering from flu, she slept heavily, woke in the morning and realized she had not heard the baby cry through the night. He was peacefully asleep. She realized that she might have been arousing him by her usual immediate response to his cries. It seemed that he could, at five months, go for several hours without a feed. Parents of babies who have had severe colic often fail to adjust to their babies' changed needs after the colic has disappeared.

The next time Mother and baby came in Patrick, now five months old, looked around the room; Mother sat in silence as he turned to look at her, at me and at the window. She said to him, 'Have you sorted out where you are?' before telling me of the intervening fortnight. It is of interest to note here that Sylvester-Bradley and Trevarthen (1978) have written of the stage from about four months at which mothers talk to babies of external matters of interest, not just of the emotions between themselves and the baby. As Patrick started to sleep through the night, he and Mother were freed to enjoy such conversations with each other. In fact the sleep problem was solved when Mother became able to step back from Patrick sufficiently to let Father in to help both of them with it. She asked Father to go in to Patrick in the night instead of herself. Within a few days of this change Patrick was sleeping through the night.

We have seen the disturbance caused to Patrick's feeding in part by the fantasies his mother had about breast-feeding. Another mother said that it was difficult for her to know how to soothe her second baby, a boy. She had felt easily able to get close to the first baby, who was a girl. Possibly this mother was defending herself against sexualized feelings stirred up by the physical contact with her male child. Unable to let herself express ordinary parental intimacy, she stayed at an awkward distance from him; he presumably did not feel properly held. He cried a great deal, day and night and mother felt at a loss what to do.

THE EXPERIENCE OF FEEDING

In their pioneering study, 'Night waking in early infancy', Moore and Ucko (1957) looked at many variables to find what distinguished the babies described by them as settlers from the non-settlers (their use of these terms is in fact questionable) at the age of thirteen weeks.

> Differences between settlers and non-settlers had been sought, but not found, in total duration of feeds (time in mother's arms) and in actual sucking time. It then occurred to us to take the difference between these as a measure of the time given by mother to the baby for contact and play, over and above what he needs for feeding . . . This quantity which we have called 'excess nursing time', estimated at the three-month interview, turns out to discriminate very significantly between babies who settled by thirteen weeks and those who did not . . . Whereas the babies that received least nursing had the greatest tendency to wake, those that received a rather excessive amount were the next most wakeful group, while those that had between 10 and 20 minutes in addition to their feeding time settled best. (p. 340)

Moore and Ucko conclude: 'apparently for most children an adequate amount of contact with mother is an important factor conducing to the establishment of the sleeping rhythm' (p. 340).

We are now in a position to take this argument a good deal further. It is no accident that Moore and Ucko identified this important contact time between mother and baby as being connected with feed time. The amount of time and also the affective tone of time before, during and after a feed is when the key emotions between mother and baby are stirred up, experienced and dealt with. Both mother and baby are dealing with a micro-cosm of life and death fears, anxieties and fantasies at every feed. With a successful feed they get through this; reassurance comes from the actual experience of a task accomplished. What then is the resolution of this experience? One outcome is for the baby to fall asleep at the breast and be put down while asleep. The mother can then feel a unity with the sleeping baby, satiated by the milk she has given him, whether from her own breast or from the bottle. Another way a feed might end is when a satisfied but still alert baby wants contact with Mother in another way and wants to play with her. Even a baby who falls asleep at the end of the feed may seek and take part in play-time with the mother during pauses in the feed. What are the uses of such play-time?

A feed is a gratification of an instinctual need; it is also a sensual experience and a learning experience. As the baby satisfies his hunger, he is also touching, seeing, smelling his mother and her breast. He is putting together sensations, expectations, memories, and so on. Daniel Stern (1985) notes how from a very young age cross-sensory impressions are built up. Citing Meltzoff and Bos-ton's (1979) research study, he shows how babies at only three weeks who had been given either knobbly teats or smooth teats to suck while blindfolded were able, after they were unblindfolded, to pick out by sight the teat they had previously sucked but never seen. We can see from this that all the time experiences are being put together and that the perceptions derived from one sense modality can also be derived from another. As the baby sucks, his hand may be stroking the breast or clutching it. A visual impression of the shape of the breast, of Mother's neck, her cheek, adds to the tactile feel of these parts, to their smell and then to sensations of the nipple in his mouth which is followed by warm milk in the stomach.

Taking this further, we see how in pauses during the feed or in time afterwards the baby is able to do several things: firstly, to go on exploring Mother's body, away from the urgency of taking in the milk; secondly, he can assimilate the experience and deal with the *idea* of having had a feed and the *idea* of a mother who is there to feed him, but also exists in addition to this function. Part of the idea that grows in this time is of mother and baby as two separate beings who have been wordlessly together and are now about to move apart. It could well be that how a mother and baby manage this time influences and is significant for how they will manage the separation aspect of the baby falling asleep. If on the one hand the feed is carried out only as a necessary routine piece of care, with no time allowed for exploratory playing, then there is no period of transition for the baby to change from the *idea* of being fed to the *idea* of the end of the feed. If on the other hand a mother plays excessively long, it may be because she is not able to face with the baby that 'all good things come to an end' and cannot bear the small separations that happen many times daily.

One mother of a baby girl, Elaine, was an example of a mother spending what could be thought of as an excessive length of time over feeds. She was thinking of going back to work when Elaine was six months old. Although absorbed in her career she thought of this present time at home with her baby as very precious and was full of doubts about whether to go back so soon or not. Elaine slept badly and Mother had to feed her often during the night. An observer noticed how, during the day, she hardly seemed able to put Elaine down after a feed. She would play with her for long periods and even bath her in the middle of the feed, so that to the observer it was almost like two feeds very close together. However, by this long gap in the middle of the feed it seemed as though Mother was spinning out the length of time she could be very intimately involved with her daughter; Elaine's sleep problems seemed to be a further sharp illustration of the difficulties in timing separation.

A mother who, according to Moore and Ucko, gets this timing right, seems to be offering a useful transitional time for learning and co-ordinating. It is relevant here to think about the nature of the transitional objects that help babies to move away from their mothers. Winnicott has emphasized the need for these to be looked at, touched and smelt. I think this follows from an earlier necessity for the *mother* to be looked at, touched and smelt by the baby, who is then no longer occupied with feeding, though still immersed in the instinctual feelings of the feed. Moore and Ucko also show that 'the frequency of sucking fingers or fist shows . . . a relationship to unbroken sleep which is probably but not certainly significant' (1957, p. 338) and comment similarly on sucking dummies. It seems as though sucking after a feed, something that is done by the baby with his own body, can have the same useful effect on the sleeping ability of the baby as does the playing time with Mother.

The quality of the mother's participation in the feed is also vital. We have seen (and will look at in detail in Chapter 13) the effects of mother's depression or other states of mind on the baby's sleeping.

But nowhere is her state of mind so apparent as when feeding her baby. Babies are acutely sensitive at this time to how much their mother is able to be occupied with them. Bion's term of the mother's 'reverie' to describe this ability is particularly vivid.

In one example of this, a baby of only four weeks was being breast-fed. Mother looked at the baby and talked to him gently. Then, while still looking at the baby, she started to talk to a visitor. The baby lost the rhythm of sucking, lost the nipple from his mouth and started crying. Mother talked to him again and he re-found the nipple. Thus the baby needed to be thought about as well as simply looked at, as he fed.

This extreme need to be sensitive to the baby during feeding perhaps matches the need to be sensitive to a baby's sleep rhythms. Another way of putting it is that *managing* to establish a rhythm of feeding can carry over to a rhythm of sleep.

THE RELATIONSHIP BETWEEN BREAST-FEEDING AND NIGHT WAKING

Paret (1983) made some very interesting discoveries about the relationship of breast-feeding and weaning to night waking. At nine months she found that eight out of 11 babies described as 'wakers' were still being breast-fed, while only ten out of 23 'sleepers' were still on the breast. She notes that this is an important difference but not statistically significant. However, to add to the weight of her findings she shows that among those still breast-feeding, the good sleepers had taken many more steps in the weaning process than had the wakers. Only one of the eight waking babies still being breast-fed had begun the process of being weaned, whereas half of the ten sleepers still on the breast were already down to one feeding a day. Also in another larger sample of babies, whereas twelve out of a group of 26 wakers were still on the breast, only one of 20 good sleepers were being breast-fed. She found that the good sleepers did not need to be nursed or rocked to sleep before being put down and in general were further along in the weaning process. Paret notes that, if the mother continuously provides for the baby with her bodily presence, then the baby will be dependent on her at night as well as during the day.

FATHERS

As we will see in Chapter 11, the father has a crucial part to play in helping mothers and babies, first in establishing confidence in feeding and later in helping them with weaning. One of the problems for sensitive, involved fathers is in working out how much good fathering of tiny babies should be a continuance of the way the mother is with the baby and how much he should offer something different.

An essential aspect of breast-feeding is its exclusive intimacy between mother and baby. The range of feelings induced in other members of the family, from vicarious pleasure to envy, is one of the ordinary dramas of family life. Weaning means that both mother and baby become emotionally and physically more available to the rest of the family. Fathers can be felt either as supportive of this new stage or as destructive of the previous intimacy, according to the dynamics of the family. Equally a mother who clings on belatedly to breast-feeding may be jealously guarding her own relationship with the baby at the expense of the rest of the family or be showing her own difficulty in managing a more than two-person relationship.

Bottle-fed babies and their parents do not escape all these problems about feeding and weaning. If a mother has slipped into giving endless bottles, Father may find himself being used as part of a chain of feeding. Or by contrast he may be able to bring in a fresh point of view, that perhaps the baby could survive without all these bottles. Fathers, by being able to share in bottle-feeding, are often able to help mothers and babies out of an impasse.

WEANING AS SEPARATION

A pattern of dissatisfaction between mother and baby in feeding can lead both to sleep problems and also to weaning difficulties. Problems about ending a feed in order to go to sleep and ending the feeding situation altogether in order to wean may stem not so much from a highly-valued situation which both sides are loath to give up, but from an ambivalent, unsatisfactory one that has never been quite right. The difficulty in stopping may be an illustration of a feeling of not having got it right yet.

Some mothers and babies get into a circular problem. If they need to be together, how can it then be right to separate? Conversely if there has to be a separation, how can they be together first? Alternatively how does being together contain the germs of separating out later? Does initial satisfaction provide an experience that can last, as Klein suggests? Winnicott (1971) sums this up as a process of disillusionment. He says about feeding: 'If things go well, in this gradual disillusionment the stage is set for the frustrations that we gather together under the word "weaning" ' (p. 13).

One mother about to return to work part-time kept angrily telling her nine-month-old baby not to suck his thumb. She was starting to wean him and it seemed as though the sight of him sucking reminded her of his vulnerability and his need still to suck at the breast. In a way she could not win; it was bound to be painful for her. Either she was reminded of how important sucking at the breast still was for him at the point when she was about to start weaning him or, if it seemed that sucking his thumb had become an acceptable substitute for the breast, perhaps she would have to bear the pain of feeling that her baby had no further need of her breast.

THE EXPERIENCE OF WEANING FOR MOTHER
Weaning leaves a mother with a different experience of her own body in relation both to her baby and to her husband. During breast-feeding some mothers may use their babies as a shield to protect them from unwanted sexuality. By inadvertently allowing the baby too large an access to her own space, she can leave herself feeling that there is not enough to share with her husband. One mother told me that breast-feeding was as satisfying as sexual intercourse and a lot less trouble. When talking to a mother weaning her fourth baby, I said sympathetically, 'You want your body back.' She replied, 'I want my mind back.' Many mothers at this stage feel the same – they want to reclaim their own solitary mental life (finding time, for example, to read again) as well as their bodies. At the point of weaning a baby a mother may not even have walked anywhere unencumbered for eighteen months. She may not have been out since before she was pregnant without carrying a baby either inside or outside her body, pushing a pram or carrying shopping.

So weaning may be experienced by some mothers as a regaining of their individualities and the free use of their bodies or it may seem like the signal to conceive the next baby and continue with the cycle of child-bearing. For mothers weaning what they expect to be their last baby, regret and relief may be closely intertwined.

THE FAILURE TO WEAN
When weaning is described by a mother as impossible to manage and the mother and baby seem caught in something unbearable, then the cause may be quite serious. One reason for prolonged breast-feeding may be that the breast-feeding has become sexualized and this can have a lasting effect on the child's development of sexual relationships.

171

One father, consulting about the family's problems, described himself as an 'addict' for eroticized stroking by his wife, but was usually impotent when they tried to have sexual intercourse. He connected the beginning of his addiction with his own childhood, when his father, a coal-miner, used to get up at five o'clock in the morning to go to work. He, as a little boy, would for several years then slip into his mother's bed and for two hours Mother caressed and stroked his body and let him suck at her breast. Not only was he deprived of two necessary hours of sleep, including the REM time of the last part of the night, but he also became inextricably confused and guilty about the feelings stirred up by this stroking. In adult life he was still addicted to being stroked and inhibited, seemingly because of the connection it had with his mother, from letting it lead into full sexual intercourse. We can also see the difficulty of identifying with full male sexual potency for a man who as a little boy felt that he had supplanted his father in his mother's bed. What is painfully clear is the possible outcome of a sexualized experience at the breast. There was a collusion between the mother and son, so that no one else knew of the morning's sucking. As an adult he still woke early every morning and felt he never dreamt. It seemed as though the process of symbolizing had been interfered with early in his life by the over-stimulating experiences of the morning, as well as by the significant loss of REM sleep.

This over-stimulation is the clue to when breast-feeding is continuing as an inappropriate eroticized experience. When mothers and babies come with this problem, both usually seem agitated and preoccupied with each other all the time. My impression is that it is more often mothers and boy babies who have got themselves into this state, though we can see that mothers and little girls might also be in a state of mutually aroused erotic feeling.

One family demonstrated these sexualized feelings to me vividly. Firstly, their referral was dramatic and somewhat out of place. It came in a late-evening phone call to me at home from a psychiatric colleague. When I met them, the mother of the two-and-a-half-year-old boy, Jonathan, declared to me that it was impossible to wean him. Constantly during our meeting Jonathan lifted his mother's jumper with a proprietorial air and burrowed underneath to have a suck at her breast. Mother was embarrassed, but she also had a triumphant air. Father tried to tell Jonathan that this was not the right time to feed. Mother impatiently brushed him aside and said that he did not tell Jonathan in the right way. This incident seemed to me to demonstrate that in this family Jonathan had indeed supplanted his father in having access to Mother. The parents in fact went on to tell me of their severe marital problems. Throughout this meeting Jonathan roamed the room restlessly, rarely able to settle to play. Mother reported that Jonathan woke continually in the night to have a brief suck at her breast. It seemed as though he too, like the father in the previous illustration, had no time to have the dreams that, as we saw in Chapter 6, might have helped him sort out his oedipal conflicts. Similarly he had no time for the daydreams of solitary masturbation which might have led on to symbolic play during the day.

It is important to emphasize that extremes of this kind are not always the reason for failure to wean. Often, as we have seen, it is simply an issue of difficulty or delay in separating, with a mother either deciding not to make this break between herself and her baby yet or feeling unable to tackle it. Both mother and baby may be satisfied by the continuance of breast-feeding without it doing harm to the child's future development, including the ability to separate emotionally later on.

We have seen how negotiating feeding and sleeping rhythms are among the most important interchanges between mothers and babies. Feeding of necessity changes as babies move from breast or bottle to increasingly eating solid food and drinking from a cup. These changes in the physiological ability to chew, digest and metabolize various foods also represent a change in the distancing between mother and baby, which in itself has emotional repercussions. A baby sitting up in his high chair, biting at a rusk or banging his spoon on the table, looking at his mother and babbling to her, is in a different relationship to her from a baby who is held close to her breast, her nipple in his mouth. We can guess that his 'thoughts' about her have also developed into a different form. His thoughts as he lies in his cot awake or his dreams as he sleeps will include the images of these different experiences. A baby falling asleep or dreaming as he sleeps is thus in a state which is partly a response to his feeding and weaning.

CHAPTER TEN

PARENTS' OWN CHILDHOOD EXPERIENCES

NINE-MONTH-OLD Bruce made a great fuss about going to sleep when his mother put him to bed, though he settled easily for Father or the au pair. Mother said to me challengingly, 'Don't tell me to leave him to cry.' After we had talked about this for a while I asked, 'Were *you* left to cry?' Mother burst into tears and told me of her mother's fixed views that babies should not be picked up when they cried. I remarked that her views seemed to be as fixed as her mother's, though their content was different. Mother was one of twins, but it sounded as though her mother had tried to solve the dilemma of which baby to attend to first, by delaying going to either. Whatever had in fact happened in the past, this mother's memory now was of herself as a baby being left to cry in vain. It seemed as though Bruce's cries sounded like her own cries then, as unbearable in her son in the present as in her memory of her own childhood. Perhaps also contained in Mother's determination to act differently from her own mother was a reproach. It was as if she was saying, 'This is how babies *should* be treated.'

It is clear from this that parents' experience of how they were looked after help determine how they look after their baby. Raphael-Leff (1982) has described how the period of pregnancy is often used by expectant mothers to muse over their memories of their own childhood. Part of this preparation period is of course one of preparing psychologically to become a mother. Memories are drawn upon and one consequence of this time may be what Dana Breen (1975) described as a reconciliation with the mother's own mother. Clulow (1982) has remarked that 'the birth of a first baby is a significant moment of generational change'. At this point it can be seen whether past legacies are handed on unchanged or whether 'there is room for a creative response to the challenge of a new family life' (p. xxvii).

Bound up with all this is the need for people to have a confirmation of themselves as parents from their own parents. For Bruce's mother this lack of confirmation from her own mother was a crucial factor. When Bruce was born, her husband's parents were pleasantly supportive and visited almost at once, but her own mother felt unable to attempt the long journey and did not visit for several weeks. It seemed to me that Bruce's mother did not have the seal of approval from the person whose opinion mattered to her most at this time. Perhaps the two, Grandmother and Mother, missed a particular moment of reconciliation that might have happened between them about the shortcomings of the past. Perhaps also Grandmother's 'mistiming' of this first crucial visit re-evoked in Mother the bitterness she felt at Grandmother's 'mistiming' of attention to her baby self in the past.

Gareth's mother, as we saw in Chapter 3, went through a traumatic experience at the time of her baby's birth which affected things later. She had had a very good relationship with her mother, but two weeks before her baby was due there was an earthquake in her home country. She went into labour on hearing the news and for four days after Gareth's birth did not know whether her parents and the rest of the family were alive or dead. It is not difficult to see how unbearable this experience was for her. The family were in fact safe and Grandmother visited a few weeks later, but Gareth's mother said wistfully that all her sisters had had her there from the beginning. Mother regretfully told me how difficult the beginning had been. Her account is so gripping that I quote it again from Chapter 3: 'Every time I was changing him he was screaming. I didn't know what to do. I couldn't relax. My husband said I was like a machine. After my parents had been I realized Gareth had been aware of everything.'

It seemed as though this mother's realistic fear of her parents' death at the time of her baby's birth had not been dispelled until she actually saw her parents. Not only did she not have her mother's help and reassurance about her new baby, she had also had to deal with the shock of her parents' possible death. The preoccupation this caused in her got in the way of being able to notice and respond to the baby.

The examples of Bruce and Gareth's mothers show how important is the mother's relationship with her own mother, particularly at the time of childbirth. Judith Trowell (1983), writing on the effects of emergency Caesarean sections, comments on factors that may partially determine whether this procedure is carried out. She cites Kennell et al. (1980) who argue that 'the presence of a familiar adult female can reduce the length of labour by half'. We can guess that this adult female represents the mother's need for mothering during the actual process of labour, though it is important to recognize this need as being for symbolic mothering – the familiar female is rarely the actual mother. Further, it may be the quality of the internalized relationship the mother has with her own mother that affects her at the birth of her baby. Grandmother may in fact be absent through distance or death, but be vividly present in the mind of the child-bearing mother. Equally important of course is the father's presence at the birth, both as a support to the mother and in his own right, as the father of the baby.

Gareth was nine months old, when his parents came to see me about his sleep problems. It seemed clear that Mother's irresolution and lack of confidence about how to deal with Gareth still stemmed from her disastrous experience in the first few days of his life. This was compounded by the fact that Father had had unhappy times in his own childhood. As well as the individual effects all this had had on them there were also disagreements between these two parents about how to solve the problems with Gareth.

I suspect that quite often strongly-held differences of opinion between husband and wife about how to deal with aspects of child-rearing may stem from unsatisfactorily resolved experiences with their own parents. ('Beating never hurt me', is the sort of example that easily springs to mind.) Parents are unable to negotiate with each other and work out the relative usefulness of each point of view, because their fixed reactions are based on a denial of what their own childhood was really like. Because they cannot argue out within themselves what the past was like, they cannot argue with each other about what to do now.

Amy's parents were a good example of this. Both parents had suffered mistreatment of one kind or another from their own parents. Mother was cynical about her background, but Father clung to an idealized view that not only was his mother's neglect of him understandable in the circumstances (which it was), but also that it had not harmed him in any way. Because he could not look at the thought that it *might* have done so, he was unable to work at forgiving her. Amy's father was left feeling in a muddled way that his mother must have been right in her dismissal of her children's needs. He uneasily felt that he wanted Amy to have something different, but he did not know what. He and his wife had indecisive arguments about what to do for the best; neither had an inner certainty to bring to the discussions.

Parents with deprived backgrounds have a good chance of doing better with their own children, if they can remember their child-hood clearly. They need to be able to recall the feelings about what happened, not just the factual circumstances. Those who may be doomed to reproduce the behaviour of their own parents are those who have no memory of their childhood and those who idealize it (Main *et al.*, 1985).

Stanley's parents had similar problems. Stanley could not get to sleep without hours of one or other parent sitting with him and he woke often in the night. As we talked about the difficulties, it emerged that each parent had real torments at the thought of leaving him to get to sleep on his own. Equally they were at loggerheads with each other about any possible changes in the routine they had all three devised for themselves.

I discovered first that Mother's own mother had died suddenly, when she was in her early twenties. The experience of this bereave-ment being unbearable still underlay her feelings, although she had achieved much in her life since. She was successful profession-ally and her marriage, though full of complications, was a going concern. It seemed to me that the ultimate separation that was felt to be unbearable, her mother's death, coloured her attempt every night to put her baby down to sleep. She could not bear the separation from him; much more important she could not bear it *for* him.

Father brought other problems from childhood. After we had met three or four times, he dreamt that Stanley (who could not yet talk) said to him, 'Why don't you show me how to get to sleep?'. This dream (as we saw in Chapter 6) evoked memories of himself as a little boy, also unable to get to sleep, and Father now said that he felt *his* father had been unable to help *him*. We are again left with the dilemma so many people have: how to pass on to their children what they did not get from their parents. (We are reminded of the example that pet lambs, brought up away from their own mothers, do not make good mothers themselves.)

These two parents both had problems about what to pass on to their child from their own parents. Stanley's father felt his father had not known what to do in crucial situations; Stanley's mother still felt the loss of her own mother.

THE DEATH OF MOTHER'S MOTHER
Many of the mothers and fathers I see had their own parents die before the birth of their first baby; in their flounderings about what to do this loss is often obvious. (We will see later, in Chapter 13,

that mothers whose own mothers died before they were eleven are vulnerable to depression (Brown and Harris, 1978) and perhaps particularly postnatal depression.)

It is important to separate out the various consequences for a mother of her mother's death. In the immediate present we have a mother who lacks the chance to have her mothering of her baby confirmed by her own mother. She may feel her mother's death more acutely at her baby's birth than at any time since it happened. Becoming a mother puts her emotionally into contact with herself as a baby, as Dinora Pines (1982) has shown us. Not having a real mother there may leave her with her own infantile feelings stirred up; and without a chance to have these symbolically satisfied by some attention from her mother, the feelings remain undealt with.

However, a mother who has lost her mother through death can be helped by having time to talk over her memories of her mother and of the mothering that she did get from her. If her mother died when she was young, then talking about her experience of growing up without her can help to bridge the gap from the time of the death to her own baby now and revive what memories she has of when her mother was alive. Talking about what her own mother would have thought of the baby seems to give the mother a chance to think of her mother as approving and confirming the new mother and baby's existence.

Talking in this way may then help the mother to feel more able to use other older figures – her father, stepmother, mother- or father-in-law or other relations – as supportive to her in her new role. It does appear that a father's death does not have the same specific high-risk effect on mothers undergoing childbirth as does a mother's death. However, any bereavement during the actual pregnancy can have a confusing and adverse effect.

PARENTS' DEPRIVATION

It is not too fanciful to reverse the idea of parents telling their children what to do and suggest that babies 'tell' their parents how to look after them. Parents in difficulties are often ones who have missed the cues from their babies.

Main *et al.* (1985) have argued that adults secure about their relationships with their own parents are able to pick up signals from their babies about their needs. Insecure adults have to ignore the signals, otherwise they put themselves in the painful situation of remembering their own attachment needs which were not met in childhood.

When parents start to tell me about their own unmet needs, it seems that even in this brief work one of the features that helps change can be to experience *me* as the parent who does not notice and listen. One mother told me very painfully of a frightening incident that had happened in her teens. She had never been able to tell her mother about it. The next week she was convinced that I had forgotten what I had told her. The therapeutic vehicle was not only that I was the sort of person who *could* be confided in, but also that I was felt to be someone who *could not*. Working out her distrust, based on the real experience of her mother, enabled her to take another step and separate out what *her* son thought of her now. She decided that perhaps she could let him know that she *did* listen to and remember about him. With this idea of remembering in her mind, her little boy became less anxious in the night and slept better.

Judith's parents, both in therapy, provided examples of parents' childhood difficulties getting in the way of their relationship with their own child. Judith's mother came to see me, referred by her own therapist. Judith's acute sleeping difficulties were causing the whole family to have very disturbed nights. Both parents felt they could not stand it any longer and were furious with each other to the point that the marriage was in danger. On the first occasion the mother came with one-year-old Judith, she poured out a bitter account of her own difficult and deprived early life. It sounded as though her mother, and an influential aunt, had been both neglectful of her and also later on ambitious for her, in a way that made her feel that she was not valued for herself, but only for the prestige that she might bring to the family by being successful professionally. As I got to know this mother better, I was sure this account was factually correct and not her own misperception of her mother's and aunt's behaviour. She came over as angry, unsure of herself, untidily dressed, obviously *very* tired, but also as intelligent, very warm to her baby and surprisingly open to new ways of thinking after an initial quibbling response to every remark of mine.

At the parents' own suggestion, Father also came the second time. He was suffering from the recent death of his analyst, but a consultation with a psychiatrist had helped him deal with some of his feelings about this. He felt that in this process he was also retrospectively mourning his parents properly for the first time. He also had a tale to tell of neglect and misunderstanding in his childhood.

I saw these parents three times before a holiday and there was an immediate improvement in the baby's nights. In fact this improvement had started with the referral and it seemed as though even the prospect of support in their problems enabled them in turn to start to help Judith.

The problem was that Judith cried out repeatedly in the night and one or other parent, usually Mother, would go in to comfort her, often give her a bottle of milk and stay till she settled down again. These parents were sensitive to the fears they felt she was expressing and were perhaps especially open to her emotional state. Because they themselves were personally open and vulnerable at this time, having explored their own infancies in their therapy, they were well able to understand Judith's fears. However, it seemed as though they were less able to contain and mitigate these fears. The brief, focused work with me could respond to a different timetable from the longer-term work of their therapy.

In order to give them something to hold on to between sessions, I suggested that they read Winnicott's *The Child, the Family and the Outside World* (1964). In the last session before the holiday I had lost my voice. I decided not to cancel the session, as I did not otherwise feel ill. It seemed important with this family not to disappear when crucial work was going on. (It is difficult to decide whether this 'the show must go on' policy is helpful in the end to patients or not.) In any case I had to whisper and Mother was able to voice her fears that her destructiveness and exhausting of possible help was the cause of my disability.

We started again after the holidays with a new contract that Father would be part of all sessions, so that they could work as a family. The focus shifted from the fears that Judith might be feeling. It seemed as though the parents had first had to be sensitive to these fears, in a way that their own parents had not been for them. With no memory of their own fears being listened to and understood, they did not know what to do next when they received the impact of Judith's fears; they simply felt overwhelmed by them. Repeatedly going in to her in the night was less a comforting response to Judith than a panic reaction of their own. As we talked about all this, they started to feel more in control.

They thought about a setting of limits and Mother having rights herself, that is, to stay in bed and to sleep. We were able to start looking at her negative feelings towards Judith. As she started to acknowledge these feelings, she realized that previously she had thought of any negative thoughts as being entirely destructive.

Because of this she could never risk saying 'no' to Judith, however appropriate the 'no' might be. Father was very supportive to Mother, as she worked all this out, and she began to have more confidence in her mothering abilities and to set tentative limits.

One week the family came in, settled themselves down in somewhat of a flurry and produced a bottle of milk for Judith. They said that now she was not having milk at night she needed it during the day. I said they seemed to be telling me in a backwards sort of way that the nights had changed. They told me, beaming, that Judith was waking up only once or twice a night. If she woke up before the parents' bedtime, Mother would go in to her and firmly tell her it was night-time and time to go to sleep. After the parents got to bed themselves they did not go to her, but called to her from their bed. Judith would cry for a few minutes and go back to sleep. Both parents were delighted with this success. What accounted for this change? Of course the parents' new commonsensical, clear and firm manner with Judith was in itself reassuring to her. She was not abandoned by them, she knew they were there and listening, but the limits were set. How did the parents get to the point where this behaviour on their part was possible? If in the first place I had simply mapped out advice on these lines, they would, I am sure, have thought I had not understood the problem at all. What I think was effective was the combination, within this relatively brief, focused work, of both parents telling me something of their childhood, while I also saw them with their child and connected all this through their actual relationship with me.

I must emphasize that Mother had been left very much torn to pieces by her childhood experiences. It took several years of her own very good therapy to help her repair this. But it was essential for me also to know about this, so as to be able to connect it with her feelings about her baby now. The necessary stages were these: firstly, she told me about her own relationship with her mother and some actual childhood experiences; secondly, I noticed her anger, both in telling me about her mother and in her reactions to my comments; then we had the episode of my lost voice, when she was able to talk about the destructiveness she felt in herself – the aftermath of a mother who had actually been destructive of her daughter's individuality and real creativity. When Mother saw that I was hearing all this, with no damage to myself besides a temporarily lost voice, it all seemed less dangerous.

At this point it was appropriate for me to show my appreciation of the real warmth between Mother and Judith. Having really dared to look with her at her worst fears about herself as a damaging mother, it was not now empty reassurance for me to confirm a new belief in herself as a good mother. Father's presence was of course essential in underlining this. There was also a chance for Mother and Father to look at ways in which anger with each other had made the problem worse.

The next stage was to look at Mother's difficulty in giving up her picture of herself as a deprived baby with nothing good to hang on to. If she were able to give something good to Judith, she might have to acknowledge that somewhere she got something for herself and would therefore have to lose some of the anger and resentment which were so much part of her. I thought that going through all this with me, in our sessions together, led her to a trust that it need not invalidate the truth of her early experiences if she did allow things to get better now.

I met this mother several years after this piece of work and found she had developed a real cutting wit, a brilliant kind of black humour. This seemed to be a creative way of expressing the anger still inside her and was much valued by her husband and daughter as well as by her own growing professional circle.

Parents who have felt very undermined by their own parents may easily feel criticized by their babies. Judith's mother felt reproached at times by the look in her complaining daughter's eye.

Penny's mother on the other hand felt criticism rather differently. She had started to feed her baby less often and was pleased that she slept for longer. She then panicked, took Penny into bed with her and told me it all sounded too theoretical, that what 'the authorities' said was not always right. I said it sounded as though I was being a 'theoretical authority', not realizing what she and her daughter really needed and simply criticizing her for what she was doing. She agreed and we thought about how devastating criticism appeared to her. I then suggested that perhaps taking her daughter even closer to her in the night than before, having her in bed with her, was a way of stopping the baby's criticisms of her mother's attempts to put more distance between the two of them. Mother took this up enthusiastically and offered me another twist of the generations. She volunteered that perhaps she could not stand being 'criticized' by her daughter, because it would remind her of how vehemently she had criticized *her* mother.

MOTHERS WITH SLEEP PROBLEMS

Giorgis *et al.* (1987) found in their study of babies with sleep problems that 26 percent of mothers had families with sleep troubles, while only 10 percent of fathers did. Of the mothers themselves 16 percent of mothers of sleepless babies also had sleep problems. The really fascinating figure that emerges from this is that in the contrasting group of babies without sleep problems, the figures for mothers' families and fathers' families with sleep problems was the same, namely 10 percent in each case. From this it seems that the influence of a mother who has experienced sleep problems in her own family of origin is high. However, the personal effect of the mother's own sleep problems is not so great. Of the babies who slept well 13.3 percent of their mothers had disturbed sleep, not so very different from the 16 percent of mothers of non-sleeping babies with disturbed sleep themselves.

The case of Jesse and his mother shows how a baby's sleep problems can connect with the mother's own sleeplessness as a child. Jesse at nine months was waking often during the night and had to be put to sleep by Mother. It emerged that he was breast-fed for four weeks and then Mother stopped, because she felt she was not giving him enough. At four months Mother had *never* left him – when she tried to leave him with her mother while she went out for the evening with Father, Jesse was beside himself with emotion. Father described how the veins stood out on his scalp.

Jesse's mother had volunteered that she herself had been unable to sleep and that her sister had similar problems with her children. When I asked Father, he said there was no such trouble in his family. He added that his mother had been able to get him to sleep and his first wife had been able to get his children from his first marriage to sleep. I commented on his assumption that getting children to sleep was only a mother's job! Jesse's mother confirmed what seemed to be both her own and her baby's belief – that without her presence Jesse could neither get to sleep nor manage during the day.

I asked more about her own sleep problem. She initially said she had had a happy childhood. Then she told me that when she was born her father was in hospital with TB. She was the first child and she and her mother lived in Grandmother's house. An aunt and her children were also there. Everyone seemed to be critical of her mother's handling of her little girl, so that it was an extra strain trying to keep her quiet. It seemed to me that this mother's own mother, separated from her husband and afraid that he would die, might have clung to her baby for comfort. Perhaps the baby had become one of the vigilant babies, feeling responsible for mothering their own mothers and displaying 'reverse attachment' behaviour (see Chapter 12).

Jesse's mother told me that when she was three her father came out of hospital; the parents moved into their own home and had another baby. She reported being able to sleep from then on and said she was surprised, because she would have expected a new baby to have had the opposite effect. I suggested that the relief of having her father back safely, and the family together for the first time as a going concern, might have been more influential than jealousy of the baby. The relief was perhaps her own and also a reflection of her mother's. Jesse's mother agreed that here was a key to her own sleeplessness and started to think how it might connect with Jesse's problems. It did seem as though her inability, to an unusual degree, to let herself and her son be out of each other's sight might have its origins in her own childhood overshadowed by her father's illness.

Despite this weighting from the past it seemed a good time to start work on the present problem. Although he was unable to let his mother out of his sight, Jesse was starting to use words and therefore presumably concepts that could include that of separation. He could say 'Mamma' and 'Dadda' and also 'bye-bye'. In Chapter 7 I suggested that absence is necessary to stimulate thought. Although Jesse had not yet managed to be absent from his 'Mamma', his use of words to name his parents might indicate a readiness to hold people in mind when they were not there. Following this suggestion, Mother reported some improvement in Jesse's sleep.

However, perhaps the most interesting outcome of this piece of work was that at the end of our first meeting, Mother, intrigued by the connections we had made, planned to talk it over with her own mother. Next week she told me how helpful she and her mother had found it to talk together.

RECALLING CHILDHOOD

Sometimes I find that asking mothers questions about their own childhood makes them realize the gaps in their knowledge. When their mothers are still alive and in touch, then the conversation between mother and daughter can fulfil many functions. It not only provides information or confirmation for the mother about her own early experience, it is also a vehicle for the two mothers to share feelings about what has happened in the past and what is happening now. In Fraiberg's (1980) vivid description, 'In every nursery there are ghosts. They are the visitors from the unremembered past of the parents' (p. 164).

A mother who is being helped therapeutically to consider her childhood may also be able to help her own mother recall and voice regrets about the past. The understanding that can be engendered by this between grandmother and mother has infinitely more value than insights that remain in the consulting-room.

However, Pound *et al.* (1985) warn us that good relationships in the present between the mother and her own mother may come too late to undo the present effect on their parenting of the grandmother's past deficiencies: 'Low evaluation of her own mother was also strongly associated with child problems even though most women's *current* relationship with their mothers was quite friendly, and they had, as it were, forgiven them for their past shortcomings.'

Her own mother's obstetric history can be a crucial factor in the mother's relationship to the child-bearing aspect of her own body. Women whose own mothers had miscarriages and still births may grow up with their mother's confusion, anger and distress about the birth and death their bodies have produced tearing around in their own bodies.

One such mother felt guilty about her own survival and not only guilty but apprehensive about the survival of her baby. She felt she had no right to be spared the grief her mother had suffered. She checked so continually on her baby in the night that he was in fact unable to sleep. The agonizing effects of cot deaths can also spread through extended families. Women whose sisters have suffered in this way talk of their guilt and fears and not surprisingly may also have sleepless babies. Mothers also may feel guilty about their own child-bearing coinciding with their mother's menopause, as though their ability to have babies has destroyed their mother's ability to do so.

In listening to parents' experiences, it is also useful to notice the way in which they talk about them. Main *et al.* (1985) have shown that the way parents talk about their relationships with their parents in a single hour-long interview can enable a prediction to be made of the baby's response to the parents in a stress situation. They used Ainsworth and Wittig's Strange Situation Test, described in Chapter 8, to show how babies' behaviour, when briefly separated and then reunited with their mothers, connects with the adults' own upbringing.

Strikingly, they found that there are characteristic ways in which parents describe their own childhood experience which connect with the kind of attachment their baby has with them. Parents whose babies had insecure attachments can be classified into three types. Firstly, those who deny and devalue the importance of attachment; these parents have babies who avoid them. Secondly, there are parents who continue to be preoccupied with what has gone on between themselves and their own parents; they have babies who are ambivalently preoccupied with them and may angrily insist on attention. Thirdly, there are traumatized parents who have suffered deaths or separations; they may have babies showing disorganized behaviour.

In contrast to this, parents with securely attached babies are able to talk about their own childhood in a coherent manner. I find Main *et al.*'s comment that 'coherency in the discussion is the best predictor of security' extremely interesting. Their pinpointing of incoherency as being diagnostic of the quality of insecurity fits well with my own experience of being told by parents what I describe as a jumble of unassimilated material.

Main *et al.* consider the manner in which a parent tells their history as well as its content; it is also relevant that this information is gathered within an hour-long interview. Their observations diagnose the relationship between parent and baby. In brief work I also make the assumption that the *telling* of the incoherent story within the framework of one or two hour-long sessions, plus the putting together of the story by the listener, are themselves therapeutic. In other words I think that some of the parents I see become less incoherent by the reviving of their incoherent story – the work does in fact make some sense of the past and connects it to their relationship with their baby in the present.

It is worth ending by referring again to Fraiberg *et al.*'s (1980) belief that the affect of childhood experiences must be remembered in order for ill-treatment or neglect not to be reproduced yet again for the parent's own child. This is also a comforting thought for workers facing an inter-generational sequence of unhappy childhoods. Things can be changed by remembering and bearing the pain. I also think that the effectiveness of this sometimes lies in the therapist bearing the transference of the emotions evoked by the memories. In such cases the therapist cannot just pleasantly enjoy being an 'understanding mother' for the first time in the parent's own experience. The therapist must also stand being experienced as though she was the mother who *did not understand*, before she can know what the parent really needs to say.

CHAPTER ELEVEN

FATHER'S ROLE,
THE PARENTS' MARRIAGE,
SINGLE PARENTS AND
WORKING MOTHERS

 S THE TITLE INDICATES, this chapter covers a variety of themes. It examines how both relationships and external circumstances can affect parents' handling of their baby. Firstly, we see how parents' interaction with each other influences their baby. Following on from this, we see some of the possible repercussions when the father is absent, temporarily or permanently, and the complex issues for working mothers. We also look at how the external factors of a family's circumstances are, as we might expect, dealt with according to the personalities and relationships within the family.

In my work either mothers alone or both parents are seen, according to their own choice; very rarely do fathers come alone. The quality of the marriage does not seem to determine who is worked with. Fathers who do not come to the Baby Clinic may be as much, or as little, supportive at home as those who do. The baby of course is nearly always there as well.

Where there are two parents, I always invite both to come. Mothers often say that it is difficult for their husband to take time off work and come on their own the first time. After a visit where they see the style of help I am offering, many of them encourage their husbands to come the next time. It is worth noting that I have not yet worked with any fathers bringing up small children on their own.

Although I do not think the success rate is altered by whether both parents come to the Clinic, the content of the work can certainly be very different. When only mother comes, the theme is very often centred on the mothering she had herself and its influence on her as a mother now, on her physical and emotional experience of pregnancy, childbirth and breast-feeding. The absent father may be represented as supportive and understanding of all this, with mother relating our conversations to him each week, or he may be pictured as not understanding or even hostile to the thoughts mother is developing about herself and the baby. When both parents do come, then each has a chance to look at the present problem in terms of their own childhood experience. They also have a chance to work out with a third party conflicts between them about their philosophies of what to do about their baby. My presence as this other person can be experienced as supportive, provocative or as both.

The use of me is thus different when one or when two parents come to the Clinic. Either can be seen as a helpful way to intervene in a particular family or on the contrary as a way of falling in with the defences and denials of that family's system.

When I do see a mother without the father, it can be truly helpful to work with her, centring on her emotional problems of mothering. She may use me to work through some of her unre-solved feelings about her mother. I often think that, even in the relatively brief time-scale of this kind of therapy, some very deep connections are made. The pitfall of working with only the mother is that a partnership between me and the mother, with the baby in between, can actually seem to have the effect of excluding the father. I make this situation explicit, hoping by doing so to break up the collusive element.

I have also sometimes worked at this emotional level with a mother in the presence of her husband and have found this can be liberating for both partners. It does not usually have the effect of making the father feel excluded; on the contrary it opens up into the marriage a vocabulary for talking about intense emotions. Both parents may be able to start telling each other more about what they feel and what they have undergone. In joint work when parents are in conflict over what to do about the baby and are upholding different ways of child-rearing, they may be amazed to discover where the other's attitude evolves from in their own childhood. Mutual planning of how to deal with the baby's sleep and other problems becomes much easier, when the origin of their disagreements has been opened up. Where joint work does not seem useful is when parents are at loggerheads and not in sym-pathy enough to look at the causes. Some may accept referral for marital or family therapy; in other cases it may be worth doing some limited work with the mother alone, if she claims that the care of the children is in any case left to her.

To give a brief example, Edward's parents came with a conflict between them about how to deal with him. Edward always cried when he was put in his cot. Mother wanted to leave him to get himself to sleep, Father felt he should always be picked up and held until he fell asleep. Father had been left to cry himself, in a way that left him with traumatic memories. In his insistence that Edward should never be left he seemed to be expressing how unbearable his own memories were. He was making his wife stay with the baby, when he had been unable to make his mother stay with him. In a sense he was being as tyrannical with his wife, in making her stay with the baby, as his own mother had been by her neglect of him. His own mother had not read the signs that he needed her and had not known that he was frightened when he was left alone in his room. Equally dogmatically Father did not read the signs of what Edward really needed now; more importantly he did not allow his wife to use *her* judgement of how to carry out her mothering, of when to be with Edward and when to be apart from him.

FATHER'S ROLE

Let us now turn to the wider question of a father's role in the rearing of babies. I am defining a dual role here: firstly, the direct relationship between father and baby and secondly, the sense in which the father is supportive of the original mother–baby couple.

Fathers can be also supportive of mothers in not letting babies and small children exploit their mothering. They can help with establishing a cut-off point. Many mothers feel unsure that they have given their babies enough good mothering during the day and so let the baby go on asking for more during the night. Father, helping the mother to feel that she has done what is reasonable during the day and that nothing more is owing to the baby, can be startlingly effective.

Judith's father (described earlier in Chapter 10) was a case in point. Here it was vital for Mother to know that she had her husband's confidence before she had the courage to say 'no' to Judith at night. It would not have been enough in their case for Father himself simply to say 'no' to Judith, though this was the vital first move. Father said 'no' himself and also helped Mother to regain her own authority and limits.

We have seen from several examples in Chapter 9 the struggles mothers have between their wish to continue the intimacy of breast-feeding and conversely to hasten their child's independence. At best fathers can remind mothers of how the baby has grown, help her clear her conservative vision and help her find the authority within herself to be more separate from her baby and to share the baby more with father and the rest of the family. At worst this position of the father's can be felt as an envious intrusion into an intimacy that only mother and baby can share.

Father may also provide a protection for a baby whose mother is depressed or having other difficulties. Guedeney and Kreisler (1987) say the father can help by being 'an effective substitute for a very depressed or withdrawn mother, or by limiting the influence of mother's phobias on the child' (p. 311).

The quality of the marital relationship is also a protective factor against depression. Brown and Harris (1978) have shown that a woman without an intimate relationship with a husband or boy-friend is much more likely to break down. If this intimate relation-ship is protective for the mother, it is also of importance for the baby. When parents have an estranged relationship, the baby's experience will not only be of a mother in difficulties with being emotionally available to him, but he will also sense that his parents are not performing this for each other.

Strong feelings abound in families. We have seen how the problem of separation for the baby at night is rooted in the com-plexity of his tie to the mother. Another issue which is almost universal is the oedipal situation, where the baby's reason for not sleeping seems to be an anxiety or protest about the parents being together and excluding the child. A baby who cries frequently and requires the attention of one of his parents is very effectively keeping them apart. Often parents are suffering the consequences of this, but have not really thought of it as a cause. They will have become resigned to broken nights, have got used to a small child between them in bed or are often even sleeping separately so that one of them can get an undisturbed night's sleep.

The effect on a marriage can be disastrous and the stress can affect a whole family. Sometimes this aspect of the problem is obvious at once. For example, Jim's parents were quite explicit about the blight on their sexual relationship. They were ready to take this on at once in our work and to look at the mutual misun-derstandings of each other's needs which had led them to the 'musical beds' of the night. Having previously been allowed his pick of the family's beds, Jim was surprised to find himself firmly put into his own bed and told to stay there. He was no longer the centre of interest in the night, as his parents worked out their sexual hesitations and with amusement and pride reported each week's discoveries to me.

In another family, Melanie's parents came to this understanding at a totally different pace. We had worked for some weeks on Melanie's highjacking of the nights. Here there was some painstaking work to be done on Mother's ability to separate herself from Melanie and the need for Father to support this. This work was slow, but very successful. The parents came and told me of a whole week of almost unbroken nights. I remarked on how subdued they both appeared. The success had fallen rather flat. I followed my hunch and asked how they were getting on sexually. Father told me it was a non-event. Mother had been too exhausted by the broken nights and had only recently weaned the demanding Melanie. She said, as do many other mothers in this situation, that she felt she wanted her body to herself. It took meetings over several months for us to talk about how she would achieve this and find her own individuality again. Expressing sexuality as *part of* individuality and not as a loss of it again can be quite a problem. An easy answer for a mother is to be 'too tired' for sex and a baby's jealousy can compound the tendency.

In both these cases it is also important to spell out that a marital relationship, which in its sexual aspects excludes the child, is in fact just as vital for the child himself as for his parents. A child who by his jealousy manages to keep his parents apart is himself deprived of being able to grow within their flourishing relationship. He will bring less knowledge of emotional involvement to his own marriage in later years. It is worth confronting his immediate jealousy now for this end. In fact parents with a troubled marriage, who have been sleeping separately while their child has had sleep problems, are particularly vulnerable when they come together again. Focusing on the child has given them a respite from dealing with their own problems.

It can often be overlooked that evenings may be just as important for parents as the night as a time together, sometimes as their preferred time for sexual intercourse, but in any case as a time to relax together after the day's work. It may be as necessary for parents to claim this time for themselves as later in the night. The evening can then be used for parents to become attuned to each other after the separate activities of the day. But even this can easily slip away from them under the stress of a baby's demands.

One major source of jealousy is of course that of older children towards younger ones in the family. Father can play a major role in dealing with this. Adam, a three-year-old boy who had always slept badly (see also Daws, 1985), became even more difficult after the

192

birth of a new baby who slept in the parents' bedroom. Every night Adam came and got into the parents' bed. In many families this would be an acceptable solution for a while, but Adam, having got into his parents' bed, was unable to settle down. He slept restlessly, kicked his parents and woke them and himself many times during the night. It seemed as though the disturbing feelings which led him to seek their bed were not relieved by being with them; they seemed in fact to be accentuated. Adam's parents decided to try to keep him in his own bed. They explained to him that Father would come to him if he called, but that he was not allowed out of his bed. They offered him a small car as a reward for staying in his bed. On the first two nights he stayed in his bed throughout the night, calling out for Father a couple of times and falling asleep again while Father stayed with him. On the third night he slept throughout the night and came into the parents' bedroom in the morning, saying to his father, 'You've been a very good boy. You stayed in your bed all night. I shall buy you a new pair of cuff-links.' This father indeed deserved a reward for the firmness which relieved his son of the torment of jealousy of both parents and new baby which he was unable to get away from in the parents' room.

Another small child, David, aged two and a quarter, took a long time to settle in the evenings, continually reappearing downstairs. Eventually the parents realized what was on his mind. They talked to him about the new baby they were expecting and told David he did not need to keep on checking if anything was happening; the new baby would not just suddenly appear. David settled much more easily from then on. A week after his baby sister was born, David again could not settle to sleep. Father talked to him and David said, 'More baby coming.' Father told him not to worry, there weren't any more babies coming. David said, 'Nicholas got two.' Ten months previously his friend Nicholas's mother had had twins. 'I told him that he was right, but we weren't having twins.' 'Where's Gregory?' asked David. Father told me: 'Gregory was in fact the name we had chosen if the baby was a boy. I explained and David settled.'

This little story shows the importance of listening carefully to exactly what is troubling a child. It would have been easy for Father to assume that it was the birth of the actual baby sister that was now disturbing David and keeping him awake. Father's finding out that his worry was the imagined arrival of yet another new member of the family was an instant relief to David; he could stop being on guard and let himself go to sleep.

This father and son understood each other well. David had a period at about twelve months of waking distraught and being very angry with Father – hitting at him either if Father picked him up and held him or through the bars of his cot. On one such occasion Father said to him, 'David, why are you so angry with Daddy?' David stopped hitting out at his father, gave him a kiss and lay down to sleep. The relief of something being put into words, to a little boy who had as yet very few words of his own, is interesting. With little information we can only speculate as to why David was so angry with his father – was it something going on between them or was the anger perhaps a displacement from the complicated emotions going on with his mother who had recently weaned him? Whatever the cause it was the *acknowledgement* of the anger that David needed from his father.

As in many families sleep problems re-emerged at times of stress. After the family moved house David, now nearly three, was again wakeful. Father bought him a clock and pointed out on the clock the time when he could come in to his parents in the morning. After a few genuine mistakes David got the idea within a week. He then appeared one night, half an hour after going to bed, and said, 'It's pointing to the seven, Daddy', with a twinkle in his eye. The joke between David and his father shows a much more creative internalization by David of the new rule than a solemn acceptance of it might have done.

We see how enjoyably this father interacts with his son and how he helps him through times of stress or change in the family. A crucial element in families is whether the father can be different from the mother, act in a complementary way to her and be able to rescue mother and child from too heightened an emotion.

One topic, full of hidden perils, is whether the father takes turns or not in getting up for a baby in the night. This is a very complex subject. When a mother is breast-feeding, obviously only she can feed the baby. She may enjoy this exclusivity and wake up quite pleasurably to feed the baby, matching her own sleep rhythms to the baby's. Father may also get up, sometimes to be part of an enjoyable social time or to support Mother. Sometimes more destructive forces are at work – either a father cannot tolerate the exclusive mother–baby feeding or conversely the mother cannot bear Father to sleep while she is awake.

After weaning or if a feed is not needed, either parent can go to the baby. Gordon Scott (personal communication, 1988) has noticed that many mothers complain that fathers cannot wake up properly and perform clumsily, if they do get up to a baby in the night. Is this a reluctance to be helpful or is it that mothers are more able to attune their own sleep–wake rhythms to the baby's and are able to wake as the baby does?

If, however, a baby is waking too frequently, where does the father fit in? It may be that Father is needed to help Mother limit the baby's demands, to say when enough is enough. It may be that Father can reassure Mother that the baby could go for longer between feeds or that his wakings do not mean he is in need of anything. Father can reinterpret the baby's signals to a mother who is feeling anxious, so that she has a chance to understand them in a less urgent way. However, mothers may use fathers to displace on to them annoyance about being woken by the baby. Instead of being firm themselves with the baby about what is going on, they may be angry with Father either for not providing the firmness or on the contrary for not similarly leaping to attention whenever the baby makes a sound.

Fathers can be supportive by confirming to a mother that it is the baby who is 'fussy', difficult or unreasonable and help with the problem of trying to understand what to do. One mother rather movingly described how she was able to let Father help, after some months of excluding him. She wrote to me:

> Actually our method for getting Charles to sleep through the night seems to have worked – unless it's just a coincidence. S carried on going into him, instead of me, for a week. He would pick Charles up and give him a cuddle and a drink of water and then put him back into bed and firmly leave the room. To begin with, this had to be repeated several times a night but by about the 5th night he was only waking once, and after a week started to sleep right through! I can't believe it was that simple in the end! Though I think it was a question of timing really – I had reached a point where I was prepared to let S intervene. Before then I always felt I had to be the one to go to him in the night.

This mother, a friend of mine, had read an earlier paper on sleep problems. She said: 'I identified immediately with the mothers who feel uncertain that they have given their babies enough good mothering during the day and therefore give in to their demands far more during the night.'

What we see in this fascinating account of family dynamics is how something vital changes in the interactions between all three. Mother says that at first she was not sure about being a 'good-enough' mother and had to keep giving more; she could not allow Father to help her set limits. In such cases saying 'no' is felt to be being a 'bad' parent; Mother is unable to do this herself. She may put into Father this aspect of parenting, but also stop him from effecting it. These two parents, in fact very appreciative of each other's qualities, were able to change from this way of operating before it became too fixed. Perhaps as Mother became able to admit to her own wish to say 'no' to the baby, she was able to let Father take over from her. In addition Father was allowed to be a comforter to the baby and enjoy the intimacy that comes from this.

Father's role of course changes with the age of the baby. Small breast-fed babies need their mothers to some extent exclusively. Fathers come increasingly into their own with weaning and may be especially needed to help mothers and babies separate.

With older children, the need for a partnership of parents being firm is obvious. Mothers may seem to rely too much on fathers to provide the firmness, letting themselves be the indulgent, 'caring' parent and leaving Father to do the 'heavy' parenting. On the other hand a somewhat surprising pitfall for parents can be when each parent tries to be too much like the other and act in the same way towards the child.

One pair of high-powered professional parents each worked part-time and looked after their twenty-month-old daughter Maria in turn. She seemed happy during the day, but refused to settle to sleep at night. They told me in detail how consistent they were in their handling of her. It emerged as they talked that in their busy work/baby-minding schedules each of these parents whizzed in and out, not particularly saying 'hello' or 'goodbye' to Maria, because they did not feel she was going to miss one parent, left as she always was with the other. I suggested to them that Maria might actually be quite angry at this lack of ceremony and at their assumption that one parent was the same as or as good as the other at any time. Perhaps to Maria this was not so. I said I thought she was being politely co-operative during the day, but letting them know at night that she felt somewhat pushed around. These parents started to be more careful to signal what was happening to their daughter and also, to their own relief, to behave more spontaneously, so that their style of looking after her corresponded more to their own natural ways. They were able to be different in style from each other and Maria was able to have a slightly different experience with each of them. This was perhaps easier for Maria to understand; at any rate she began sleeping better.

Such issues can be particularly troubling for parents with strongly held views of not wanting to behave in sexist and stereotyped ways with their own children, which they feel marked their own childhoods. This is especially relevant where parents' own mothers have unfairly carried most of the responsibility for bringing up children and the parents do not want to perpetuate the pattern.

The constructive wish to share and enjoy time and contact with children and not define rigidly the roles of either a mother or a father can, however, sometimes become confused with not recognizing individual personality or indeed even biological differences and the creative tension between these differences which is a major component of a live marriage. The change towards recognizing this was a great relief to Maria and her parents.

THE ABSENCE OF FATHER

Father's importance means that his absence will of course have repercussions. When I saw one-year-old Joanna, mentioned in Chapter 6, she had been sleeping badly since she was six weeks old, when her father had been away for a brief period. It seemed as though the difficulties had started then because of her mother's own panic at this separation and her resentment with Father for not being there to support her.

Karen's mother also had a strong reaction to father's business trips. Karen had slept badly for some time, but her mother felt doubly unable to deal with this when Father was away, partly because she herself slept so badly then. She lay awake, worrying about burglars. I suggested that this fear might have its origin in her anger with Father for being away. She was rejecting her absent husband, so that in her fantasy if he came back he would be an intruder. This formulation was shocking and also made instant sense to both Mother and Father. It also came in the context of Mother thinking of herself as an exile from her own large, warm family. Often in Father's absences she and Karen went to stay with the grandparents. Neither had trouble sleeping there.

Karen's sleep problems had started when she was five months old, when Mother went back to work. Karen was happy with the baby-sitter Mother left her with, but stopped sleeping at night. Mother continued breast-feeding Karen and the nights were one long agony of Karen refusing to let go of the breast. When she and her mother came to see me, Karen was ten months old. She and Mother were both beautiful, brightly dressed, brightly smiling, but underneath Mother at least was feeling desperate.

We thought about the possible connection between Mother's lack of sense of herself on her own and Karen's problem of separating from her at night. It seemed reasonable that Karen had protested when Mother left her at five months to go back to work. Mother felt it was an unsuccessful experiment; it had not really suited either of them and she had given up work as soon as it was possible. Why, however, was Karen still playing out this tragic role of the baby who must never be left? It occurred to Mother that in some subtle way she was letting Karen dramatize her own feeling that it was unbearable to be left. She started setting some limits which Karen accepted. Most importantly Mother decided that in Father's forthcoming absence she was going to stick it out on her own with Karen for the first week of his trip. We agreed that she could telephone me, but we did not arrange a meeting (I always saw these parents together). She did not phone me and managed to keep the improvement going during this week. My interpretation to Mother that 'burglars' were in part the representation of her own anger left her feeling much less of a helpless victim; acknowledging this anger gave her added strength and allowed her to start experimenting with a picture of herself as a competent adult woman who could look after her daughter on her own. This new competence came over convincingly to her daughter, who perhaps now felt safe enough to sleep. Karen was perhaps an example also of the inverted attachment described in the next chapter, where babies' wakefulness is produced by feeling responsible for looking after their mothers.

MARITAL CONFLICT

Marital conflict can of course in itself cause sleep problems. It is obvious that overt rows and shouting can keep a child anxiously awake. Much more subtle signs of marital discord are also noticeable to babies and young children, for whom a major part of their world is the awareness of their parents' emotions. We have seen how an intimate relationship with the father is one of the protective factors for a mother against depression. If this is missing, she is more vulnerable to depression. The baby then experiences his mother's uneasy state of mind and also his parents' inability to be close to each other. This can make the world feel like an arid place in which it is hard to find the comfort of sleep.

SINGLE PARENTS

Single parents are particularly vulnerable, when there is no one easily available to support them. Many parents in this situation are also aware that they are unsure whether they really want their small child to go off to bed and leave them alone. The parent may be torn between needing a respite from a child's demands and dreading loneliness. Andrea Pound (personal communciation, 1985) has pointed out that difficulties in a child going off to bed may be an unconscious protest by both child and parent about the missing parent who is not there to help and that perhaps what both are doing is keeping a place open for this absent parent.

One family illustrated, albeit dramatically, some of the problems of single-parent families (see also Daws, 1985). Just before the summer holiday a five-year-old girl, Dawn, and her eight-months-pregnant mother were referred to me. Dawn was not sleeping and was refusing to go to school. Dawn's father had left her mother some years before and the expected baby's father had just left after beating up the mother violently.

In the first session I got Mother to tell me some of this story in front of Dawn. I listened and commented that Dawn was also listening, while she played with toys. I then asked about Dawn's sleeping difficulties and Mother told me of her reluctance to go to sleep and of her nightmares. I talked about what I thought was Dawn's worry about Mother after all the dreadful experiences. Dawn listened carefully. I then asked Dawn herself to tell me of her recurrent nightmare. She crossed the room, stood in front of me and told it to me at great length. I had not become attuned to her speech and could not understand anything that she had said. However, it was obvious that Mother could; she was listening as avidly as Dawn had earlier listened to her. I solemnly said that the dream was very frightening and that Dawn should tell her mother every morning what her dreams had been about.

Next week they reported to me that there had been no nightmares. Dawn had gone to bed easily each night and slept well. That week Dawn told me in vivid detail of the time the mother's boyfriend had smashed up the flat. Mother told me that she had not been able to get Dawn to talk about it at all before. I said it seemed to need an outside person to help them both talk about such things.

Pathetically, Dawn and her mother could both have used me not just as an outside listener, but as a missing father. We talked about Dawn staying home from school to look after her mother and about how bossy she had become. When I once said to her that she was a little girl and that she didn't decide what happened, that Mummy decided, she said to me, 'No, you decide'.

WORKING MOTHERS

Working mothers may also have difficulties of this kind (see also Daws, 1985). They and their babies may actually need more time together to become reunited after the day's separation, but this may merge into a guilty reluctance to face the baby's feelings about being put down. One professional mother found that her one-year-old boy, Henry, was having great difficulty in sleeping, when she started back at work. She then realized that one problem was in her way of separating from him in the daytime. She had been taking him to the child-minder, waiting until he was happily settled and playing and then slipping out of the room without saying goodbye to him. This mother had gone back to work reluctantly and found the separation from her little boy very painful. She realized she was saving herself the pain of saying goodbye to him during the day, but had to have the confrontation with him at night instead. When she managed to let him know in the mornings that she was going away, he was able to make his protest to her at the appropriate time and not displace it to the evenings. He also perhaps felt more generally secure, by always knowing when his mother was leaving him and when she was not. With this settled between them his mother was able to look at her feelings about leaving him and found them to be more complex than she had imagined. She had previously not owned that *she* was leaving her son; she had thought the *job* was taking her away from him. Once she had worked out that her son perceived her as leaving him, she became more able to feel this herself. She took the responsibility for the separation and became more able to enjoy her job, while still regretting the time away from her son.

Another working mother found herself with a different version of this problem. Coming back home after a day's separation from her baby and toddler, she found herself puzzling about how hard it seemed to be to cuddle them and talk to them. It was easy to do things for them – cook their supper, get the bath ready, even sit down and look at a book with them – but it always seemed as though there had to be something else to relate to the children through. She could not just physically touch and play with them. She then realized that this extended to the perfunctory way she put them to bed. Thinking all this over, she decided that feeling and showing the children that she knew she mattered to them most seemed to make the separation of the day more painful. If books and toys came first, then the baby-minder could provide these just as well as her. When she began to acknowledge that it really was painful to be away from her children through the day, she could have a reunion that was more satisfying for them all. Bedtime became more of a time for cuddles and games and both children started to sleep better.

Perhaps the greatest stress for working mothers is not having the freedom to attune exclusively to the baby's sleep rhythms but having also to be subject to the alarm clock. Mother and baby have the problem of working out a sleep–wake rhythm with limited time available to them to do it.

Several mothers have told me that the prospect of going back to work has broken in to their experience of the early weeks, even when they were actually able to be full-time with their babies. They were not able to be totally in the present, because of the future separation looming ahead. Brazelton (1988) has found similarly that in a prenatal interview when parents anticipate the pressures of having to return to work 'too early', they guard against talking about the future baby as a person or about themselves as parents. They talk instead about the concrete problems of timetables and finding substitute care for the baby. He suggests that they are already defending themselves against too intense an attachment, because of the pain of separating prematurely from the new baby. Brazelton implies that the impending return to work robs parents and baby of some intimacy ahead of the actual separation. He cites three months as being 'too early', but I have seen parents similarly suffer with later dates for the return to work.

This gives us an interesting glimpse into the way time is experienced by mothers and babies together. Freud has said that the unconscious is timeless. It seems as though the experience of the early weeks of babyhood needs to be timeless and thus infinite to be fully enjoyed by both mother and baby. Just as, in memory, the summers of our childhood seem to be endless, so mother and baby need to share a 'timeless time' together. If they are able to have this, then the mother can also, as Stern and Winnicott depict, look at her baby and imagine him growing into future stages of development.

When a separation that seems premature is imminent, mothers often seem unable to comprehend the phases and cycles of needing to be close and ability to move apart that they and the baby might otherwise naturally have. Most important, they may attribute sepa-

201

ration from the baby as only due to the job that takes them away. Put outside their relationship, there is no way to absorb it and deal with it as part of self and baby starting to move away from each other.

There is considerable debate about whether working leads to a lower incidence of depression in mothers. Brown and Harris (1978) have suggested that it does. However, Moss and Plewis (1977) dispute the beneficial effects for mothers of going out to work:

> Brown identified employment as offering some protection against the onset of depression in women, possibly by increasing their sense of self-esteem. But in our study no such positive relationship was observed. This may be because the experience of employment, and therefore the protection it affords through supporting a sense of self-esteem, varies among women. Data from our study, for instance, suggests that women employed full-time in manual jobs are less likely to be satisfied with their employment experience than those employed part-time, especially in non-manual jobs. (p. 649)

Although there was no significant relationship between employment and distress, there was one between distress and the desire to start work expressed by women at home full-time at the time of the survey. Moss and Plewis also quote Ginsberg's (1976) study of women with pre-school children which showed that women with conflicting feelings about being full-time mothers and housewives – that is, feeling a duty to stay at home, but feeling dissatisfied with this and wanting to work – were four times as likely to have been prescribed sedatives, tranquillizers and other similar medication in the previous year as those who experienced no such conflict. It should also be taken into account that depressed women are less likely to be able to organize themselves into getting a job – the ones at work are therefore more likely not to have been depressed *before* seeking work.

Lozoff *et al.* (1985) have given unaccustomed maternal separation as a cause of sleep problems – that is, the mother's return to work may cause distress to babies rather than her being at work over a period of time. Ferber (1985b) shows that, as we might expect, the mother's unaccustomed absence in hospital having a new baby also causes sleep disturbance as one aspect of an increased aroused state. Zuckerman *et al.* (1987) did not find a significant difference in sleep problems where mother worked or was absent during the day (or at night). On the other hand Giorgis *et al.* (1987) found that 60 percent of babies with sleep problems had working mothers, compared with 41 percent of babies without such problems who had working mothers.

The conflicts for working mothers are often and variously described in terms of the opposing pull between work and home and the pain of being separated from a baby weighed in the balance with economic necessity or professional ambition. But something more serious and far-reaching has been missed in such an account of the debate.

We have seen how Daniel Stern (1985) describes the process by which mother and baby become attuned to each other. He describes the minute steps of mutual recognition and adjustment which build up to this state between them. He also describes the various stages of development of the baby's own self (see Chapter 7). Klein, Anna Freud, Mahler and Winnicott do something similar in their own various psychoanalytic languages.

I suggest that going through these stages is as crucial psychologically for the mother as for the baby. She is not simply enabling something to happen for the baby; she is also going through an integrating process in her own right, for herself, finishing a cycle that starts with conception. If she has to be absent from the baby for more than a few hours a day, or has an inflexible timetable outside the home that takes no account of herself with the baby, then this process is interfered with. This is nothing to do with the rights or wrongs of working or not, it is simply a description of what the mother will miss, to the degree that she is absent during the first year.

What the mother may feel cheated of is a triple process:

1 working out with the baby his regulation of his own physiological states;
2 witnessing the baby's own process of integration;
3 physically and emotionally absorbing and working through her own experience of labour, birth, lactation and the restarting of the menstrual cycle *in the presence of the baby*.

To give a small example: the postnatal six weeks check-up is no doubt arranged for administrative economy, but I suggest that, as it is often performed by the same doctor at the same time, it is also of emotional significance to both mother and baby. It acts as a confirmation of the interconnection between mother's and baby's states of being.

HOUSING CONDITIONS

I see many families who are badly housed and at times have to remind myself that there is some evidence that bad housing does not necessarily in itself create emotional problems in children. What I do see is that anger in parents about their bad living conditions makes it difficult for them to bring up their children in these conditions. This anger is often constructive, the only effective weapon that might change something for them, but the fury in the family and the impotent waiting for outside bureaucracy to find a solution can make it very difficult for emotional issues to be dealt with effectively within the family unit. These include the setting of limits for sleeping.

One such family lived in a one-bedroomed flat, parents and the two boys sleeping in this one bedroom. Mother came to see me about the sleep problems of the two-year-old. This family had been promised the house next door, but squatters had got in and the council seemed to be delaying evicting them. Mother was so brimming over with the need to tell me each time we met of this injustice, and of the outrageous behaviour of the squatters, that she was unable to think about how, in the meantime, to calm down her two-year-old. It is really a moot point as to what is the most effective survival behaviour in such circumstances. Is it making life more tolerable in the short term to change what it is in one's own power to do within the family or is it essential to keep looking outwards at what must be changed externally, even at the cost of keeping the status quo of the problem within the family?

In this vein I was sceptical about the referral of another family by their doctor. The referral letter mentioned their harassment by a neighbour who had just moved out. I said to the doctor that I doubted whether this was a family who would want to work on their problems.

I was therefore pleasantly surprised when I met two-year-old Alex and his parents. They poured out a horrifying story of a mad neighbour in the house next door who abused them verbally and physically, threatening Mother and baby and implying that she would set her ferocious-looking Alsatian dog on them. After the relief of having me listen to all this seriously, they then said that they thought Alex's sleeping problem was also their own problem; it had started before this neighbour moved in. With this acknowledgement here was a wonderful chance to work on the idea of how much of the trouble was caused by the horrendous external problems and how much from within the family.

The neighbour had now moved away so we looked in detail at the present family situation. Father's job in a hospital obliged him to work late on many evenings; Alex clamoured to stay up until Father came home and then wanted to stay up playing with him. Mother said she was exhausted, with no chance to rest in the evening. As we talked, it emerged that in fact Mother was in two minds whether she wanted Alex in bed or whether she needed his company in the evenings. We talked about whether Mother, although she backed Father's choice of profession, was angry about him being out till late so often. Perhaps Alex's protest was partly on her behalf.

Talking about all this cleared the air and the parents decided that Mother would put Alex firmly to bed in the evening, telling him he would see Father in the morning. They decided to give Alex a special decorated night-light, in case he was frightened on his own in his room. After only a fortnight of this they told me the nights were greatly improved. Alex settled to sleep in the evening and was awake only once in the night.

They now said that Alex's eating habits were worrying them. He ate very little and they worried about his low weight gain. From Mother's description of what food she gave Alex, it sounded as though she herself was a 'faddy' eater and I commented on how thin she was and asked *her* weight. She confirmed that she did have an eating problem herself. I asked when it had started and she recalled that it was soon after the accidental death of her elder sister, when Mother herself was ten. I pondered on the thought that Mother might have felt she did not have the right to live, that is, eat to keep herself alive, when her sister was dead. Mother then revealed that her sister had been schizophrenic and ill for some years before her death.

I felt we had come full circle to the content of the original referral. Here perhaps was a key to how to put externally based and internal precipitating factors together. I said that although Mother's fear of the mad neighbour was based on external reality, the degree to which she was shaken by it, to the extent of being unable to leave the house without Father escorting her, was produced by the fear of madness within herself and within her family. This acknowledged fear of madness within made her powerless to deal with the actual madness existing outside in this neighbour.

Another example, albeit much less extreme, of displacing feelings from inside the family on to neighbours is when parents tell me they have been unable to experiment with letting their baby cry for a little while, because of 'what the neighbours will say'. Sometimes, unfortunately, it is only too true that intolerant neighbours complain about the most innocuous noises coming from young families and the inhibitions resulting from this may be one of the causes of trouble in sleep. However, it is often worth questioning whether the disapproval from next door, real as it may be, is not also a displacement of the parents' own inability to bear some crying; or again the neighbour may also represent a fierce critical aspect of the parents themselves that feels they are getting their child care wrong. This can be similar to parents' use of professionals' opinions or of 'advice' in books on bringing up children, referred to in Chapter 2, as a way of displacing their own opinions on to others.

We have looked at how parents can either support and enhance each other's relationship with their baby or can exacerbate any difficulties. One thread that has gone through this chapter is that of disowning an aspect of the self, a part of one's character, and attributing it either to another person or to external circumstances. The result is an impoverishment of the self and a restriction of possible action.

CHAPTER TWELVE

DISTURBED SLEEP AS A PSYCHOSOMATIC PROBLEM

P SYCHOSOMATIC DISTURBANCES are malfunctions of the body activated by emotional conflict. We have seen how parents help their baby to establish his own sleep rhythms and how the baby's physiological and emotional development are bound up together. In particular we have seen how the interactions between mother and baby connected with satisfying physical needs, especially feeding and sleeping, are the ground on which emotional relationships are built up. Intimacy is established and from this grows a feeling of security and the baby's ability to be an individual, feeling himself to be separate in relation to someone who goes on knowing about him andprotecting him.

When something goes wrong with the process of separating between mother and baby, then something often also goes badly wrong with the baby's knowledge of his own body and his feelings about his body. Psychosomatic symptoms are one aspect of this. Sleep disturbances are basically a psychosomatic problem.

PSYCHOSOMATIC DISTURBANCES

Joyce McDougall, a New Zealand psychoanalyst who has worked in France for many years with the very active group of psychosoma-tists there, has done much work on the theoretical concepts used in this field. In her paper 'The psychosoma and the psychoanalytic process' (1974) she refers to the work of Fain and Kreisler (1970) on babies suffering from serious psychosomatic disturbances in the first months of life. One important group is comprised of infants who are only able to sleep if rocked continually in their mothers' arms, otherwise they suffer from almost total insomnia. Fain and Kreisler's studies suggest that these mothers have partially failed in their function as a protective shield against exciting stimuli. This is paradoxically because they have overexercised the protective func-tion. Instead of developing a primitive form of psychic activity akin to dreaming, which permits most babies to sleep peacefully after feeding, these babies require the mother herself to be the guardian of sleep. There is here a breakdown of the capacity to re-create a good internal state of being in symbolic form and it is linked to an allied failure to develop autoerotic activity. Fain and Kreisler's observations led them to the conclusion that these babies do not have a *mère satisfaisante* ('satisfying mother'), but a *mère calmante* ('tranquillizing mother'). The mother, because of her own problems, cannot permit her baby to create a 'primary identification' which will enable him to sleep without continual contact with her. There seems here to be a dysfunction of imagining, mental 'playing', or some inability to dramatize about feelings.

Following from Fain and Kreisler's observations, McDougall suggests that these mothers are performing an addictive function. The baby comes to need the mother, as an addict needs his drug. There is total dependence on an external object to deal with situations which in normal human behaviour can be handled by self-regulatory psychological means.

In two later works (1985, 1986) McDougall examined psychosomatic conditions and their origins. Her ideas on the 'psychosomatic personality' problem were inspired by her French psychoanalytic colleagues, who have used the concept of 'operational thinking' which is akin to the concept of 'alexithymia' originated by Nemiah and Sifneos (1970) in Boston. Alexithymia (from the Greek *a* = without, *lexis* = word, *thumos* = heart or affectivity) refers to the state of patients who have difficulty both in describing their affective state and in distinguishing one affect from another. Such patients are dominated by operational thinking, or the way to *do* things, and are out of touch with feelings about their own psychic reality.

McDougall uses ideas from Krystal (1978) to show how psychosomatic conditions can arise in this situation of being out of touch with feelings. Affects are connecting links; they are both psyche and soma. One of their functions is appraisal. They alert the mind to situations requiring readiness and mental action.

> If these signals do not achieve mental representation then the emotional arousal runs the risk of only alerting the body which is likely to respond with psychosomatic dysfunctioning, since the soma, following its own specific biological law, will frequently react as though defending itself against *physical* rather than psychological dangers. (1985, p. 370, author's italics)

We may all at times 'fail to contain and reflect upon the experiences that besiege us' (1986, p. 100) and may then be likely to fall ill. Infants tend to show conflict in psychosomatic terms and the fundamental functions of breathing, digestion, evacuation or sleeping can be affected by conflicts that started and really belong within personal and emotional relationships.

McDougall (1985) suggests that failure to face psychic pains causes not only psychosomatic illness, but also leads to 'addictive personality organization'. This happens when individuals plunge into *action* to dispel emotional pain, rather than containing and working on it mentally. Drugs, alcohol and addictive use of sexuality are all examples of 'action symptoms'. The temporary relief offered by addictive behaviour allows the basic psychic conflict to be ejected from consciousness. Refusal to face mental pain in this way notably increases vulnerability to psychosomatic illness.

The addictive personality arises partly from a failure to use transitional phenomena. Winnicott (1971) has shown how the ability to use transitional phenomena follows from the ability to internalize the early, close mother–baby relationship. The use of a transitional object then allows the process of internalization to gather speed, as the baby has a symbol to use in place of the mother. According to McDougall (1985, p. 371) people unable to use transitional phenomena may later use 'pathological transitional objects' in the form of addictive substances or relationships. These addictive patterns are not only an escape from mental pain and psychic conflict, but are also magical attempts to fill the void in the inner world. The addictive personality structure almost always seems allied to psychosomatic dysfunction.

In *Theatres of the Mind* (1986) McDougall begins to show us what lies behind alexithymic symptoms and psychosomatic tendencies. She says that an infant's earliest external reality is the mother's physical presence. The baby is also affected by the mother's emotional state, including feelings the mother herself is not consciously aware of. The way in which she relates to her child's body will influence his somatic functioning, vitality and affectivity. Many of McDougall's alexithymic/psychosomatic patients talk of their bodies as though they did not really possess them or their bodily functions. It seems as though they still unconsciously belong to the mother. Children of such mothers may also conceive of their emotions as not being truly their own possessions but their mother's (Krystal, 1978).

If a mother's way of relating to her pre-verbal infant's bodily

functions, gestures and affective storms is of cardinal importance in the organization of early psychic life, it must be remembered that as direct bodily communication gives way to symbolic
communication and the acquisition of language, it is also the
mother who first names the child's affects and thus provides the
potential for thinking or not thinking about feelings. (1986, p.
100)

McDougall goes on to suggest that such parents may give considerable attention to physical pain, but are totally uninterested in any
expression of mental pain. Their children are likely to be unable to
communicate or get any confirmation of their emotional state of
mind.

By putting these various formulations of McDougall's together,
we can see how they fit in with sleep problems in infants. Firstly,
some parents are unable to divest themselves of being the only
means of getting their baby to sleep. They feel they can only be the
'guardians of sleep' for their baby when they are physically present;
the baby has no chance to internalize them in their absence. They
are *mères calmantes*, or addictive mothers.

Next, we see how a failure to provide a confirmation for a baby
of his emotional states leaves him unable to take charge of his own
feelings. This process of confirmation takes place in the early
months, chiefly non-verbally, though most mothers will 'talk' to
even tiny babies as a way of expressing their own intuitions about
their baby's emotions. At later stages it is necessary to name these
emotions to help a child know what he is feeling. McDougall shows
how the parents she describes are able to deal with physical actions,
while ignoring emotions and experiences.

Thirdly, it seems that the child's ability to deal with physical
sensations and pain is equally impoverished by the failure to help
the child differentiate his experiences from those of his mother.
The joke, 'A sweater is a garment a little boy puts on when his
mother feels cold', is an example that comes to mind. To spoil a
joke by pulling it apart, I suggest that here there is no exchange
about whether the little boy himself feels cold or not. The implication of this for sleep problems is that we may have a baby who
cannot trust his own bodily signals to know whether or not he wants
to go to sleep and has to check back continually with his mother. It
is worth surmising also that, if such a baby is sleepless in the night,
his mother is unable to communicate a wish of her own to sleep and
hence provide an 'atmosphere' of sleep.

People who work on shifts and have to sleep during the day often report the difficulty of changing their sleep rhythms. They may also describe the feeling of having to sleep at the 'wrong time', when everyone else is awake. For most of us part of the background of being asleep is to be part of a sleeping world. One of the special pleasures of adolescence is in overturning such general perceptions, going to bed and getting up at quite different times from parents and other boring, ordinary people. A baby wakeful during the night is unable to join in with the generally shared perception of 'ordinariness' or has not been offered it. Of vital importance is the way the mother relates to the child's father. This determines what she expects of her child and, particularly at night-time, whether she gives priority to her relationship with the father or with the child.

DISTURBED ATTACHMENT

Mary-Sue Moore (1989) explains the origin of some psychosomatic symptoms in terms of disturbed attachment. When attachment develops normally, a child feels protected by his attachment figure and can sleep within the security of this relationship. When there has not been a straightforward building up of this attachment, the child may be left feeling anxious and this in turn can have a damaging effect on the ability to sleep. Moore writes about an anxiety-related sleep dysfunction that includes an alteration in both physiological sleep stages and dream function. In this dysfunction a perceived failure in the protective role of an attachment figure plays a key role.

In explaining how this comes about, Moore reminds us of the cyclical nature of sleep, with dreaming sleep (REM) occurring about every ninety to one hundred minutes during the night, the longer periods happening later in the night. You will remember from Chapter 4 that overall, deepest, slow-wave, Stage 4 sleep occurs during the initial third of the night, while most dreaming sleep occurs during the last third of the night. We have known for some time of the crucial need for dreaming time for our mental health. Moore has collated recent evidence to show the equal importance of Stage 4, the deepest level of sleep in the early part of the night, for the maintenance of psychosomatic functioning.

Anxiety affects sleep because anxious individuals take a longer time to fall asleep, sleep more lightly and have more frequent awakenings than those who are not anxious. McDonald *et al.* (1976) have shown that unusual 'electrodermal storming during slow-wave (Stage 4) sleep is *positively* correlated with anxiety and stress, and *negatively* correlated with *amount* of Stage 3–4 sleep . . . if one function of storming is to reduce the amount of Stage 3–4 sleep this might have survival value in the presence of environmental threat' (author's italics). Moore expands on the nature of this threat and explains that the deeply unconscious state which occurs during Stage 4 sleep renders the individual vulnerable to external threat. Anxious and depressed individuals psychically perceive themselves to be in such danger and thus cannot fall deeply asleep.

We have seen in Chapter 8 that attachment plays a part in allowing sleep and that disturbances in attachment connect with disturbed sleep. Moore highlights for us the protective role of an attachment figure. Threats can be surmounted if there is sufficient 'protection' for child or adult. In contrast to this an individual who does not feel protected when undergoing stressful or traumatic events will feel chronic anxiety and possibly a 'pervasive sense of helplessness and depression'.

Following Bowlby (1973) Moore argues that where parents are themselves anxious about the availability of their own attachment figures, they may unconsciously invert the normal parent–child relationship and require that the child be the parent figure to the mother. In cases of inverted attachment roles it is the child's responsibility to remain available to the mother; it is the mother or attachment figure who might wander off or be hurt, abandoning the child. Thus a child in this situation has the primary responsibility for remaining aware of the environment – including the whereabouts of the mother. Deep sleep precludes any awareness of the environment and might be experienced as threatening to the attachment bond.

In normal attachment, according to Moore, mothers of young children do not go 'off duty' during the night. They sleep lightly (McKenna, 1988) and are conscious of not wanting to fall into deep sleep. This wish is so strong that as Pound *et al.* (1985) comment, even depressed mothers given anti-depressant medication do not usually take it, because they cannot risk being unable to hear their child in the night. This being so, the normal readiness of mothers to wake up when their child needs them is echoed in the young child who, in the reverse process, cannot sleep deeply when he feels he is responsible for his mother.

This inverted attachment need not always seem to be morbid. A.A. Milne, in the poem 'Disobedience' (1924), describes for posterity the three-year-old in charge of his mother:

> James James
> Morrison Morrison
> Weatherby George Dupree
> Took great
> Care of his Mother,
> Though he was only three.
> James James
> Said to his Mother,
> 'Mother,' he said, said he;
> 'You must never go down to the end of the town, if
>   you don't go down with me.'

His mother disobeyed these instructions and 'Hasn't been heard of since'. We can see how the child learning to move away from his attachment figure (James James is pictured on his tricycle) needs to be sure that she will not move away from him. The reasonable desire for security can change imperceptibly to a tyrannical demand that the mother remain available and interested only in him.

To return to a more scientific description of inverted attachment, Moore says that one of the characteristics of this state may be a discrepancy between the affect of the mother and her external behaviour. The mother who comes into the child's bedroom ostensibly to soothe him may in fact herself be angry and disturbed, so that she has to be calmed by the child. The child feels anxious both on his own account and on behalf of his mother. His anxieties are not dealt with and a vicious circle may be set up. The unmet needs of the child make it hard for him to sleep. He has a disturbed Stage 4 sleep that may lead to increased somatization which in such cases may mean more night waking. The cycle can be endless.

As Moore shows, disturbed attachment relationships may have bodily repercussions, for example asthma and allergies. Going back to McDougall's (1974) formulation of the addictive function, the mothers of some asthmatic and allergic children appeared, in the circumstances Moore described, to allow their children no satisfactions that were obtained away from direct contact with themselves. Autoerotic activity and the capacity for psychic development was blocked in these children. Here also the mother may be insufficiently interested in other aspects of her life, particularly her love-life, to wish the baby to go off peacefully to sleep, leaving her free for other preoccupations; she then overdoes her role as a protective shield, keeping the baby tied to her. Kales *et al.* (1970) found that compared to normal children of the same ages, asthmatic children had a significant reduction in Stage 4 sleep. In the sample studied no asthma attacks occurred during the first third of the night (i.e. during Stage 4 sleep). It appears, however, that these children were unable to let go into enough deep Stage 4 sleep, which might itself have provided a protective factor against the asthma.

This leads us to the fascinating question of the function of Stage 4 sleep, which is perhaps best answered by default. We have seen how anxiety of various kinds can lead to a loss of Stage 4 sleep. What are the results of this loss?

Moore refers to psycho-social work on low-growth children who have less Stage 4 sleep which connects with the finding that it is in the initial period of deepest sleep (Stage 4) that a significant percentage of daily growth hormone is normally produced (Sasfin *et al.*, 1969; Riley, 1985). Thus children who have failed to thrive in abusive homes, that is, situations where they have not been or not felt safe, have started to grow when removed to foster homes, where their sleep pattern changes. This does not of course mean that all low-growth children are in unsafe home situations, but it may be that many low-growth children have, for external or internal reasons, a feeling of needing to be 'vigilant' and have not had enough Stage 4 sleep. Some of these children have been helped by psychotherapy.

Recent research findings reveal that important restorative immune system functions occur during slow-wave sleep and not during REM or lighter stages of sleep. A major repercussion of insufficient Stage 4 sleep is therefore that the effectiveness of the immune system is reduced. Of interest here are Guedeney and Kreisler's (1987) preliminary findings that half of the children referred to them at the IPSO (a hospital department for the psychological assessment and treatment of children with severe somatic disorders) in 1985 for severe sleep problems had associated diseases, such as infantile colic, allergy, otitis. It is crucial to note that Guedeney and Kreisler did not feel that colic and so on *caused* the sleep problem, but that they were *associated* with it. We might therefore conclude that the disturbed sleep itself had interfered with immunity in such a way that these children were vulnerable to their various other disorders. This is a good example of how, as we have seen in this chapter, mind and body influence each other to produce 'psychosomatic' conditions.

It should be noted here that I have not taken up fully in this book the issue of child abuse, especially in its sexual aspect. I have not recounted major examples of this, because the parents who consult me over a period of time about their babies' sleep problems seem to have had less dire instances of family dysfunction on their minds. However, I do think that some families coming to see me only once, and failing to turn up again without further explanation, may have felt worried that I would 'discover' something they were either not ready to talk about or felt that I was not the person to tell. When families have broken off prematurely, I have sometimes had an intuition and told their doctor or health visitor of my misgivings about possible sexual abuse. It also seems evident that some of the more bizarre sleeping arrangements in families, reported as an aspect of a child's sleep problem, may be in fact symptoms of other forms of family dysfunctions.

CHAPTER THIRTEEN

MOTHER'S DEPRESSION
AND OTHER STATES OF HEALTH

OW DO MOTHERS' own conditions, be they physical, mental or psychosomatic, fit in with their children's well-being and with their sleep?

PREGNANCY

It is increasingly understood that events in pregnancy and the mother's health during pregnancy affect both mother and baby after the birth. Guedeney and Kreisler (1987) show that in 18 cases of severe sleep disorders dating from the early weeks, seven mothers had had somatic disorders (four of which were a threat to the pregnancy) and nine others a noticeable depression during pregnancy. Interestingly, they suggest that these figures, obtained by asking questions of the mothers themselves, imply that mothers do attribute the cause of their baby's sleep disorder to their own state before his birth. They also show that anxiety during pregnancy is related to a high level of activity in the baby after birth and to the onset of sleep disorders.

We can see that there is a connection between the vulnerability of mothers to somatic disorders and their babies' tendency to very early sleep problems. As we have seen in Chapters 4 and 5, the weeks after birth show that the attainment of sleep patterns is a sensitive balance of regulation of the baby's neurophysiological states with the emotional interaction between mother and baby. If a mother has a somatic disorder during pregnancy, her physical condition may affect her emotional response to her baby or, reversing this, she may be converting her emotional ambivalence about the baby into a somatic form. The chain of bodily expressions of conflict may then be passed on to the baby. He may respond to his mother's ambivalence and to her way of expressing it and also pick up from her that emotions are best expressed in bodily form.

Some mothers feel 'used up' by the foetus and exploited by its residence in their bodies. Such a mother might come to terms with her baby after its birth and feel that she has enough reserves for it after all, or she might continue with her feeling of being drained by her baby's needs. In any case we could guess that, just as the babies of mothers who had disorders threatening their pregnancy have early sleep problems, so the babies of mothers who feel drained by the pregnancy might also be among those with sleep difficulties.

As we saw in Chapter 7, the events of the birth itself can cause difficulties in the relationship between mother and baby. Blurton-Jones *et al.* (1978) show that adverse events during the birth lead to increased night waking. Night waking has also been found to be associated with length of labour and the time until the first cry (Barnes, 1975).

MOTHER'S SLEEPLESSNESS AFTER THE BIRTH

The mother's own ability to sleep is also significant and insomnia in the mother can be one of the earliest signs of post-partum depression (Karacan and Williams, 1970). They note that insomnia starts before the onset of the psychosis and that clinical symptoms first appear during this period of sleep disturbance. From a nineteenth-century article in the *Lancet* (Savage, 1896) they quote the colourful term 'miserable sleeplessness', which has become a classic description of this kind of insomnia.

It is important to realize that this sleeplessness is not only an early symptom of the post-partum depression, but also that the failure to sleep itself increases the mother's vulnerability to such a depression. The loss of sleep and its restorative function, particularly of Stage 4 and D sleep, means that the restructuring necessary to take in the physiological and emotional upheaval of giving birth takes place insufficiently. Sleep helps in an integrating process; loss of sleep means the mother is more vulnerable to a feeling of disintegration. The lack of sleep also makes it more difficult for her to relate to the baby and impairs the process by which mothers can usually feel themselves recovering from the birth through the emotional interchange with their baby. Insomnia is thus both the result and the cause of serious post-partum depression.

MOTHER'S ECZEMA

There are many ways, some obvious, some more subtle, by which a mother's state of health affects her baby. We can speculate about this from a clinical example of a mother and baby who both had eczema. Was it an inherited condition, either as a physiological allergic reaction or as a family tendency to somatize? Or was it transmitted by psychological communication? And what effect did the eczema have on their relationship?

Mother and baby Simon, whom we saw in Chapter 9, both suffered from eczema, Mother said her eczema was related to a milk allergy and to stress. Simon seemed to share the milk allergy and, when mother had any milk product in her diet, it affected her breast-milk and the baby. This mother attributed the origin of her eczema mainly to stress. She told me of her own difficult family life and said that on a recent visit to her parents her eczema, dormant for several months, had reappeared.

When Simon was born, Mother was isolated and this was a time when she particularly mourned and resented not having the backing and understanding of her mother. Her eczema flared up. Crucial in the relationship between Mother and Simon was how the eczema then affected them both; Mother found it very difficult to hold Simon, when her own skin was so vulnerable. When Simon himself was affected by eczema, he likewise did not want to be held. Simon cried much of the time, day and night. Out of the mutually unsatisfied needs of this mother and baby couple a situation arose where, once their eczema had subsided, holding seemed the only solution. For this baby, who had little continuous sleep, we can also imagine that he was deprived of much needed Stage 4 sleep and that his vulnerability to the eczema was increased by this.

Mother and baby suffered at times from similar uncomfortable states of mind and body. There is often a clear connection between how both mother and baby feel and of course how a mother behaves towards her child affects him directly. A mother who is over-stimulating, for example, will naturally tend to have an active, excited child who also may not sleep (Guedeney and Kreisler, 1987).

As we saw in Chapter 1, Lozoff *et al.* (1985), in looking at the causes of sleep problems, cite five different kinds of precipitating factors that range from external events to maternal mood. They describe how stress in the family (accident or illness, unaccustomed absence of the mother during the day, maternal depressed mood, co-sleeping with parents and maternal ambivalence towards the child) are experiences significantly differentiating children with sleep problems from those without, especially when the five factors are associated. They claim that 'specifically, disturbance of sleep seems to occur in children where mother's psychological attention had been withdrawn from them' (p. 481).

POSTNATAL DEPRESSION

This is one of the prime situations in which a mother may be emotionally distant, at least in part, from her baby. At least one in ten mothers experience depression after giving birth to a baby (Cox *et al.*, 1982). It has also been shown that over 30 percent of mothers of pre-school children may be suffering from depression (Richman, 1976).

Although these two categories overlap, there are also important differentiations to be made. Postnatal depression can be seen partly as a reaction to the event of giving birth and to having a vulnerable new baby to care for. It can also include the reaction to the situation of being a mother, possibly isolated, at home. Depression in mothers of pre-school children may include those mothers who have not yet recovered from traumatic reactions to giving birth and can also include new sufferers who represent a response over time to adverse conditions.

Postnatal depression is so widespread that at one time it was thought of as a 'natural' reaction to birth, perhaps due to hormonal changes. It seems now as though it can be partly a reactive response either to trauma or to adverse social situations, that mothers without support are vulnerable to it and that providing support greatly helps recovery from it.

Difficult births may provoke a postnatal depression, by leaving a mother feeling shocked, upset and inadequate at not having given birth 'properly'. I have previously suggested that difficult births often lead to sleep problems in the baby. One of the routes by which this happens is that depression ensuing from the birth experience makes it harder for the mother to be in touch with the baby's sleep rhythms.

Brown and Harris (1978) have argued that depression is a social phenomenon. They found that at least a quarter of working-class women with children living in London suffer from a depressive disorder. By contrast crofters in the Outer Hebrides are apparently practically free of depression and London middle-class women have a much smaller incidence of depression than do working-class women. They suggest, however, that bad housing and other difficult conditions, which working-class women are more likely to be subject to, are *provoking* agents and not the only cause of depression.

There is in fact a second set of factors. If a woman does not have an intimate relationship with a husband and or boyfriend, one in which she feels she can confide and trust, she is much more likely to break down in the presence of a major life-event or difficulty. Similarly she is also at greater risk if she has three or more children under fifteen at home; if she is unemployed, and if she lost her mother (but not her father) before the age of eleven. We call these *vulnerability factors* although more optimistically they can be seen in a reverse way and called protective factors. None is capable of producing depression on their own, but they greatly increase chances of breakdown in the presence of a provoking agent. (Brown and Harris, p. 229)

Some of these vulnerability factors to depression apply particularly to postnatal depression. We have seen earlier (Chapter 10) that the lack of a confiding relationship and the loss of the mother's own mother have an effect on mothering ability. Other important factors are the impact of being responsible for the life of a vulnerable new baby, the social isolation of many mothers, the low esteem accorded to child-rearing and the loss of identity for mothers who have given up their jobs, lost touch with friends at work or friends without babies.

Even though it is clear from Brown and Harris's findings that there are sociological factors determining which mothers may be depressed, it is vital for us to think of each depression as having individual meaning. The content of each mother's depressive thoughts are hers and hers alone. Brown and Harris have cited vulnerability factors, such as the death of a mother, and although this has statistical significance, it is essential to know about the personal route by which such a loss leads to a depression now.

It is also significant that the birth of a baby may itself reawaken feelings about the loss of the mother. The mother's own infantile feelings are stirred up by the experience of her new baby's needs. Mourning needs to be done in various stages through life and bereavement reactions are provoked at each new life-event, including childbirth. Also relevant are the universal feelings of loss of the unborn baby that are experienced in giving birth to a baby. Sometimes the real baby outside cannot make up for the loss of the 'ideal' baby that belonged only to the mother inside herself. The change from being an individual to being a parent should also not be underestimated as another focus for the feeling of loss.

Time spent by professionals with a vulnerable mother before and after the birth dramatically reduces depression (Holden *et al.*, 1989). Much of this may be simply providing what is missing in the mother's own social network. A crucial facet of any help seems to be the opportunity to talk through the details of the baby's birth; the mother often needs to relate this to one of the workers involved in some stage of the pregnancy or the baby's birth, either in the antenatal care, the labour or postnatal care. The person who listens may equally be the doctor, the midwife or the health visitor, but part of the process for the mother of absorbing the experience of labour is facilitated by this narrative.

All mothers may need this chance to talk, but a few are in particular need of it. By noting that a motherless mother-to-be is vulnerable, professionals may be alerted to the fact that it is import-ant to spend time in listening to the mother's experiences. Although this cannot replace the interest of an actual grand-mother, there can still be a real possibility for the mother to have a confirmation of herself as a mother from these exchanges with the worker. Talking about the mother that she has lost and her memories of having been mothered herself is particularly valuable. Doing this reminds her of what she has inside herself from her mother to pass on to her baby, as well as allowing her to think about her loss in the context of being a mother herself. This process may also help the mother move on and find a substitute 'mother' in her family, neighbours or friends, who will take a continuous interest in her and her baby.

This brings us to the critical effect a mother's depression may have on her baby. Lozoff *et al.* (1985) suggest that sleep problems may ensue when the mother is emotionally unresponsive to the baby and I will be quoting several other workers who confirm that this does affect the baby's sleep. I will then look at work on the nature of a depressed mother's relationship with her baby and try to reconstruct the way in which this influences the baby's sleep.

THE EFFECTS OF MATERNAL DEPRESSION
ON A BABY'S SLEEP

In assessing the effects of a mother's depression on the child, Guedeney and Kreisler (1987) ask: what is more puzzling for the child, the mother's motor and mental retardation or her mood disorder and emotional flatness? They suggest that this emotional flatness is an important and painful element in depression, ham-pering attunement of feelings between mother and child and sub-sequently damaging the mother's ability to match the infant's own interactional rhythm and thus to understand his sleep rhythm.

Soulé (in a personal communication to Guedeney, 1986)

remarked on the mother who can say to her baby, 'I understand your sleep.' Guedeney (1989) contrasts this with a depressed mother who is preoccupied with fantasies about the baby which get in the way of her being able to perceive the real baby and its needs. Such a mother does not understand her baby's sleep.

Zuckerman *et al.* (1987) have also identified an association between mothers' depressed feelings and children with sleeping problems. They say that previous studies did not allow any inference to be made as to whether children's sleeping difficulties cause mothers to feel depressed or whether mothers' depressed feelings affect their handling of their children, resulting in sleep problems.

> The longitudinal nature of this study allowed us to demonstrate that mothers' depressed feelings do not appear to be a *consequence* of children's sleep problems between eight months and three years of age. This conclusion is reached because of the similarities of newly identified maternal depression at three years whether or not the child had a sleep problem at eight months. (p. 669)

Anecdotally I know of instances of mothers who do claim to have become ill and depressed *because* of their babies' sleeplessness. It is, however, possible that some of these were actually suffering from undiagnosed postnatal depression early on and did not really notice at the time whether their general feeling of *malaise* started before or after their baby kept them awake at night.

Zuckerman *et al.* suggest that depressed mothers may be awake more often themselves and are thus more aware of their children's night waking, whether the child cries or not. They also surmise that some mothers may have been depressed and had recovered by the time of their study of babies at eight months. Thus unrecorded depressions might have influenced some other of the sleep problems seen at eight months. Looking at cause and effect, they suggest 'that stressful life-events do not affect children directly, but rather are indicated by mother's affect and changes in her responsibility and caretaking' (1987).

THE EFFECT OF POSTNATAL DEPRESSION ON INFANT DEVELOPMENT

In her study of the effect of postnatal depression on infant development, Lynne Murray (1988) describes how mothers and babies normally interact with each other when the baby is between six and twelve weeks old. At a time when the infant is not yet able to make much use of physical objects 'he will be captivated by the attention of a solicitous person'. Mother and baby spend long periods looking at each other and 'each partner's experience of being in relation to the other appears to exist as an end in itself'. In work which was a startling breakthrough in our knowledge of how early communication between mothers and babies starts Colwyn Trevarthen (1974) described the reciprocal 'conversations' which mothers and two-month-old babies appear to have with each other and he recorded these on video. Murray refers to his work to show how much mothers and babies who are in good health look at each other and respond to each other. She observes that a depressed mother's ability to focus on her infant is impaired.

In order to gain some idea of the effects such a difficulty in focusing might have, studies on the effects of contrived disruptions of normal infant–mother couples were carried out. These studies included setting up 'perturbations' in ordinary communications between mothers and babies. The normal looking at each other and normal response from one to the other was made to go awry in these tests. In one perturbation the mother became still and expressionless for a period of forty-five seconds, while continuing to look at her baby; in the second perturbation the timing, not the form, of the mother's acts in relation to the infant's were interfered with by using the 'Double Closed-Circuit Television Technique'.

In this system mother and infant each sees a full-face life-size video image of the other where perfect eye to eye contact is possible. When the images are relayed in real or 'live' time the two are able to interact in a normal, mutually responsive fashion. But if the mother's image is replayed to the infant after an interval of some 30 seconds, the interaction is perturbed, the infant sees and hears the same maternal behaviour that occurred during the Live sequence, but in the Replay sequence the mother's communication is unrelated to her infant's behaviour. (Murray, 1988, p. 17)

Not surprisingly the responses of the babies to these two tests were that they quickly became disturbed. Thirty seconds of mistiming between a mother and baby is a serious matter. The baby's reaction to being shown a blank-faced mother was of protest followed by withdrawal, with his gaze averted from the mother's face; the reaction to the replay sequence was puzzlement or confusion.

The results of perturbation studies show how sensitive two-
and three-month-old infants are to the quality of their
mother's communication. Infants can not only discriminate
subtle variations in maternal behaviour, but their distress
when the mother behaves inappropriately and their apparent
protests or efforts to solicit communication are also evidence
for a strong motivation for the particular forms of interpersonal engagement that mothers spontaneously provide in
normal face to face encounters. (p. 179)

As a result of being, over a period of time, with a post-partum
depressed mother – who may indeed either have a blank face or
mistime her signals to her baby – the baby will devise some kind of
behaviour to deal with the mother's inattention. One reaction may
be to give up trying to get her attention and instead withdraw and
he may then go on being withdrawn after the mother has recovered from her depression. Mother and baby will therefore
continue to be out of touch with each other. We can see how this
may then stop them being in touch about sleep rhythms.

It is important to consider depression in the mother not only as a
state of mind that impairs her ability to focus on the child. It may
be useful sometimes to start the other way round with the hypothesis that some psychologically vulnerable mothers are thrown into a
state of depression by their very attempts to focus on their child.
To such mothers the life and death communications from a new-
born baby, both as direct bodily needs and as emotional signals, are
terrifying and unbearable and some mothers may switch off into a
state of not noticing the intensity of the baby's communications. As
we have seen, Main *et al.* (1985) have observed that some mothers
cannot notice their babies' signals because they remind them of
their own unmet needs as babies. Depression and withdrawal in the
mother may sometimes be an extreme version of this inability to
notice, because noticing is so painful.

EXPERIMENTALLY INDUCED MOTHER–INFANT
DETACHMENT

Hanuš and Mechthild Papousek (1975) have looked at infants'
reactions to their mothers' 'incomprehensible' actions. In their
study we can see, by default, how important the understanding of
each other's behaviour is for mother and baby. The Papouseks
looked at sequences of behaviour in which the mother–child interaction became erratic and thus 'incomprehensible' for the child.

224

They analysed the capacity of four-month-old infants for 'comprehending' their mothers' behaviour and asked the specific question: how do infants react to the deliberate omission from a behaviour chain of an important segment containing key information?

> In the first experiment the mother was asked to leave her child six times for 15 seconds each time and to act in the same way she would act at home when leaving her child for a short time. All mothers tended to employ similar routines on leaving (stepwise separation under control of eye contact, verbal repetitions, etc.) and on returning they experienced no difficulties in renewing happy contact with their children.
>
> In the next experiment, with a different group of infants, the mother was required to leave her child without any preparations when overhead lights were turned off for 3 seconds, and then to return under the same conditions after 15 seconds. This 'incomprehensible' disappearance and reappearance of the mother produced rather conspicuous changes in the child's behaviour . . . At first the infant reacted cheerfully to his mother on her return. Although still rather quiet during her absence, after her later reappearance the child gradually rejected the renewal of contact with his mother more and more strongly. Thereafter the mother's efforts to renew contact only intensified the baby's turning away; in some of these infants such renewals even led to listless or whining rejection of the mother. Control experiments in yet another study showed that the short periods of darkness as such did not produce changes of this type. These experiences surprised the mothers as well as the observer, and we noted with some relief that the children's relationship with their mothers recovered quickly after the experiments ended! (p. 257)

I have quoted the Papouseks' study at some length, because of the particular relevance that this examination of the result of a mother's unheralded departure in the dark has for our study of sleep disturbances. What it shows is the importance for babies of clear messages about the mother's intentions. The first part of the Papouseks' study, where mothers, when the lights are on, leave their children briefly, in their own natural way, tells us what most mothers routinely do in these circumstances. The ordinary means these mothers used, visual and verbal, communicated an intention to the baby which appeared to make the absence manageable for him. We could add that it seems as though this prepared absence

225

also contained the idea of the mother's return. An incomprehensible disappearance and reappearance destroyed both the infant's cognitive attempts to learn about intention and of course the mother's trustworthiness.

This rather odd little test shows the possible effect on an infant in his own home if his parents are unable to signal their comings and goings to him at night. The problem for the baby may not be so much in being left but in *not knowing* when the parent is going to leave and when, or why, she will return. This reminds us that one very ordinary situation that can lead to sleep problems is when a baby wakes up and finds himself, unprepared, with a baby-sitter instead of with his parents. After such an experience many babies will wake on subsequent evenings to check who is there and who is not or they may wake later in the night to see whether their parents have returned.

DEPRESSED MOTHERS AND THEIR BABIES

Pound *et al.* (1985) have looked in detail at depressed mothers and their children and found that they tended to have more problems with their children (though they also discovered that quite a number of children in the control group also had noticeable problems, particularly in sleeping).

It requires little imagination to see that spending most of one's life with a mother who is irritable, anxious, exhausted and weepy rather than calm and good-humoured is likely to affect one's view of her, oneself, and life in general. However, much will depend on whether she is irritated particularly by her child, her husband or the neighbours, whether she worries about his safety or health or paying the bills, or whether she blames him for her unhappiness or alternatively uses him as a comforter in a hard world. (Pound *et al.*, 1988, p. 243)

Pound *et al.* also came across a group of depressed mothers whose sensitivity to their children's needs was *not* affected by their depression. In spite of their problems these mothers were able to enjoy their relationship with their babies, play with them and contain their emotions and for many of them the baby was the best thing in their lives. Some of the depressed mothers also reported changes in their child's behaviour when they themselves were particularly low. 'Most became less active and more clinging and often attempted to comfort the mother in a very touching way, for

example, by bringing her their teddy bear to make her feel better'
(p. 243).

Summing up, the authors argue that whether a mother's
depression leads to the child developing behaviour disorders which
include sleep problems 'seems to depend mainly on whether he
and his mother maintain an intimate and satisfying relationship in
which he is not exposed to (nor provokes) high levels of hostility'
(p. 249).

MATERNAL CRITICISM AND HOSTILITY
Some mothers do pass on their own feelings of misery or low self-
esteem to their child. One form this can take is maternal criticism,
which can have a devastating effect on children. Richman *et al.*
(1982) cite this as the single most predictive factor for child disturbance, closely followed by lack of warmth; these factors were more
important than either maternal depression, marital disharmony or
environmental stress.

Maternal criticism can be thought of as a distorted perception of
the child. Such distortions by a mother in how she sees her baby
have been shown to be associated with sleep problems. In a study
by Nover *et al.* (1984) of normal mothers and infants, it was found
that the majority of mothers perceived their babies' temperaments
very similarly to the way the researchers viewed them. However, a
minority saw their babies differently, usually as being more difficult than the researchers did and their babies had a greater
tendency to sleep problems. Nover *et al.* suggest that the mothers'
misperceptions were associated with more anxiety. These mothers
were less responsive to their children and interfered more with
their play. The implication is that the mother's negative response to
the child will affect his ability to sleep. Reversing this, they also
suggest that a sleep problem could tire and anger a care-giver, so
that the negative perceptions might be the *result* of the sleep
problem.

A key factor in maternal criticism and hostility is the mother's
blaming of the child for his own problems and perhaps for her own
also. She has cut herself off from seeing problems as something
going on between the two of them. Where sleep is concerned, this
will therefore intensify a reaction that a baby who is not sleeping is
to blame.

UNTIDINESS
An interesting fact related to depression is that many mothers

consulting me about their baby's sleep problem eventually tell me how untidy their homes are. At times I have measured therapeutic success by the number of filled plastic bags taken to Oxfam or put in the dustbin.

As a general problem extreme untidiness may have many psychological meanings. When mentioned in the context of parent–baby relationships, a few are particularly relevant. In the first place of course it is a well-known sign of depression. Secondly, it may simply reflect the feeling of a new mother that there is too much to do, that she does not know what to attend to first. It may illustrate anger at being saddled with child care and household tasks. On the other hand it can also have a positive value as a lack of rigidity, a lessening of obsessional ways of coping. If extreme untidiness continues, however, it is fair to describe the chaos of the house in Joyce McDougall's (1974) terms of the disintegration experienced by the mother trying to come to terms with her own and her baby's feelings about the 'primal separation' from each other. The fragmentation that is described to me in consultations, where parents do not know which aspect of their babies' needs to attend to first, is reflected also in the objects strewn inappropriately round the house.

Another facet of extreme untidiness can be the parents' attitude to their own toilet-training and the way their own parents carried it out, stirred up by the need to toilet-train their young child. Molly's mother was a good example of this (see also Daws, 1985).

Two-year-old Molly was having sleeping difficulties and also being toilet-trained. Molly's mother told me at length how untidy her house was and how much her own mother, who was coming to stay, would disapprove. She developed this theme to tell me how she also expected her mother to criticize Molly's lack of progress in toilet-training. I asked her if she knew about her own toilet-training and indeed she did. Her mother made sure that she knew that she and her sisters had been definitively trained at about one year. I pointed out that her descriptions to me of her untidy house were not only despairing, they were also boastful. A messy baby side of herself that she felt had been cleaned up too quickly still needed to communicate with her own mother about this issue. Getting in touch with the idea of this, through the medium of our words, seemed to be sufficient to mobilize more adult motivations and she went home, intending to tidy up her kitchen before her mother's visit. Molly's toilet-training ceased to be a fraught issue and was resolved within the next few weeks.

The *result* of acute untidiness can also be similar to a psychosomatic condition. Just as a psychogenic factor can cause the body to fall into a physiological condition which has its own repercussions (that is, the individual then suffers from an illness which follows its own course, however it originated), so extreme untidiness can have its own effect and appears to the sufferer to be the *cause* of their depression and feeling of ill-being. Babies brought up in such a setting have an additional difficulty in making sense of their physical surroundings – the 'incoherence' of mothers who are unable to respond to their babies' signals appropriately. This is also a useful word to describe the ambience of extreme untidiness.

PARENTS' MENTAL ILLNESS

Pound *et al.* (1985) suggest that depression has relatively little impact on the child compared with 'the more serious hazard of long-standing psychiatric disturbance in the mother'.

Stern (1985) gives a good example of a parent's irrational behaviour. He describes a 'paranoid schizophrenic' mother who overprotects her ten-month-old daughter inappropriately. He describes a visit by the mother and baby when the baby was asleep as they arrived.

> The mother gently took her sleeping baby and began to lay her on the bed so she would stay asleep. The mother did this with enormous concentration that left us closed out. After she had ever-so-slowly eased the baby's head onto the bed, she took one of the baby's arms, which was awkwardly positioned, and with her two hands carefully guided it to a feather-like landing on the bed, as though the arm were made of eggshells and the bed made of marble. (p. 205)

Stern shows how this mother, by being over-careful, was reacting against harmful impulses in herself. Although in the instance witnessed this over-careful handling did allow the baby to remain asleep, we can see how puzzling this sort of behaviour might be to a baby building up its picture of the world from its mother's cues.

Similarly, in looking at dreams and nightmares in Chapter 6, we saw how a schizophrenic father's violent and unpredictable behaviour led to his infant son Jerry suffering from night terrors. These appeared to be a direct result of attacks that frightened and could not be made sense of by the child. The father's irrational behaviour affected the child's sleep.

229

What we have seen in this chapter is the great interest that mothers and babies have in communicating with each other. Through this communication the baby makes sense of the world. When the responses of the mother are impaired because of her own state of health, then the baby's ability to deal with the world outside and with the regulation of his own body, including sleep rhythms, may be affected.

CHAPTER FOURTEEN

PREMATURE, HANDICAPPED AND ILL BABIES AND GIFTED CHILDREN

THE CATEGORIES in the title of this chapter are obviously very disparate. They involve problems with different origins and different degrees of severity. What all have in common is that a physically based state in the baby has to be responded to by the parents. The baby's state and the parents' attempts to respond to it colour the parents' and babies' relationships. A large number of babies in all these categories have sleep problems. The disturbed sleep may be a direct result of the baby's condition. It may also result both from the parents' feelings about the baby's condition and the relationship that develops in this context.

It is obvious that parents of babies who have had something go wrong, either at the birth or later, will have suffered distress and had their confidence in themselves as parents affected. The normal ebb and flow of anxieties that parents have about their babies may be replaced by a continuous experience of anxiety that does not go away. A feeling of being responsible and having to go on being responsible for the baby is unremittingly there for some parents; for others the hospital seems to have taken over all initiative, leaving nothing for them to do.

One mother of a baby who had been in intensive care was typical of many. She told me that she herself had been sleepless in the baby's first few months. She felt she had to stay awake to keep the baby alive. We can see here an intensification of the normal process by which a mother's thinking about her baby is one part of her care for him. This mother could not stop thinking about her baby, even to go to sleep for very long herself. When a baby is in a special-care unit, looked after by professionals, there may be little chance for a mother to care physically for the baby herself. In such cases *thinking* is what she can offer her baby.

231

PREMATURE BABIES

A large number of premature babies have sleep problems. Let us look at some of the possible reasons for this. This section is based on the ideas developed by Helen Bender after some years of working as a child psychotherapist in a neonatal intensive care unit. (I rely mainly on her personal communications to me, but see also Bender, 1981, 1987 and Bender and Swan-Parente, 1983.)

Bender describes how out of the ordinary a premature birth usually is for both mother and baby. The pregnancy itself may have been difficult and even dangerous if the mother, for example, had high blood-pressure. We saw in Chapter 7 from Trowell's work that where there has been a Caesarean birth, this can affect the future relationship of mother and baby. Trowell (1982) states that unexpected Caesareans in particular have an effect, following the shock and sense of failure caused to the mother. We can guess, however, that elective Caesareans also take their toll. Even though the mother has a chance to prepare for the actual procedure, it is relevant that the Caesarean may follow a complication in the pregnancy. The direct effect on the baby of a Caesarean operation must also be taken into account, that the baby has had a more rapid change of environment than the baby who has been pushed gradually out of the womb.

A mother who has had any unexpected and traumatic experience during the birth may feel as though the 'bad' delivery is the baby's responsibility and be angry with him. Such a feeling is very difficult to acknowledge, let alone express, but it can underlie the mother's dealings with the baby, the father and hospital staff.

The premature baby's experience after the birth is certainly out of the ordinary. It is not just an intensified version of what other babies have. It is qualitatively different. The baby is in a setting which is noisy and unpredictable and seldom able to be influenced by what he feels about it. The noise level within an incubator is very high. This noise comes from the high-tech machinery to which the baby is wired up and is added to by the clatter of metal instruments. The exposed position of a baby lying connected to machinery in an incubator must obviously be a different experience from that of a baby held wrapped up by its mother, able to find its preferred position in its cot. It also feels different for the parent looking at the baby.

Normal babies soon develop an idea of predictability from the routine of their care and also are likely to have a preponderance of good experiences. Premature babies have to suffer many painful and invasive procedures and have few good experiences to hold on to. Many of the necessary treatments are shocking to the baby's system, which in any case is immature and physiologically incomplete.

A good way to describe the situation is to say that the premature baby has no rights. He is impotent, unable to influence his world. He is attended to because of the needs of his immature system, not because he himself has expressed a feeling of wanting something. Even his feeding is a passive experience; fed through a tube, his hunger goes away without him doing anything. He does not have the experience of actively seeking breast or bottle and actively sucking to acquire the milk. He also misses out on the feeling in his mouth of sucking a soft and responsive nipple or teat and instead has hard objects, the tubes, pushed into his nose or mouth. Objects are pushed or injected into him; he cannot use his hand to push away the hand that 'assaults' him.

The parents' experience, when the baby is in such a situation, comes partly from identifying with the baby, and partly from the direct effect it has on their own parenting. Parents are likely to feel helpless as a reflection of what their baby feels, but also impotent and peripheral, because in all the sophisticated technology surrounding their baby there is little for them to do.

The baby in an incubator is denied contact with his parents, he lacks the bodily contact with them, he lacks the building up of a picture of the world through anticipating and then experiencing interchanges with them. Parents are denied their reciprocal part in this. With no opportunity to care routinely for their babies, they have few ways to *be* parents except as an abstract idea. For parents who are already knocked sideways by the unexpected circumstances of the birth and their baby's ensuing difficulties, there are no easy means by which they can take reparative action and be part of what makes the baby 'better'.

Realizing this, many baby units are now changing their methods. It was in fact a major reform when beds were provided, so that parents were allowed to stay in baby units. Now more and more attempts are being made to allow and encourage parents to have physical contact and to be part of the baby's caring. Dieter Wolke (1987), however, warns that although holding by parents during the early sensitive period after birth enhances the parent–infant relationship for robust, healthy pre-term infants who can cope with handling, it is not appropriate for the fragile and ill baby, who may become distressed in his breathing and even collapse and need to be resuscitated because he just cannot cope with the handling. He says this experience may then become a trauma for the parents. Wolke points out that, left to use their own initiative, parents will in fact discriminate and handle the very sick baby less and that, if assisted by empathic nursing staff, they will take over more of the care when their baby recovers. Babies in incubators recognize their parents' touch from early on; often the parent has a special place on the baby's body where they touch. Minde *et al.* (1978) observed that these babies open their eyes more often for their parents than for others. It is poignant to think of the way in which a baby is able to know his parents from among a multiplicity of caretakers handling him.

The mutual need for parents and babies to have as much contact as possible seems to be overriding. Bender has also pointed out the value of dummies for premature babies to suck, particularly while undergoing invasive procedures. These babies have 'bad' mouth experiences, when something is rammed into it; a dummy can counteract this and provide a 'good' sucking experience. This can be both an ongoing satisfying experience and also a way for the baby of focusing and having a feeling of something to hold on to through the mouth, when having to deal with interventions. Paediatricians have also discovered that premature babies who have dummies to suck on may gain weight faster.

Sleep may be a particular problem in an intensive care unit, if it is organized in such a way that there is no quiet time and the sleep states of the baby are not respected. In premature babies under thirty-two weeks gestation the baby does not attain deep sleep states; with older babies their rhythms are often not sufficiently taken into account. A trail of people with a need to carry out procedures on behalf of the baby have their own timetable. It is rarely that this fits in with the baby's sleep rhythms, so that the baby's sleep is frequently and unpredictably disrupted. In addition to this the baby may not go to sleep and wake up in the near presence of the parent, as most ordinary babies do. A different person may be there, when the baby falls asleep and when he wakes up. We saw earlier how the negotiating of the baby's sleep rhythms was one of the main tasks between mother and baby in the early weeks; we see here how deprived both are of this crucial means of contact.

Bender suggests that with very little under their control, a premature baby may sleep as an escape from reality; or conversely wakefulness may be one of the few ways that the baby can have any influence – he may stay awake to have some kind of control over his environment.

Wolke (1987) has shown that in neonatal intensive care units (NICUs) there may be a lack of clear diurnal rhythms. Light levels, non-speech sounds and handling of babies may be similar over the 24-hour period. The lack of diurnal rhythms in the unit affects the baby's ability to develop his own rhythmicity. A control trial by Mann et al. (1986) showed that pre-term infants who were cared for in a nursery where the intensity of light and noise was reduced between 7.0 p.m. and 7.0 a.m. spent a significantly longer time sleeping, less time feeding and gained more weight after being discharged home than those housed in perpetual light and noise.

Premature babies are less able to regulate their behavioural states than full-term babies. Wolke stresses the importance for pre-term infants of obtaining sufficient deep non-REM sleep. At under thirty-two weeks gestation they spend only ten to twenty percent of their sleep time in quiet non-REM sleep. To achieve physiological stability deep non-REM sleep is essential. Wolke shows that by implementing day–night rhythms, dimming the light and reducing noise and handling at night, the infant's sleep need not be inter-fered with. The infant thus can attain sleep rhythms which allow him to have longer periods in deep sleep. This means that the baby gets accustomed to sleep for long periods during the night, with the dual gains of the immediate benefit to his development of physiological stability and the later benefits that the parents will be able to take home a baby with established sleep routines and a probable ability to sleep for periods of some length during the night.

THE RETURN HOME

Parents and babies returning home from a special-care baby unit are often in a vulnerable situation. The parent, who already feels inadequate because of the circumstances of the birth, goes on feeling this way, simply because the baby has needed intensive care, that is, more than the parent is able to give. From having felt impotent themselves and that it seemed as though their baby needed a dozen people or so to keep him alive, suddenly they are on their own. Many parents feel panic-stricken at this stage. For the first time they are fully responsible and also at liberty to follow or influence their baby's needs and rhythms for sleep or other func-tions. With no practice this freedom may be daunting.

Parents who have not been able to share actively in their baby's care may have focused their love and optimism for their baby by looking at him and thinking about him. This thinking may be a way of 'holding' a fragile baby and keeping him alive. As long as the parents do this, they feel the baby cannot slip away. The thinking may include anticipatory grief about a baby who may not survive. Whatever the elements it is difficult for parents who have taken their baby home, even though he may have become stronger, to switch gear and be able to stop this thinking and looking. Many parents report not expecting their babies to settle to sleep and not being able to leave them to do so. Martin Richards (1983) remarks on parents in this position feeling that they do not know their baby when they bring him home.

I saw one family who had experienced many of the problems described above. They had had twins, a boy and a girl, born at twenty-six weeks and each weighing under two pounds. The girl died at five days, the boy, Felix, survived but was in intensive care for the first four months of his life. In the first weeks he collapsed and had to be resuscitated several times.

Felix's parents came to see me when he was four years old, distraught about his uncontrollable outbursts and his sleeplessness. For me to know what they had been through I needed to ask them to describe in detail the experiences of Felix and his twin sister's birth, of the baby girl's death and of the events of the four months in hospital. I needed to know all this as background to how Felix was behaving now. Even more, the parents needed someone to tell their story to. All parents need to tell the story of their baby's birth. When something has gone wrong at the birth, there is even more need to do so. However, Bender points out that when the baby itself is in extreme need of care, the baby's survival becomes the only focus. Attention is of necessity on keeping the baby alive and the mother has no one, no place for telling the story of the birth. There may be a heartbreaking story that goes untold. As I got to know Felix's parents, it emerged how much·else had been left unsaid. These parents had had twins. As so often happens when one dies and one survives, the emotions, the grief for one baby and the hopes for the other, become confused. Hospital staff attempt to cheer the parents after the death by talking of the live baby. Parents themselves may fear thinking about the dead baby in case it magically affects the one they are trying to keep alive with their thoughts. Mourning for the dead baby gets set on one side and may never happen.

This mother told me of spending most of her days during these four months sitting by Felix's incubator, thinking about him. She fetched her older child after school. He was not allowed inside the unit, but stood by the door. Father joined them after work. It seemed in retrospect that, although Felix's mother had spent most of her time in the unit and had felt the staff there to be caring and helpful, there had never been the right moment to pour out her feelings about having a baby in such a vulnerable state. Perhaps she *had* done so and later forgotten she had. I suspect, however, that, glued as she was to the side of the incubator, being with her baby and willing him to live, no one perceived her as being distanced enough to talk about her feelings, in contrast to just having them. It was not until this belated opportunity to talk to me came that Mother and Father were able to put their feelings in perspective.

Felix's parents told me of the distress and exhaustion of the first four months, when they absorbed the situation of having a baby who might not survive. Also in their minds was the worry about how normally he would develop. When they brought him home, they felt overwhelmed by his vulnerability. They continually expected him to collapse and did not feel they could safely take their eyes off him. Felix slept in fits and starts, mostly in the parents' bed. Even there he was restless, kicking and bumping into his parents. During the day he had constant explosions and tantrums; the parents could rarely take him out without incident. He could not tolerate any new experience and often bit and ripped up his own clothes, toys, bedding, etc. All this had continued day and night for the four years until they came to the Clinic. Felix now started at school and to his parents' surprise and relief settled down well. His behaviour at school was quite different from at home. He was able to respond to the school's matter-of-fact firmness and control his outbursts. In other ways he was tentative and fearful, but able to use staff to help him last through the day.

This confirmation that Felix could survive in the outside world made an enormous impact on his parents. They started to think seriously about his problems being in relation to themselves and the early experience they had all shared. Their thoughts went in two directions: firstly, that Felix's behaviour must have been at least in part a reflection or communication of his early experiences in intensive care and secondly, that their handling of him reflected their own confused reactions to all this.

They started to connect Felix's rejection of anything new with the repeated unpredictable interventions in intensive care; his present explosions and anger might represent a feeling of not being able to tolerate what was happening to him, of having no focus for explaining it and holding it together for himself. For their own part they thought about how, with their fragile picture of him, they had not been able to look after him in a firm, consistent way. They had always worried that he would collapse. They had responded to him in an immediate panicky way; no firm routine had been built up for him to fit in with. They then confessed, perhaps for the first time, the anger they themselves felt and the unfairness of having a baby like Felix. At the back of their minds continued the fear that he was even now not really 'normal'. Their doctor then arranged more tests that showed he was not brain-damaged. They now worked out that Felix's outbursts had seemed so extreme that they felt he must be damaged and ordinary parenting could not reach him. They were then able to agree to my suggestion that at times they might have wished Felix had not been born.

These acknowledgements seemed to lift an enormous weight from them. They were firstly able to remind themselves that they were successful parents with their older son. Then they started to talk with Felix about the experiences in the hospital and about the sister who had died. They were able to speculate on what it might feel like to Felix to be the survivor when his twin sister had died. They did not discuss this directly with him, but thinking about the confusions or guilt he might have experienced about being the one who held on to life helped them feel they understood him better. They showed him the marks on his body from transfusions, blood-gas tests and drips. They had broached this before and wondered if it was necessary to do it again. This time he appeared to understand and take in what they were saying much more clearly. It occurred to them that talking from time to time about the overwhelming central circumstances of Felix's existence would help them all to take it in. They noticed at once that he was calmer and more able to take part in conversations about everyday matters.

Father decided to be firmer with Felix and found that during his outbursts he could hold him until his rage subsided, preventing the orgy of destruction that he had previously felt was unstoppable. Possibly acknowledging their own anger at the situation allowed both parents to separate anger from firmness and hold him without doing harm. Felix not only got over these outbursts quicker, he also had fewer of them.

It seemed time to look at the sleep problems. Felix would only go to bed with the parents in their bed. The parents decided that even though Felix would end up in their bed later, he must start off in his own bed. Father lay beside him for hours till he got to sleep. Later in the night Felix would wake and call until Father fetched him to the parents' bed. This was a small first step, but it seemed to alter some perception in Felix. He had always woken up again 'swearing'. Now, though he still woke and called for Father, he was not so angry and explosive in his words. As we thought about the next changes to make, Mother poignantly described Felix's position as he slept. His leg had to poke out from under the duvet and he lay with his arms spread outwards above his head on the pillow. She said he looked as he had done in hospital in the incubator.

We talked about the feeling the parents had had then of their helplessness in not being able to pick up their baby, cuddle him and wrap him up. His exposed sleeping position now seemed a continuation of this unreachability. I suggested that Felix need not still be a child beyond their reach; that what they as parents did could now make a difference. Perhaps setting limits for Felix could be a way of wrapping him around with their care. Furthermore he was now a little boy who could understand words. At bedtime Father could perhaps stay with him for a while, tell him he was going out and would come back again. The parents had tried to make up for the unreachable time by going on being physically there for Felix. I suggested that being *reliably* there was more important now than being *always* there. Expected and understood separations might be what was necessary now. If Felix had slept well when he was with his parents, these thoughts would not have been relevant. In such a case he might have been communicating that he needed still more of his parents' presence before being separate from them. But Felix's anger and disturbance, even when he was in their bed, might have been a sign that he needed to find a bearable way to be able to leave them, not to go on being with them. At the time of writing this issue is still not resolved between Felix and his parents.

BABIES BORN AFTER STILL BIRTHS
One of the griefs that Felix's parents had to bear was the death of Felix's twin sister five days after her birth. They had to cope with their anxiety about Felix's survival and try to deal with their mourning for the dead twin all at the same time. Felix also grew up with his own confused feelings about the death that took place so close to his own birth.

The paradoxical problem for families in such a situation can be that because they do not want to confuse their feelings about the live baby with their grief about the dead one, mourning gets put on one side and may never properly be done. Because there has not been the time and space really to feel the grief about the death, this grief may in fact stay around, unrecognized, for years.

Babies born after still births may be in a similar position. Bourne and Lewis (1984) have shown how 'After a perinatal death everyone hopes the next pregnancy will set things right' (p. 31). However, the mourning of still birth and genuine recovery are difficult processes that require time and, if the next pregnancy starts before the mourning process has had enough time to take place, then the new pregnancy can cut short the mourning for the last baby, predisposing the mother to mental disturbance. Bourne and Lewis show how difficult it is in fact to mourn a still birth and how difficult it is also for professionals to help with this task. They describe how a still birth is experienced as a 'non-event' by parents. Instead of the expected baby there is nothing, just a feeling of emptiness.

> Beyond ordinary pain and disappointment, still birth is complicated by extraordinary sensations of confusion and unreality as birth and death have been fused. After months of expectation and growing fullness, there is sudden emptiness with nothing to show, a stupefying non-event. (Even after a live birth women have a sense of emptiness and sadness mingled with their joy.) Women complain that, after a still birth, people expect them to go on as if nothing had happened. The mother feels the stigmata of disease although she usually has no illness. She feels ashamed, inferior, and guilty without reason. If the baby's body is whisked away to an unknown grave, the reality may be yet harder to grasp. (Bourne and Lewis, 1984, p. 31)

It is important for the parents to have memories on which to base their mourning. They need a chance to see and to hold the dead baby, to have photographs taken, to have a proper funeral and also to name the baby. The more that the dead baby has a real identity the easier it is to mourn it. If the mourning has been helped along in this way, then there is less risk of the next pregnancy producing a confusion between the dead baby and the expected one. Although parents will still be more likely to be anxious and depressed than the average expectant parents, the new pregnancy offers consolation and fulfilment. Bourne and Lewis stress the importance of not giving the name chosen for the dead baby to the 'replacement' baby, in order that the new baby does not inherit a feeling of simply stepping into the shoes of the other.

After the birth parents may be puzzled by their reactions to the new live baby. They may be overwhelmed by sadness in the middle of their joy; painful memories of the dead baby will be reawakened and at times they may confuse the live baby with memories of the dead baby. Telling parents in advance that they may feel like this gives them 'permission' to be confused and afraid.

There is thus a chain of circumstances which can lead from the experience of still birth to subsequent difficulties in the care of later, live babies. Parents who have lost confidence in their child-bearing capacities, who are anxious and confused, will have difficulty in understanding and responding to their baby's signals. We can see how sleep problems sometimes develop out of this confusion of past and present.

COT DEATHS

As with parents who have had still births, parents who have lost a baby through a cot death have the traumatic event of the death itself to deal with, as well as the loss of their baby. If these parents have a later baby, almost universally they are unable to leave the baby to himself during the night. Quite understandably their need to keep checking whether the baby is still alive is uppermost in their minds and may in fact continually disturb the baby. This in itself may be a relief; an awake baby is an alive baby.

We looked earlier in Chapter 8 at parents' ordinarily ambivalent feelings about their babies and saw that the hostile part of this ambivalence can be expressed as death fears. Most parents have the good fortune that their babies survive. For parents whose babies do not survive it can feel as though it was indeed the ambivalence that caused the death. Irrational it might be, but it can be part of the conscious and unconscious feelings that make up the parents' grief.

One such mother, with a sleepless nine-month-old, had earlier had twins who had died from cot deaths a few weeks after their birth. She told me, dry-eyed and factually, the story of their deaths. She said that if she started to cry, she would never be able to stop. The acute unbearableness of the two babies' deaths, a grief beyond the relief of tears, was there every night as she put her live baby to bed. It did seem as though sleep and death were still entangled in her mind.

HANDICAPPED BABIES

Mentally and physically handicapped babies also have severe sleep problems in many cases. It has been shown that behaviour problems, including sleep disturbance, cause stress in mothers caring for handicapped children (Quine and Pahl, 1985) and is one of the reasons for requests for long-term care (Carter, 1984).

Clements *et al.* (1986) show that sleeping difficulties occur with considerable frequency amongst mentally handicapped children of all ages. There is a strong association with serious daytime behavioural difficulties, such as tantrums and destructiveness. There is also a specific link between self-injury and night waking and there have been speculations about a bio-rhythmic component to self-injurious behaviour.

Here again we can see that there may be both a failure in the functioning of the central nervous system to attain the normal development of sleep stages and, in addition to this, a disturbance in the relationship between parents and infants because of the way in which the handicap influences the normal negotiating of sleep rhythms. We can see how the need for parents to adapt their parenting to the different circumstances of a handicapped child's development can in itself impair the ordinary parenting approaches that the handicapped child still needs. Providing for special needs may mean that ordinary ones go unmet. Furthermore the lack of response or skewed response by a handicapped child to general spontaneous parenting has a very dispiriting effect on parents and stops them being able to go on offering it.

Tracy, aged five, was a little girl who had had a difficult birth. She was mentally handicapped and had had a great deal of treatment for the many facets of her condition. The diagnosis of Tracy's condition was uncertain and it was difficult for Tracy's parents, in recounting the story of her first year, to know which elements in the course of her illness and its treatment were the provokers of the various aspects of her state and her behaviour. However, it seemed clear that her birth had been normal until the last fifteen minutes of labour, when the cord became wrapped round her neck and she became blue. Her father felt that her illness started at that point. It gradually emerged that Tracy's development was slow and she had epileptic fits. She had always been a crying baby, but at seven and a half months she had a hernia operation and her crying increased greatly after that. She started having some shaking movements which were like sleep jerks. At this point she had a wiped-out vacant look. She was put on steroids at eleven months and after a month of taking these she suddenly stopped shaking. Her mother said it was like an iron curtain lifting. She would smile and look at people. Although her fits resumed, she was never so detached again. However, because she was full of adrenalin she was always active and hungry, never still.

How all this fitted in with Tracy's sleep pattern is complex. Mother said that even on the day of her birth Tracy was wakeful. She was born, with the traumatic last stages described above, at midday. That night a nurse took her away from Mother's side, because she would not go to sleep. She spent the entire night on her tummy being rocked. Throughout the first few months she was difficult to settle and had to be wheeled in her pram round and round the garden to send her to sleep. The movement would send her to sleep, but she might wake as the pram was bumped up the stairs back into the house.

After her hernia operation she cried and cried in hospital and her shaking started shortly afterwards. When she went on the steroids which cured the shaking, the effect seemed to be acutely stimulating. She hardly slept at all and Mother's memory was of her and Father being with Tracy all the time. Tracy remained on the steroids for six months and after she came off them some sleep patterns started to develop. Even so she was awake between one o'clock and three o'clock every night. Mother would go and get into bed with her, they had given Tracy a double bed for this purpose, and would lie with her as Tracy sucked her breast. At eighteen months, in order to achieve some separation, they bought her a cot. Tracy did not like the cot and would cry angrily while lying in it. One night Mother became so angry herself in response to this crying that she shut the door and left her to cry. After that Tracy would never go in the cot again and Mother reverted to using the double bed for her. However, Mother's next attempt to get Tracy to be separate from her was more successful. At two years and four months Mother weaned Tracy by asking Grandmother, who was staying, to lie with Tracy for these two wakeful hours in the night.

Looking back at this time, Mother observed that most mentally handicapped babies do not go through all this. She felt that the explanation lay in the assaults on Tracy's body. She had had painful injections daily from a home care team who visited at home. Mother held her during these injections and fed her afterwards to help her recover.

It seemed to me that the origin of Tracy's sleep disturbance and failure to establish sleep rhythms lay initially in the irritability of her central nervous system and the stimulation from medication. Following from that, what psychological elements can we see in her sleeplessness? The element of reaction to painful procedures, such as the injections, perhaps bridges two kinds of responses and includes a psychological as well as a physiological response.

Even for a little girl as physically assailed as Tracy was we can see strong connections with emotional processes in Tracy's responses to her parents' attempts to manage her and mitigate her condition. Tracy's mother felt that her baby survived because of the breast-feeding, which they kept going throughout the traumatic events of the first couple of years. During the time of Tracy's operation, her injections and the worst of her fits, they maintained a relationship through the breast-feeding. Without this Mother felt that Tracy would have turned in on herself, as so many severely handicapped children do. By keeping the breast-feeding going, Mother kept this closeness with Tracy; the adverse effect of this from Mother's point of view was that Tracy needed Mother in a continuous sort of way. To fall asleep she needed a person lying touching her, preferably (though not essentially) Mother and her breast. Mother felt trapped. It was also presumably not really satisfactory to Tracy, judging by the way in which, when sleeping in the parents' bed, she slept fitfully and pushed aggressively against them.

However, things changed. As Tracy grew and attained speech, a sleep routine became established. Tracy became able to take part in a bedtime routine which meant that Mother had to stay *near* her room while Tracy went to sleep, but no longer had to lie with her. When she woke in the night, she still went into the parents' bed. At this point her sister asked Tracy, 'Why do you get into Mummy and Daddy's bed?', and she replied, 'Because I feel lonely'. Here we see how much Tracy had developed. This self-awareness is a totally different state of being from the inconsolable baby who had to be held or pushed in her pram without stopping. We can also see how the parents' sensitivity to Tracy's needs and their wish to be there for her constantly, if that was what she wanted, then produced its own problems. Mother's capacity to remain available to Tracy day and night was probably a major factor in bringing Tracy out of her apparently unreachable state. However, being so available also meant that Mother at times felt unbearably trapped. What also needs to be recognized is that at some point Mother changed in her policy of being always available to Tracy to one of firmly setting up a bedtime routine and gradually expecting Tracy to take more responsibility for getting to sleep herself, with Mother moving by steps away from her side.

It seems that both these stages (of being always available and gradually moving away) are essential ones. What is particularly difficult for the parents of handicapped children, who may need their parents more than do normal children, is to work out when the child needs and is ready to be more separate. Many parents miss the cues, which are much less apparent than in other children. Tracy's mother in fact said that Tracy never initiated anything new and all changes had to be lengthily negotiated with her.

How did a little girl like Tracy get from the stage where she seemed, paradoxically, to be both unreachable and also to need her mother's constant presence and holding to become the child who could be separate enough and able to conceptualize enough actually to say that she was lonely? It seems quite plain that her mother's availability was crucial. Perhaps also the moments of rejection, as when Mother shut the door and left Tracy in her cot, were necessary in order to signal to Tracy that Mother had needs of her own. With hindsight this mother might perhaps have been less devoted and insisted earlier to Tracy that she existed outside of their mother–baby relationship. If she had done so, she might not have had to dramatize her feelings so intensely, as when she had to get away to leave Tracy to cry in her cot. Mother also described how Tracy's very skilled and sensitive speech therapist played a vital part in helping Tracy find the words to express her emotions.

In thinking about the meaning of Tracy's difficulty in getting to sleep, her father guessed that she might be fearful of the hypna-gogic stage (the transitional stage of losing consciousness while falling asleep) – that this might be for her like the losing of consciousness of her fits. In thinking of her as making these comparisons and fighting sleep as a response to her fear, we are seeing her as no longer just swept along by neurological processes, but as having a sense of her own ability to protect herself. Tracy had come a long way.

There was also, if Tracy's parents were correct in their connec-tion, an unassimilable shock for Tracy from the hernia operation. Her parents attributed the onset of her shaking to the operation. Also important is that before the operation she had attained a pre-verbal 'babble'. She lost this after the operation and reverted to an insistent early-baby cry. Not till Grandmother went away when she was seventeen months did she say her first words, 'bye-bye'.

ILL BABIES

Parents of ill babies also have the problem of finding a balance between giving their baby the care he needs and divining the moment to allow him to work out his own bodily processes. One mother whose baby had recently recovered from a severe illness told me how impossible it was to look after a baby *and* do the washing. She had a washing-machine and at first I puzzled over what she meant. It emerged as we talked that when her baby was seriously ill, she had thought about him all the time, willing him to stay alive. This had succeeded, in the sense that he had survived and was now well and flourishing. But what his mother had been unable to do was to switch off from this total preoccupation with him and belief that he could not survive if she stopped thinking about him. This carried over to other areas of responsibility, even the washing-machine. She could not, so to speak, bundle the clothes in and let it get on with 'doing the washing'. She went on thinking about the washing-machine and this conflicted with thinking about her son; she could not manage both.

Parents of ill children have to deal with anxieties about their children's illness. They also may have to deal both with separations, when babies and young children have to be in hospital and, if the parents are unable to be with him, with the repercussions from the separation when the child is back home.

James Robertson and Bowlby worked in the 1950s on the effects of separation on young children during limited stays in residential nurseries and hospitals. Bowlby (1961) says of their findings that a child of fifteen to thirty months who has not been previously parted from his mother will show a predictable sequence of behaviour. The phases of this can be described as protest, despair and detachment.

At first with tears and anger he demands his mother back and seems hopeful he will succeed in getting her. This is the phase of protest and may last several days. Later he becomes quieter, but to the discerning eye it is clear that as much as ever he remains preoccupied with his absent mother and still yearns for her return, but his hopes have faded and he is in the phase of despair. Often these two phases alternate: hope turns to despair and despair to renewed hope. Eventually, however, a greater change occurs. He seems to forget his mother so that when she comes for him he remains curiously uninterested in her, and may seem even not to recognize her. This is the third phase –

that of detachment. In each of these phases the child is prone to tantrums and episodes of destructive behaviour, often of a disquietingly violent kind. (p. 48)

What was discovered when this work was done was the seriousness of the effects on a young child of being away from his parents in hospital. This involved the child both being away from family and home and also having to deal with frightening situations and possible painful treatment without the emotional protection of his parents. Before the careful observations of James and Joyce Robertson (Robertson, James, 1958; Robertson, James and Joyce, film series, 1967–75) the phases of behaviour described above, ending with the phase of 'detachment', were usually misread as indicating that the child had 'settled in' to the hospital. Hospital policy throughout the world was consequently insensitive on this problem.

On the child's return home after such an experience it was then observed that the longer the stay in hospital, and particularly the longer an unvisited stay, the longer it took the child to re-establish relationships at home. The child would at first be unresponsive and undemanding. When this broke, the intense ambivalence of his feelings for his mother was shown in intense clinging and anxiety. These findings brought about a change of policy in hospitals, instigated in Britain by the Platt Report (1959), so that now most children's wards allow and encourage parents to stay with their young children where possible.

If there has been a separation, one of the consequences on coming home may be sleep disturbances. The child may need to reassure himself of his parents' presence and they themselves may be anxious to spend as much time as possible with him. The ambivalence of the reunion between parent and child may be played out through a sleep disturbance. The child may 'blame' the parents for allowing both the separation and any painful experience in hospital; parents may feel reciprocally guilty.

In some instances children who sleep badly at home may actually sleep better in hospital. Occasionally children are taken into hospital for observation for acute sleep disturbances. If the child does sleep better there, then we may guess at some family disturbance and that this is one of the 'vigilant' children, described by Moore (1989), who do not feel protected by their parents. Similarly some children, sleeping in a laboratory for research purposes, may sleep better with the 'protection' of the researchers.

At fourteen months Claudia, who had severe sleep problems, was admitted to hospital because of a low weight gain. Her mother went into hospital and slept with her and while in hospital Claudia slept very well. It seemed as though both Claudia and her mother felt protected by the hospital and that this feeling of protection was able to override the uncertainties the two of them felt together at home. Claudia had also slept well when staying with Mother in Mother's parents' home. The hospital seems to have had the same parenting quality as the grandparents for this mother–baby couple.

Hospital procedures need not lead to sleep problems. In one family two little girls needed operations and splints for a congenital dislocation of the hips at the end of their first year. Mother or Father stayed in hospital much of the time with each baby. Both babies ate little and had unsettled sleep while in hospital and for the first few nights at home again, but they both settled back quickly into their sleep patterns, even though they were in plaster casts for a couple of months. It seems as though a basic feeling of security in these babies was not destroyed, even by the experience of the operations and the ensuing immobilization. Mother or Father's almost continual presence must have helped keep this feeling of security going. Other children, however, will feel unbearably helpless and may have frightening dreams of being attacked, which disturb their sleep in such a situation.

GIFTED CHILDREN

I have included issues about gifted children in this chapter about children with special needs because, although the circumstances of special need are very different, there is in common a situation where parents are 'responding to a difference' in their child from the normal run of children. As we have seen, this affects the parents' handling of their child and their ability to respond to the universal and ordinary aspects of their children's needs.

Gifted children are often thought to need less sleep. Joan Freeman (1979) has interestingly demonstrated in her research study, 'The Gulbenkian project on gifted children', that 'sleep was not a function of giftedness but of social expectation' (p. 122). In this study children who had not been measured as gifted, but were seen by their parents as being gifted, were compared with two control groups, the first of similar intelligence to the 'designated' gifted group and the second group chosen at random as far as their intellectual ability was concerned. The target group was found to be hyperactive and to sleep poorly compared with both control groups, that is, children of parents who had joined the National Association for Gifted Children appeared to be the ones with sleep problems.

In looking at the early development of such children, alertness at birth is an important aspect. Freeman says:

It was only the target children who were described as more alert at birth in comparison with the control groups. This is a feature of children which has been mentioned as an early indication of their giftedness by Gesell (1950) and others. However, no differences in early alertness were reported between the high IQ children and the moderate IQ children, nor between the adjustment groups.

It cannot be said therefore, on the evidence from this study, that children who are intellectually gifted are objectively more alert at birth. It is possible that a high proportion of the target parents were anticipating a very bright child, even before the baby's birth and readily accepted their own and the nurses' description of their babies as 'bright' or 'clever' in support of this. No one has ever investigated how often new-born babies are complimented in this way, but this present research may have provided some evidence as to how seriously such remarks may be taken by some parents. (p. 221)

What Freeman's findings suggest is that parents who associate 'alertness' in their babies with desired giftedness may encourage and stimulate alertness in their babies to the detriment of more peaceful ways of being. I would surmise that such babies may be encouraged both to interact with parents and be spurred on to activity of all kinds in a way that does not allow enough of the kind of relaxation that develops into the drowsiness necessary before a baby can fall asleep. In this vein the parent may continue to encourage 'ambitious' play, which consists of accurate building, puzzles, etc., and not give the child adequate opportunity for play involving less motor co-ordination, particularly reflective play. Playing with sand or water or apparent aimless sorting through of small toys can allow the dreaming play which helps the small child to sift through in his mind the conflicts and experiences of the day. In particular a small child who is occupied with learning new skills for much of the day needs time to absorb the changes in himself that this new learning represents. Such reflective time enables him to start to process the anxieties that taking on new experiences

249

brings. By beginning this process during the day, there is less backlog of anxiety to be dealt with at night. The small child's REM time can then effectively deal with the consolidating of new learning that Hartmann (1973) describes and he is less likely to be disturbed in the night by arousals of anxiety.

From this it would follow that 'bright' children in fact need as much or even more sleep than the average child, in order to assimilate new knowledge and achievements and metabolize them into the personality without them being a cause of anxiety. The clever children who are always anxious about possible future failure may be those who have not had enough sleep to metabolize the changes of past learning and to keep their confidence going. The remedy would seem to be more time spent in non-learning activity, so as to allow relaxation that leads to sleep.

We have seen in this chapter how illnesses and adversities concerning their children affect the confidence and self-esteem of parents and can seriously influence their handling of their children in a way that impairs the establishment of sleep rhythms. Anything that means the child is perceived as unusual by the parents, including giftedness (which might seem to be an asset, not a disability), may start off a chain of responses which leads to sleep difficulties.

CONCLUSION

THIS BOOK has been about reflecting, about putting difficulties into the context of both past and present experiences and relationships. It is about the need for several kinds of theoretical knowledge on which to base our thoughts about the nature of infants' sleep problems, even though it can be difficult to put these different approaches together. It is also about the way in which dreams put us in touch both with what is going on in our minds now and with our memories of the past, and how they help us organize our experiences.

I more or less started with a dream of my own, to illustrate my principal theme of the connections in thought between parents and their children; and I also end with one.

The night before starting to write on the sleep problems of infants, I dreamt that I had a baby who was waking and feeding repeatedly in the night. I was confused and despairing of how to sort it out. This baby obviously represents in part the sleepless inner-city London babies that I have thought about. What is also illustrated is the integrative process that a dream carries out (together with the hidden wish-fulfilment!) that allowed me to some extent to translate my jumbled thoughts and experiences into the structure of a book. As one appreciative parent said, 'It worked like a dream.'

SUGGESTED READING FOR PARENTS

Some of the parents I work with find it useful to read these books:

Douglas, J. and Richman, N. (1984) *My Child Won't Sleep*. Harmondsworth: Penguin.
This is simple and helpful and parents find the advice effective.

Haslam, D. (1984) *Sleepless Children*. London: Piatkus.
Friendly and reassuring, but impoverished in my view by its dismissal of psychoanalytic thinking about dreams.

Weissbluth, M. (1987) *Sleep Well*. London: Unwin Paperbacks.
An informative book, but while at times very knowledgeable about emotional factors, it also contains oversimplified behavioural advice.

Ferber, R. (1985) *Solve Your Child's Sleep Problems: A Practical and Comprehensive Guide for Parents*. London: Dorling Kindersley, 1986.
This is much liked by parents, both for the degree of information it gives in readable but non-patronizing form and for the easily understandable suggestions about how to make changes; a sympathetic approach to both parent and child.

Gray, P. (1987) *Crying Baby: How to Cope*. London:Wisebuy.
Deals with parents' feelings, as well as giving information and advice.

Scott, G. (1986) *Coping with Your Night Waking Baby*. (New edition by Gordon Scott and Martin Richards, 1989.) Obtainable from Child Care and Development Group, University of Cambridge, Free School Lane, Cambridge CB2 3RF.
This book was part of a research project comparing the usefulness for parents of reading the book with other kinds of help. Parents have reported that its informative and undogmatic approach has helped them understand and feel more confident in dealing with their child's problem.

BIBLIOGRAPHY

All books are published in London unless otherwise indicated:

Ablon, S.L. and Mack, J.F. (1979) 'Sleep disorders', in J. Noshpitz, ed. *Basic Handbook of Child Psychiatry*, vol. 2. New York: Basic, pp. 643–60.

Ainsworth, M.D.S. and Wittig, B.A. (1969) 'Attachment and exploration: behaviour of one-year-olds in a strange situation', in B.H. Foss, ed. *Determinants of Infant Behaviour*, vol. 4. Methuen, pp. 111–36.

Ainsworth, M.D.S., Blehar, M.C., Waters, E. and Wall, S. (1978) *Patterns of Attachment: A Psychological Study of the Strange Situation*. Hillsdale, NJ: Lawrence Erlbaum.

Als, H., Tronick, E., Lester, B.M. and Brazelton, T.B. (1979) 'Specific neonatal measures: the Brazelton Neonatal Behavioural Scale', Chapter 6 in J. Osofsky, ed. *Handbook of Infant Development*. New York: Wiley, pp. 185–215.

Anders, J.F., Keener, M., Bowe, T.R. and Shoaff, B.A. (1983) 'A longitudinal study of night-time sleep–wake patterns in infants from birth to one year', in J.D. Call, E.G. Galenson and R.L. Tyson, eds *Frontiers of Infant Psychiatry*. New York: Basic, pp. 150–70.

Aserinsky, E. and Kleitman, N. (1955) 'A motility cycle in sleeping infants as manifested by ocular and gross bodily activity', *J. Applied Physiology* 8:11–13.

Association of Sleep Disorders Center (1979) 'Diagnostic terminology', *Sleep* 2:1–137.

Balint, E. and Norell, J.S., eds (1973) *Six Minutes for the Patient*. Tavistock.

Barnes, F. (1975) 'Accidents in the first three years of life', *Child Care Health and Development* 1:421–33.

Bell, S.M. and Ainsworth, M.D.S. (1972) 'Infant crying and maternal responsiveness', *Child Development* 43:1171–90.

Bender, H. (1981) 'Experiences in running a nursing staff group in a hospital intensive care unit', *J. Child Psychotherapy* 7:152–9.

——(1987) 'Psychological aspects of prematurity and of neonatal intensive care: a working report', in P.G. Fedor-Freybergh and

V. Vogel, eds *Prenatal and Perinatal Psychology and Medicine: Encounter with the Unborn*. Carnforth: Parthenon, 1988, pp. 235–48.

Bender, H. and Swan-Parente, A. (1983) 'Psychological and psychotherapeutic support of staff and parents in an intensive care baby unit', in J.A. Davis, M.P.H. Richards and N.R.C. Robertson, eds *Parent–Baby Attachment in Premature Infants*. Beckenham: Croom Helm, pp. 165–76.

Berg, W.K. and Berg, K.M. (1987) 'Psycho-physiological development in infancy: state, startle and attention', in J. Osofsky, ed. *Handbook of Infant Development*, 2nd edn. New York: Wiley, pp. 238–317.

Bernal, J. (1973) 'Night waking in infants during the first year', *Developmental Medicine and Child Neurology*, 15:760–9.

Bick, E. (1964) 'Notes on infant observation in psychoanalytic training', *Int. J. Psycho-Anal.* 45:558–66.

Bion, W.R. (1962a) 'A theory of thinking', *Int. J. Psycho-Anal.* 43:306–14; reprinted in *Second Thoughts: Selected Papers on Psycho-Analysis*. New York: Jason Aronson, 1967, pp. 110–19.

——(1962b) *Learning from Experience*. Heinemann.

Blurton-Jones, N., Rosetti Ferreira, C., Farquar Brown, M. and MacDonald, L. (1978) 'The association between perinatal factors and later night waking', *Developmental Medicine and Child Neurology* 20:427–34.

Bourne, S. and Lewis, E. (1984) 'Pregnancy after still birth or neonatal death: psychological risks and management', *Lancet* July: 31–3.

Bowlby, J. (1961) 'Childhood mourning and its implications for psychiatry', *Am. J. Psychiatry* 118:481–98; reprinted in Bowlby (1979), pp. 44–66.

——(1969) *Attachment and Loss*, vol. 1, *Attachment*. Hogarth.

——(1973) *Attachment and Loss*, vol. 2, *Separation*. Hogarth.

——(1979) *The Making and Breaking of Affectional Bonds*. Tavistock.

Brackbill, Y. (1973) 'Continuous stimulation reduces arousal level: stability of the effects over time', *Child Development* 44:43–6.

Brazelton, T.B. (1973) 'Neonatal Behavioural Assessment Scale', *Clinics in Developmental Medicine* 88. Spastics International Medical Publications, 1984, pp. 1–125.

——(1988) 'Stress for families today', *Infant Mental Health J.* 9:65–71.

Breen, D. (1975) *The Birth of a First Child*. Tavistock.

Broughton, R. (1968) 'Sleep disorders: disorders of arousal?', *Science* 159:1070–8.

Brown, G. (1978) 'Depression: a sociological view', in D. Tuckett and J.H. Kaufert, eds *Basic Readings in Medical Sociology*. Tavistock, 1987, pp. 225–34.

Brown, G. and Harris, T. (1978) *Social Origins of Depression*. Tavistock.

Carter, J. (1984) 'Why are the mentally handicapped admitted to hospital? A ten-year survey', *Br. J. Psychiatry* 145:283–8.

Caudill, W. and Plath, D.W. (1966) 'Who sleeps by whom? Parent–child involvement in urban Japanese families', *Psychiatry* 29:344–66.

Chisholm, J. and Richards, M. (1978) 'Swaddling, cradleboards and the development of children', *Early Human Development* 2/3:255–75.

Clements, J., Wing, L. and Dunn, G. (1986) 'Sleep problems in handicapped children', *J. Child Psychology and Psychiatry* 27:399–407.

Clulow, C. (1982) *'To Have and to Hold': The First Baby and Preparing Couples for Parenthood*. Aberdeen: Aberdeen University Press.

Coons, S. (1987) 'Development of sleep and wakefulness during the first six months of life', in C. Guilleminault, ed. *Sleep and its Disorders in Children*. New York: Raven, pp. 17–27.

Cox, J.L., Connor, Y.M. and Kendall, R.E. (1982) 'Prospective study of the psychiatric disorders of childbirth', *Br. J. Psychiatry* 140:111–17.

Crowell, J., Keener, M., Ginsberg, N. and Anders, T. (1987) 'Sleep habits in toddlers eighteen to thirty-six months old', *J. Amer. Academy of Child Adolescent Psychiatry* 26:510–15.

Cunningham, N., Anisfield, E., Casper, V. and Nozyce, M. (1987) 'Infant-carrying, breast-feeding and mother–infant relations', *Lancet* February 14:379.

Davis, M. and Wallbridge, D. (1981) *Boundary and Space: Introduction to the Work of D.W. Winnicott*. Karnac.

Daws, D. (1985) 'Sleeping problems in babies and young children', *J. Child Psychotherapy* 11, 2:87–95.

Desmond, M.M., Rudolph, A.J. and Phitaksphraiwan, P. (1966) 'The transitional care nursery: a mechanism of a preventative medicine', *Pediatric Clinics of North America* 13:651–68.

Douglas, J. and Richman, N. (1984) *My Child Won't Sleep*. Harmondsworth: Penguin.

Dunn, J. (1977) *Distress and Comfort*. Fontana; Open Books.

Emde, R. (1984) 'The affective self: continuities and transforma-
tions from infancy', in J.D. Call, E.G. Galenson and R.L. Tyson,
eds *Frontiers of Infant Psychiatry*, vol. 2. New York: Basic, pp.
38–54.

——(1988) 'Introduction: reflections on mothering and on re-
experiencing the early relationship experience', *Infant Mental
Health J.* 9:4–9.

Emde, R. and Robinson, J. (1979) 'The first two months: recent
research in developmental psychobiology and the changing view
of the new-born', in J. Noshpitz, ed. *Basic Handbook of Child
Psychiatry*, vol. 1. New York: Basic, pp. 72–105.

Fain, N. and Kreisler, L. (1970) 'Discussions sur la genèse des
fonctions representatives', *Revue Française Psychanal.*
34:285–306.

Ferber, R. (1985a) *Solve Your Child's Sleep Problems: A Practical and
Comprehensive Guide for Parents*. Dorling Kindersley, 1986.

——(1985b) 'Sleep disorders in infants and children', in T.L. Riley,
ed. *Clinical Aspects of Sleep and Sleep Disturbances*. Butterworth,
pp. 113–57.

——(1987) 'The sleepless child', in C. Guilleminault, ed. *Sleep and
its Disorders in Children*. New York: Raven, pp. 141–63.

Field, T. (1985) 'Attachment as psychobiological attunement', in M.
Reite and T. Field, eds *The Psychobiology of Attachment and Separation*. Academic, pp. 415–54.

Foulkes, D. (1983) 'Dream ontology and dream psychophysiology',
in M. Chase and E.D. Weitzman, eds *Sleep Disorders Basic and
Clinical Research*. SP Medical and Scientific, pp. 347–62.

Fraiberg, S. (1950) 'On sleep disturbance of early childhood', *Psychoanal. Study Child* 5:285–307.

——(1959) *The Magic Years*. Methuen, 1968.

Fraiberg, S., ed. (1980) *Clinical Studies in Infant Mental Health*.
Tavistock.

Fraiberg, S., Adelson, E. and Shapiro, V. (1980) 'Ghosts in the
nursery', in Fraiberg (1980), pp. 387–421.

Freeman, J. (1979) *Gifted Children*. Lancaster: MTP.

Freud, Anna (1953) 'Some remarks on infant observation', in *The
Writings of Anna Freud*, vol. 4. New York: International
Universities Press, pp. 569–88.

——(1966) *Normality and Pathology in Children*. Hogarth.

Freud, S. (1900) *The Interpretation of Dreams*, in James Strachey, ed.
*The Standard Edition of the Complete Psychological Works of Sigmund
Freud*, 24 vols. Hogarth, 1953, vol. 4, pp. 509–622.

——(1916–17) *Introductory Lectures on Psycho-Analysis*. S.E. 15.

——(1920) *Beyond the Pleasure Principle*. S.E. 18, pp. 3–64.

Gesell, A. (1950) *The First Five Years of Life*. Methuen.

Ginsberg, S. (1976) 'Women, work and conflict', in N. Fonda and P. Moss, eds *Mothers in Employment*. Uxbridge: Brunel University, pp. 75–88.

Giorgis, F.G., Camuffo, M. and Cascioli, P. (1987) 'Influenza dei disturbi precoci del sonno sullo sviluppo cognitivo', in *Atti dell' VIII Convegno di Neurologia Infantile*, Istituto di Neuropsichiatria Infantile. Universitá la Sapienza, Roma, pp. 1–10.

Glasser, R. (1986) *Growing up in the Gorbals*. Chatto & Windus.

Guedeney, A. (1989) 'Les Troubles de l'endormissement et du sommeil au cours des trois premiers semestres de la vie', in B. Cramer, ed. *Proceedings of World Infant Psychiatry Congress, Stockholm, 1986*. Paris: Eshail.

Guedeney, A. and Kreisler, L. (1987) 'Sleep disorders in the first eighteen months of life: hypothesis on the role of mother–child emotional exchanges', *Infant Mental Health J.* 8:307–18.

Harlow, H.F. (1961) 'The development of affectional patterns in infant monkeys', in B.M. Foss, ed. *Determinants of Infant Behaviour*, vol. 1. Methuen/New York: Wiley, pp. 75–97.

Harlow, H.F. and Zimmermann, R.R. (1959) 'Affectional responses in the infant monkey', *Science* 130–421.

Harris, M. (1975) *Thinking about Infants and Young Children*. Perth: Clunie.

Hartmann, E. (1973) *The Functions of Sleep*. New Haven, CT: Yale University Press.

——(1984) *The Nightmare*. New York: Basic.

Haslam, D. (1984) *Sleepless Children*. Piatkus.

Holden, J.M., Sagovsky, R. and Cox, J.L. (1989) 'Counselling in a general practice setting: a controlled study of health visitor intervention in the treatment of postnatal depression', *Br. Med. J.*, in press.

Hopkins, J. (1986) 'Solving the mystery of monsters: steps towards the recovery from trauma', *J. Child Psychotherapy* 12: 61–71.

Hunziker, V.A. and Barr, R.G. (1986) 'Increased carrying reduces infant crying: a randomized controlled trial', *Pediatrics* 77:641–8.

Illingworth, R.S. (1954) 'Three months' colic', *Archives of Disease in Childhood* 29:167–74.

Jones, E. (1910) *On the Nightmare*. Hogarth, 1931.

Kahn, J.H. and Wright, S.E. (1980) *Human Growth and the Development of Personality*. Oxford: Pergamon.

Kales, A., Kales, J., Sly, R., Scharf, M., Tjiauw-Ling, T. and Preston, T. (1970) 'Sleep patterns of asthmatic children: all-night electroencephalographic studies', *J. of Allergy* 46:300–8.

Karacan, I. and Williams, R.L. (1970) 'The relationship of sleep disturbances to psychopathology', in E. Hartmann, ed. *Sleep and Dreaming*. Boston, MA: Little, Brown, pp. 93–111.

Kennell, J.H., Voos, D.K. and Klaus, M.H. (1979) 'Parent–infant bonding', in J. Osofsky, ed. *Handbook of Infant Development*. New York: Wiley, pp. 786–98.

Kennell, J.H., Klaus, M.H., Urrutia, J., Robertson, S. and Sosa, R. (1980) 'The effect of a supportive comparison of perinatal problems, length of labor and mother–infant interaction', *New England J. Medicine*. 303:597–600.

Kirkland, J. (1985) *Crying and Babies: Helping Families Cope*. Croom Helm.

Klaus, M.H. and Kennell, J.H. (1976) *Maternal–Infant Bonding: The Impact of Early Separation or Loss on Family Development*. 2nd edn, *Parent–Infant Bonding*. St. Louis, MO: Mosby, 1982.

Klein, M. (1932) 'The psychological foundations of child analysis', in *The Psycho-Analysis of Children*. Hogarth, pp. 3–15.

——(1959) 'Our adult world and its roots in infancy', in *Envy and Gratitude and Other Works*. Hogarth, 1980, pp. 247–63.

——(1963) 'On the sense of loneliness', in *Envy and Gratitude and Other Works*. Hogarth, 1980, pp. 300–13.

Kreisler, L. (1974) 'Insomnie de premier semestre', in L. Kreisler, M. Fain and M. Soule, eds *L'Enfant et son corps*. Paris: Presses Universitaires de France, pp. 70–99.

Krystal, H. (1978) 'Self-representation and the capacity for self-care', *Annual of Psychoanalysis* 6:206–46.

Leach, P. (1977) *Baby and Child*. Harmondsworth: Penguin, 1980.

Lebovici, S. (1980) 'L'experience du psychoanalyste chez l'enfant et chez l'adulte devant le modèle de la nervose infantile et de la nervose de transfert', *Revue Française Psychanal*. 44:733–857.

Lipton, E., Steinschneider, A. and Richmond, J. (1965) 'Swaddling: a child care practice: historical, cultural and experimental observations', *J. Pediatrics* 35:519–67.

Lozoff, B., Wolf, A.W. and Davis, N.S. (1984) 'Co-sleeping in urban families with young children in the United States', *J. Pediatrics* 74:171–82.

——(1985) 'Sleep problems seen in pediatric practice', *J. Pediatrics* 75:477–83.

Magagna, J. (1986) 'Night Terrors in Latency Children'. Paper given at the 11th International Congress of the International Association for Child and Adolescent Psychiatry. Paris, July 1986. Obtainable from Hospital for Sick Children, Great Ormond Street, London WC1N 3JH.

Mahler, M. (1975) *The Psychological Birth of the Human Infant: Symbiosis and Individuation*. Maresfield Library, 1985.

Main, M. (1989) 'Parental aversion to physical contact with the infant: stability, consequences and reasons', in T.B. Brazelton, ed. *Touch: The Foundation of Experience*. New York: International Universities Press, in press.

Main, M. and Solomon, J. (1986) 'Discovery of an insecure-disorganized/disoriented attachment pattern', in T.B. Brazelton and M.W. Yogman, eds *Affective Development in Infancy*. Norwood, NJ: Ablex, pp. 95–124.

Main, M., Kaplan, N and Cassidy, J. (1985) 'Security in infancy, childhood and adulthood: a move to the level of representation', in I. Bretherton and E. Waters, eds *Growing Points of Attachment Theory and Research*. Monographs of the Society for Research in Child Development, no. 209, vol. 50, pp. 66–104.

Mann, N.P., Haddow, R., Stokes, L., Goodley, S. and Rutter, N. (1986) 'Effects of night and day on pre-term infants in a newborn nursery: randomized trial', *Br. Med. J.* 293:1265–7.

Matte-Blanco, I. (1975) *The Unconscious as Infinite Sets*. Duckworth.

McDonald, D., Shallenberger, H., Koresko, R. and Kinzy, B. (1976) 'Studies of spontaneous electrodermal responses in sleep', *Psychophysiology* 13:128–34.

McDougall, J. (1974) 'The psychosoma and the psychoanalytic process', *Int. Rev. Psycho-Anal.* I:437–59.

——(1985) 'Developmental aspects of affect pathology: a contribution to the symposium: "Psychosomatic Pathology as a Developmental Failure, A Model for Research" ', *Psychiatry* 4:369–74.

——(1986) *Theatres of the Mind*. Free Association.

McKenna, J.J. (1986) 'An anthropological perspective on the sudden infant death syndrome (SIDS): the role of parental breathing cues and speech breathing adaptations', *Medical Anthropology* 10:9–92.

McKenna, J., Mosco, S. and Dungy, C. (1989) 'Synchronous and asynchronous aspects of sleep, awake and arousal patterns of co-sleeping human mother–infant pairs: a preliminary physiological study with implications for the study of sudden infant death syndrome (SIDS)', *Am. J. Physical Anthropology*. In press.

Meltzer, D. (1983) *Dream-Life: A Re-Examination of the Psychoanalytic Theory and Technique*. Perth: Clunie.

Meltzoff, A.N. and Boston, W. (1979) 'Intermodal matching in human neonates', *Nature* 282:403–4.

Metcalf, D.R. (1979) 'Organizers of the psyche and the EEG development: birth through adolescence', in J. Noshpitz, ed. *Basic Handbook of Child Psychiatry*, vol. I. New York: Basic, pp. 63–71.

Miller, L., Rustin, M., Rustin, M. and Shuttleworth, J. (1989) *Closely Observed Infants*. Duckworth.

Milne, A.A. (1924) 'Disobedience', in *When We were Very Young*. Methuen.

Milner, M. (Joanna Field) (1936) *A Life of One's Own*. Los Angeles: J.P. Tarcher, 1981.

——(1950) *On Not Being Able to Paint*. Heinemann, 1957.

Minde, K., Trehub, S., Corter, C., Boukydis, C., Celhoffer, L. and Marton, P. (1978) 'Mother–child relationships in the premature nursery: an observational study', *Pediatrics* 61:373.

Moore, M.-S. (1989) 'Disturbed atachment in children: a factor in sleep disturbance, altered dream production and immune system dysfunction', *J. Child Psychotherapy* 15, I. In press.

Moore, T. and Ucko, L.E. (1957) 'Night waking in early infancy', *Archives of Disease in Early Childhood* 32:333–42.

Moss, P. and Plewis, I. (1977) 'Mental distress in mothers of pre-school children in Inner London', *Psychological Medicine* 7:641–52.

Murray, L. (1988) 'Effects of postnatal depression on infant development, direct studies of early mother–infant interaction', in K. Kumar and I. Brockington, eds *Motherhood and Mental Illness*, vol. 2. Wright, pp. 159–90.

Murray, L. and Trevarthen, C. (1985) 'Emotional regulation of interactions between two-month-olds and their mothers', in T.M. Field and N.A. Fox, eds *Social Perception in Infants*. Norwood, NJ: Ablex, pp. 177–97.

Nagera, H. (1966) 'Sleep and its disturbances approached developmentally', *Psychoanal. Study Child* 21:393–447.

Nemiah, J.C. and Sifneos, P. (1970) 'Affect and fantasy in patients with psychosomatic disorders', in O.W. Hill, ed. *Modern Trends in Psychosomatic Medicine*, vol. 2. Butterworth, pp. 26–34.

Nover, A., Shore, H.F., Timberlake, E.M. and Greenspan, S.I.

(1984) 'The relationship of maternal perception and maternal behaviour: a study of normal mothers and their infants', *Amer. J. Orthopsychiatry* 54:210–23.

O'Shaughnessy, E. (1964) 'The absent object', *J. Child Psychotherapy* 1:34–43.

Palombo, S. (1978) *Dreaming and Memory.* New York: Basic.

Papousek, H. and Papousek, M. (1975) 'Cognitive aspects of pre-verbal social interaction between human infants and adults', in *Parent–Infant Interaction.* Ciba Foundation Symposium 33. New York: Elsevier.

Paret, I. (1983) 'Night waking and its relation to mother–infant interaction in nine-month-old infants', in J.D. Call, E.G. Galenson and R.L. Tyson, eds *Frontiers of Infant Psychiatry.* New York: Basic, pp. 171–7.

Pine, F. (1986) 'The "symbiotic phase" in light of current infancy research', *Bulletin of the Menninger Clinic* 50:564–9.

Pines, D. (1982) 'The relevance of early psychic development to pregnancy and abortion', *Int. J. Psycho-Anal.* 63:311–19.

Platt Report (1959) 'The welfare of children in hospital: report of the committee', Ministry of Health, Central Health Services Council. HMSO.

Pound, A. (1982) 'Attachment and maternal depression', in C.M. Parkes and J. Stevenson Hinde, eds *The Place of Attachment in Human Behaviour.* Tavistock, pp. 118–30.

Pound, A., Cox, A., Puckering, C. and Mills, M. (1985) 'The impact of maternal depression on young children', in J. Stevenson, ed. *Recent Research in Developmental Psychopathology.* Oxford: Pergamon, pp. 3–10.

Pound, A., Puckering, C., Mills, M. and Cox, A.D. (1988) 'The impact of maternal depression on young children', *Br. J. Psychotherapy* 4:240–52.

Provence, S. and Lipton, R.C. (1962) *Infants in Institutions.* New York: International Universities Press.

Quine, L. and Pahl, J. (1985) 'Examining the causes of stress in families with severely mentally handicapped children', *Br. J. Social Work* 15:501–17.

Raphael-Leff, J. (1982) 'Psychotherapeutic needs of mothers to be', *J. Child Psychotherapy* 8: 3–13.

——(1983) 'Facilitators and regulators: two approaches to mothering', *Br. J. Med. Psychol.* 56:379–90.

——(1986) 'Facilitators and regulators: conscious and unconscious processes in pregnancy and early motherhood', *Br. J. Med. Psychol.* 59:43–55.

Rayner, E. (1981) 'Infinite experiences, affects and the characteristics of the unconscious', *Int. J. Psycho-Anal.* 62:403–12.

Richards, M. (1983) 'Parent–child relationships: some general considerations', in J.A. Davis, M.P.H. Richards and N.R.C. Robertson, eds *Parent–Baby Attachment in Premature Infants*. Beckenham: Croom Helm, pp. 3–21.

Richards, M. and Bernal, J. (1974) 'Why some babies don't sleep', *New Society* February 28:509–11.

Richman, N. (1976) 'Depression in mothers of pre-school children', *J. Child Psychology and Psychiatry* 17:75–8.

——(1981a) 'A community survey of characteristics of one- to two-year-olds with sleep disruptions', *J. Am. Academy of Child Psychiatry* 20:281–91.

——(1981b) 'Sleep problems in young children', *Archives of Disease in Childhood* 56:491–3.

Richman, N., Stevenson, J. and Graham, P. (1982) *Preschool to School – A Behavioural Study*. Academic.

Riley, T.L. (1985) 'Biological organization of sleep', in T.L. Riley, ed. *Clinical Aspects of Sleep and Sleep Disturbance*. Butterworth.

Robertson, James (1958) *Young Children in Hospital*. Tavistock.

Robertson, James and Robertson, Joyce (1967–75) Film series: *Young Children in Brief Separation*. Tavistock Institute of Human Relations. Obtainable from Concord Films Council, Ipswich, Suffolk and New York Universities Film Institute.

——(1971) 'Young children in brief separation: a fresh look', *Psychoanal. Study Child* 26:264–315.

Roffwarg, H.P., Muzio, J.N. and Dement, W.C. (1966) 'Ontogenic development of the human sleep-dream cycle', *Science* 152:604–19.

Rycroft, C. (1979) *The Innocence of Dreams*. Hogarth.

Sander, L.W. (1980) 'New knowledge about the infant from current research: implications for psychoanalysis', *J. Amer. Psychoanal. Assn* 28:181–98.

Sander, L.W., Stechler, G., Julia, H. and Burns, P. (1976) 'Primary prevention and some aspects of temporal organization in early infant–caretaker interaction', in E. Rexford, L. W. Sander and T. Shapiro, eds *Infant Psychiatry*. Yale University Press, pp. 187–204.

Sasfin, J.F., Parker, D.C. and Johnson, L.C. (1969) 'The effect of slow-wave sleep deprivation on human growth hormones released in sleep', *Life Sciences* 8:1299–1307.

Savage, G.H. (1896) 'Prevention and treatment of insanity of pregnancy and the puerperal period', *Lancet* 1:164.

Schaffer, H.R. and Emerson, P.E. (1964) 'The development of social attachments in infancy'. *Monographs Soc. Research in Child Development* 29:1–77.

Scott, G. (1986) *Coping with Your Night Waking Baby*. Obtainable from Child Care and Development Group, University of Cambridge, Free School Lane, Cambridge CB2 3RF. New edition, 1989.

Scott, W. Clifford M. (1975) 'Remembering sleep and dreams', *Int. Rev. Psycho-Anal.* 2:253–354.

Sendak, M. (1963) *Where the Wild Things Are*. Harmondsworth: Puffin; Penguin, 1970.

Sharpe, E. Freeman (1937) *Dream Analysis*. Hogarth, 1961; Maresfield, 1988.

Smith, C.R. and Steinschneider, A. (1975) 'Differential effects of prenatal rhythmic stimulation on neonatal arousal states', *Child Development* 46:578–99.

Spock, B. (1946) *Baby and Child Care*. New York: Pocket, 1957.

Stern, D. (1985) *The Interpersonal World of the Infant*. New York: Basic.

Stevenson, A. (1983) 'Poem to my Daughter' in 'The Raving Beauties', eds *In the Pink: The 'Raving Beauties'*. Women's Press, p. 38; and in A. Stevenson, *Minute by Glass Minute*, Oxford University Press, 1982.

Sylvester-Bradley, N. and Trevarthen, C. (1978) 'Baby talk as an adaptation to the infant's communication', in N. Waterson and C. Snow, eds *The Development of Communication*. Wiley.

Symington, N. (1986) *The Analytic Experience: Lectures from the Tavistock*. Free Association.

Terr, L. (1987) 'Nightmares in children', in C. Guilleminault, ed. *Sleep and its Disorders in Children*. New York: Raven, pp. 231–42.

Tomson, M. (1989) 'Mothers to wives, history of a sleep group'. Unpublished.

Trevarthen, C. (1974) 'Conversations with a two-month-old', *New Scientist* 2 May: 230–5.

Trowell, J. (1982) 'Effects of obstetric management on the mother–child relationship', in C.M. Parks and J. Stevenson Hinde, eds *The Place of Attachment in Human Behaviour*. Tavistock, pp. 79–94.

——(1983) 'Emergency Caesarean sections: a research study of

the mother–child relationship of a group of women admitted expecting a normal vaginal delivery', in *Child Abuse and Neglect* 7:387–94.

Tustin, F. (1972) *Autism and Childhood Psychosis*. Hogarth.

Weissbluth, M. (1987a) 'Sleep and the colicky infant', in C. Guilleminault, ed. *Sleep and its Disorders in Children*. New York: Raven, pp. 129–40.

——(1987b) *Sleep Well*. Unwin Paperbacks.

Winnicott, D.W. (1947) 'Further thoughts on babies as persons', Chapter 13 in Winnicott (1964), pp. 85–92.

——(1958) 'The capacity to be alone', in *The Maturational Processes and the Facilitating Environment*. Hogarth, 1965, pp. 29–36.

——(1964) *The Child, the Family and the Outside World*. Harmondsworth: Penguin.

——(1971) *Playing and Reality*. Tavistock; Harmondsworth: Penguin, 1974.

Wolff, P.H. (1974) 'The classifications of states: state and neonatal activity', in L.J. Stone, H.T. Smith and L.B. Murphy, eds *The Competent Infant*. Tavistock, pp. 257–82.

Wolke, D. (1987) 'Environmental and developmental neonatology', *J. Reproductive and Infant Psychology* 5:17–42.

Wolke, D. and St. James Roberts, I. (1987) 'Multi-method measurement of the early parent–infant system with easy and difficult new-borns', in H. Rauh and H. Steinhausen, eds *Psychobiology and Early Development*. Holland: Elsevier Science, pp. 49–70.

Zuckerman, B., Stevenson, J. and Bailey, V. (1987) 'Sleep problems in early childhood: continuities, predictive factors and behavioural correlates', *J. Pediatrics* 80:664–71.

disturbed children, fear of labelling as
48
disturbed parents 45
diurnal cycles 11
diurnal rhythms, and neonatal
intensive care units 235
doctors 32, 44, 133, 135, 156, 163, 215
Double Closed-Circuit Television
Technique 223
Douglas, J. 11, 24–5, 26, 27
dreaming play 249
dreams 62, 64, 82–6, 164, 172, 173,
199, 211
about children 2–3, 251
children's, parents' understanding
of 88–91
children's conflicts and 91–4
as continuous process 94
function 6, 39, 85, 86
manifest content 95
of parents 86–9
REM sleep 84–6
sexual wishes of 91
dummies, for premature babies 234

eating habits 205
eczema 158, 160
mother's 158, 160, 217–18
EEGs 62
Emde, R. 67, 103, 141
emergent self 115
emotional development 5
babies' 114
emotional impact, of new babies 64
emotional interaction, between
mothers and babies 216
emotional states, confirmation of 210
emotionality, of families with sleep
problems 20
emotions 3, 4
children's awareness of parents'
198
of parents 47
epileptic fits 242
ethology 121
experiences, good and bad 106, 108,
109, 110
exploration 122

facilitators, mothers as 43–4
Fain, N. 207–8
families

babies with sleep problems 4
coming for help 19–22
housing conditions 204–6
signals within 35–8
family relationships 4, 21
fathers 7, 22, 43, 106–7, 159, 177
absence 197–8
attachment to 122
deprived 179–82
dreams of 87
exclusion of 189
feeding and 169–70
presence at birth 176
role in baby-rearing 190–7
weaning, helping with 107, 169–
70, 194–5
fears
babies' 4
parents' 31
feeding 6, 149
case example 149–51
closeness and 151–4
experience of 166–9
frequency 154–5
night-time 156–60
time spent 166–8
feelings
intense 110
out of touch with 208
of parents 31–2
Ferber, Richard 26, 42, 68, 96, 97,
155, 157, 202
firmness 31–2
focused attention 63, 64, 84
foetus 103, 104
basic rest–activity cycle 67
REM sleep
food for comfort 150
foster-mothers 128
Foulkes, David 95
Fraiberg, Selma 32, 131, 136, 143,
184–5, 186
Freeman, Joan 248–9
Freud, Anna 94, 113, 141, 142, 203
Freud, Sigmund 3, 82, 83, 89, 143–4,
201
frustrations 111

games, about separation 143–4
gifted children 248–50
Giorgis, F.G. 104, 182–3, 203
Glasser, Ralph 140
good enough mother 111